ALWAYS LOOK

ON THE BRIGHT

SIDE OF LIFE

ALWAYS LOOK
ON THE BRIGHT
SIDE OF LIFE

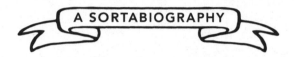

A SORTABIOGRAPHY

ERIC IDLE

Crown Archetype

New York

Photo credits appear on page 273.

Library of Congress Cataloging-in-Publication Data is available upon request.

ISBN 978-1-9848-2258-1
Ebook ISBN 978-1-9848-2260-4

Printed in the United States of America

Jacket design: Michael Morris
Jacket photographs: (portrait) AF archive/Alamy Stock Photo; (cloud) Wallace
Garrison/Photographer's Choice/Getty Images; (grail) Lord_Kuernyus/Stock/
Getty Images

10 9 8 7 6 5 4 3 2 1

First Edition

Life has a very simple plot,

First you're here

And then you're not.

CONTENTS

For Tania, Carey, and Lily

AN APOLOGY

Graham Chapman once said: "Life is rather like a yacht in the Caribbean. It's alright if you've got one." I have been traveling at the speed of life for seventy-five years now and I still don't have one, but then again, I wrote "Life's a piece of shit, when you look at it" while reminding everyone to look on the Bright Side, a line that I discovered recently is at least as old as Coleridge. This book is partly the story of that song and partly the story of a boy who became me—if you like the memoirs of a failed pessimist. I still remain foolishly optimistic, even with the threat of global warming, which worries me slightly less than personal cooling, and so I have written my recollections, before I forget everything and develop Hamnesia, which is what you get from being an old actor.

Of course I have faults, but you won't read about them here. I've glossed over all my shortcomings. That is after all the point of Autobiography. It is the case for the Defense. But I will own up to not being perfect. I have British teeth. They are like British politics: they go in all directions at once.

Writing about yourself is an odd mix of therapy and lap dancing; exciting and yet a little shameful. So here is my own pathetic addition to the celebrity memoir. On the advice of my lawyer I am leaving out the shameful bits, and on the advice of my wife the filthy bits, but as usual in my career, I will leave you wanting less.

If this isn't exactly what went down, it's certainly how it should have happened.

Look at the

bright side

always.

—SAMUEL TAYLOR COLERIDGE

1

CRUCIFIXION?

It's October 1978 and I'm being crucified. I'm thirty feet up on a cross in Tunisia singing "Always Look on the Bright Side of Life." Beneath me in a troglodyte courtyard, dug out another forty feet below ground level, an Arab woman sweeps her front yard. She never looks up. We've been here for three days. It's the final scene in *Monty Python's Life of Brian* and the song I wrote echoes across the desert to the distant hills. John Cleese has the flu. The rest of the Pythons seem fairly cheery. There are twenty-three of us on crosses and only three ladders, so between takes if you need a pee there is a desperate wait. I suppose if that's the only moan you have about being crucified, you are on the whole lucky . . .

There's something a little chilling about turning up for work and finding a cross with your name on it. Oh sure, they weren't using nails, and we had bicycle seats to perch on, but it makes you think, hanging up there for three days in your underpants, gazing out at the desert. Perhaps everyone should be crucified for a few days, because it does give you a good perspective on life. Especially if you are singing a song that references your own passing:

Just remember that the last laugh is on you . . .

And don't think the irony escaped me. I have always known this last little giggle at my expense lies somewhere in the future. I only hope there's a good turnout.

The song was supposed to be ironic, but it ended up being iconic. I mean, you can't have much less of a future to be bright about than when being crucified. But people began to sing it in real wars and in real danger. It struck a chord somehow and now people sing it everywhere. Including football matches, and funerals. Especially funerals. As of this writing, it's the number one song requested at British funerals.

So here I am, up on a cross in Tunisia singing it for the first time to Graham Chapman. How the hell did I get here?

2

A SCAR IS BORN

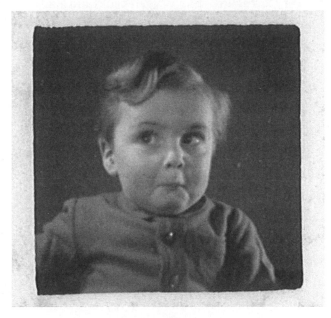

"'Oo's 'itler?"

By an odd coincidence, I was born on my birthday. In the same place as my mother, Harton Hospital, South Shields, County Durham, though luckily not at the same time. I was born plain Eric Idle. We couldn't afford a second name. There was a war on. At the time of my birth, Hitler was trying to kill me. Nothing personal, but fortunately he missed. The closest he got is one of my earliest memories: a shot-up U.S. Wellington bomber, limping home from Germany, crashing in flames in the field beside my nursery school.

"Nothing to worry about," said the nurses as they hustled us inside.

Surely the scariest words you can ever hear. Then I learned the truth from my mum: "The American pilot was looking for an emergency landing in the field. He saw the kids playing and deliberately turned away, taking the plane down."

I've always liked Americans. They're brave buggers.

So, *close,* Adolf, but no cigar.

If one of the best ways to appreciate life is to have an unhappy childhood, I was very fortunate. Things began badly and got worse. Try this for irony: my father was killed hitchhiking home from World War II. He'd been in the RAF since 1941 in the most dangerous seat of a Wellington bomber, that of the rear gunner/wireless operator, from which he emerged unscathed, and yet seven months after the war in Europe was over, he was killed in a road accident hitching home for Christmas. All over England, servicemen were waiting to be demobbed, and as the trains were full for the holidays they were told to thumb for rides, since everyone stopped for the boys in uniform. My dad got a lift in the back of a lorry load of steel. Just outside Darlington a car swerved to avoid oncoming traffic, the truck veered off the road, the load of steel shifted and crushed him. He died in hospital on Christmas Eve, my mother by his bedside. I was almost three. You can see how Christmas was never much fun in our household. I wonder if that's why I wrote the song "Fuck Christmas"?

After I was born my father was rarely home. Wars are like that. The Air Force maps they used had code words on them. I found the words *Spam Exit* in my dad's tidy handwriting. I also found a few references to myself in his tiny RAF diary for 1945; the choking words for July 7: *Eric's first paddle & trip to the Beach.*

My father's grave is in an RAF cemetery. The dead are lined up in neat white slabs, forever at attention—name, rank, serial number, and date of death: December 24, 1945. Above, the Latin words of the RAF motto: *Per Ardua ad Astra.* "Through hard work to the stars." It could be the watchword for mankind entering the Space Age. Or a young man entering show business.

It ain't 'alf cold, Dad.

My mother disappeared for a while into depression, and I was brought up by my Gran in Swinton, Lancashire. Her husband, a dentist who I called Pop, took me to the Belle Vue Circus in Manchester where, amazingly, it turned out we were circus royalty. My great-grandfather was Henry Bertrand, a famous ringmaster and circus manager in the 1880s. I still have his notepaper, with his imposing picture in white tie and tails, announcing he is the Advance Manager of *Roby's Midget Minstrels*. Only afterward did I realize that I too ended up in a circus: and a Flying one at that.

When I did a little research into him recently I found out that, incredibly, he had begun life as a comedian. Isn't that slightly too much coincidence? In my novel *The Road to Mars* I postulated that this was evidence of a comedy gene. I was joking, but now I'm not so sure. Anyway, as a child it was exciting to be taken backstage at Belle Vue Circus

MEMO. from

HENRY BERTRAND,

General Dramatic, Equestrian, and Music
Hall Manager.

Equestrian Director and Ring Master.

ADVERTISING MANAGER.

Stage Manager.   Fete and Gala
Contractor, &c.

Present Address

Permanent Address: 100, PERCY TERRACE, GATESHEAD-ON-TYNE.

CREDENTIALS AND
REFERENCES.

Hengler's Grand Cirques.

Lord John Sanger & Sons'
Royal Circus, Hippodrome,
and Menagerie.

Wulff Great Continental
Circus. London. Brighton.
and Dublin.

Geo. Gilbert's Modern Circus

Advance Manager
Roby's Midget Minstrels.

Royal English Circus,
Birmingham.   Record 10
Months' Highly Successful
Season, 1897-8.

Theatre's Royal, Sheffield,
Nottingham, Sadlers Wells.

My great-grandfather, Henry Bertrand, Ringmaster.

to meet the terrifying clowns, who were very respectful to Pop as a Bertrand and extremely friendly to me. Pop also took me to see various variety shows at the Manchester Hippodrome, where I saw the best of British Music Hall comedians: Morecambe and Wise, Robb Wilton, Jimmy Edwards, Arthur Askey, Norman Evans, Mrs. Shufflewick, Norman Wisdom, and the Crazy Gang. The most memorable thing about the variety shows were the *tableaux vivants,* where a stage full of beautiful girls stood or sat, stark naked. This was the first time I ever saw a nude woman and suddenly there were twenty-four of them. It was called "A Scene from Winter" and fake snow fell while they posed with nothing on but discreetly placed drapery. The orchestra played and someone recited a daft little poem while the girls just sat there. They weren't allowed to move. In those days, it was illegal to move around on stage naked. If they did they could be arrested, but as long as they didn't move, it was alright and everyone applauded. I remember thinking, *This is great,* and ever since then I have always been very fond of nude ladies. So that's my background in show business: circuses, clowns, comedians, and nude ladies.

In 1948, when I was five, my Gran took me to see three films in one day. I'd never seen a movie before, and I was hooked right away. We saw *Joan of Arc, The Glass Mountain,* and a Marx Brothers movie, one after the other. Twenty-four nude ladies all at once and then three movies in a day. Can you see the way my life's going? We were a pre-television generation and grew up with radio, listening to gripping series like *Journey into Space* and *Dick Barton: Special Agent!* and hilarious comedians like Al Read:

"Can you smell gas or is it me?"

There was also the incomparable *Goon Show,* a popular BBC Radio Comedy with Peter Sellers, Spike Milligan, and Harry Secombe.

The first time I ever saw TV was the coronation of Queen Elizabeth II in 1953. My school brought in a tiny eight-inch black-and-white screen and we sat around watching people walking up and down singing "Vivat Regina!" in funny costumes. They gave us lots of coronation toys, mugs, golden coaches, and paper crowns, and that morning on the radio the BBC announced we'd conquered Everest—well, a New Zealander and a Tibetan Sherpa conquered Everest, but it was a *British* expedition.

When I was five, my mother, now working as a nurse in Cheshire, sent me to school for the first time to St. George's, Wallasey, a small seaside town just a ferry ride across the River Mersey from Liverpool. One day I was missing from home. I'd met a boy called George playing on the Red Noses, the sand dunes at New Brighton. This was a very popular outing from Liverpool, and we were always playing with kids from the other side of the Mersey. George and I played happily all day, losing all sense of time. Many years later, when I met George Harrison and we became close friends, I had a very strong feeling that we had met before, and I often wondered if he was the boy who bunked off with me that day. I guess I'll never know, but when I finally got home my mother was freaked out. It was difficult for her to cope with a growing son and a full-time job, and my disappearing like that scared her. So, she accepted an offer from the RAF Benevolent Fund and put me, at the age of seven, into the Royal School Wolverhampton, which had just changed its name from the Royal Orphanage. The war had given this Victorian institution a shot in the arm, but there is no escaping the pull of irony. I was sent to a school paid for by the RAF to grow up with boys all of whom had lost their fathers in the war. We called it the "Ophny," short for Orphanage.

My first night at the school I found myself in a dormitory with a lot of crying boys. I decided not to join them. What was the point? Earlier that day, when my mother dumped me there, she simply left and disappeared. She didn't say goodbye, she just took off. Later on, she said, "Well, I didn't want to cause a fuss. You were happily play-ing so I thought I'd just slip away and *avoid a scene*." Very Northern mother, that. Above all else, avoid a scene. I still have nightmares that I'm back at the Ophny. It was very grim at the time, and is terrifying in retrospect. I was there from seven years old until I managed to escape at the age of nineteen. It was a physically abusive, bullying, harsh en-vironment for a kid. The terms were an interminable fourteen weeks. At the age of seven they seemed everlasting. *Twelve years?* You get less for murder.

In the Junior School, Miss McCartney whacked me across the hand with a wooden ruler because I didn't understand a math problem. Surprisingly, I remained bad at math. At the age of eleven I nervously entered the Senior School. Bullying was endemic. The prefects were al-lowed to whack you with slippers. The masters could beat you with canes. For severe crimes, like giggling in Prep, you could be sent to the headmaster for "six of the best." I was once sent for a beating for "silent insolence." Not even *saying* anything. I mean, what chance does that give you? The Senior School had a dormitory a hundred yards long and at night the prefects would patrol up and down. If they heard someone talking after lights out, and nobody owned up, everybody had to get out of bed and bend over their beds while they went down the line and whacked the whole dorm. And it was freezing. I was cold until I was nineteen. No wonder I moved to California.

But unhappiness is never forever. There were moments of happiness. Sardonic laughter at how, while you were being beaten, they would say, "It's for your own good."

"Oh, well why don't I do it for you then?"

I was fairly funny at school, and humor is a good defense against bullying. It's hard to hit a smaller boy when you are laughing. I got used to dealing with gangs of males and getting on with life in unpleasant circumstances while being smart at the expense of authority. Perfect training for Python.

I used to be very bitter about my school days, but now I think it was there I learned everything I needed to survive in life. It's a cruel joke to be called Idle when shoved into an English boarding school, but it does prepare you to deal with insult, and I always had several good comebacks up my sleeve. Asked about the origins of my name on a British TV show, I speculated it was from Yorkshire and came from the "idle" mechanism on the woolen looms. When I got home there was a message from George Harrison saying, "Come off it. You're just from a long line of lazy old bastards." I have since learned that the actual origin is from the English word *idel*, meaning "unused ground" or "patch of waste."

Hmm. "A patch of waste." I've been called worse . . .

When I was twelve my Gran gave me a small portable typewriter and I began writing stories: *The Mystery of the Missing Skull*, a Boadicea story, and endless war tales about heroic RAF men. I was always interested in words, because in such a sterile environment you have to create your own entertainment and explore your own brain. Reading was and still is my great escape. I also liked puppeteering with string marionettes, writing sketches, and doing funny voices, hiding in character and poking fun at the masters. We were very subversive and got huge laughs. I performed in a school musical, *Toad of Toad Hall*, where I played Second Field Mouse. I turned down the offer to play First Field Mouse as I realized Second Field Mouse had more words.

I became a folkie in a trio where I played harmonica with the Sinfield brothers on banjo and guitar, and we mainly did blues. It has always struck me as odd how we identified with the black struggle in the southern U.S., when we were very white boys in an English boarding school thousands of miles away from the Deep South, but their songs became our songs of protest too, and we sang away to Sonny Terry and Brownie McGhee. We were being repressed, and I guess the spirit of the music, the soul of it, was very close to what we felt.

Then along came rock and roll. Elvis saved our lives. He seemed to be singing directly to us. At fourteen I wanted to play guitar very badly. By fifteen I did.

Elvis was amazing. We adored him. I heard him first singing "Heartbreak Hotel" on every juke box at Butlins Holiday Camp in Skegness in the summer of 1957, while teddy boys snapped their fingers and girls jived to that haunting voice: "Well since my baby left me . . ." Back at school we gathered excitedly around the telly to see if it was true what was in the papers, that the cameras wouldn't shoot him below the waist. He danced, he jived, he shook those hips, and we heard the screams of the girls, but nothing below the waterline was shown on television. Perhaps it was the trousers. Elvis was our hero throughout my school years and we listened to him under the sheets, first on crystal sets we built ourselves, sending away for parts like cat's whiskers and tuning coils, and then finally on tiny transistor radios. Later, when Elvis was sent into the army, it cast a gloom over us all. It seemed *they* had won. *They* cut his hair and flew him off to Germany. Then Buddy Holly died. It was all too much.

At the Ophny, every Monday afternoon from the age of eleven we had to pretend we were in the army. Joining the CCF (the Combined Cadet Force) was compulsory. We're eleven years old and we're out on the playground in army boots, marching up and down the square in itchy uniforms being yelled at by professional drill sergeants from the Walsall Barracks. *What the hell's this?* I can still feel the webbing on the gaiters and smell the Blanco product with which we painted them khaki. Polishing boots and shining brasses was something we had to do not just for our own uniforms but also for a designated senior boy, because in our first year we were all "fags." In British boarding-school-speak, a *fag* is a first-year slave for a prefect, making him toast and cleaning his shoes and running his errands. If we were late we were beaten. "Character forming" is, I think, the expression. By the age of fourteen, not only could I perform arms drill and shoot a .303 Lee-Enfield rifle with reasonable accuracy, I could strip a Bren gun blindfolded. Then they'd drop us in the Welsh mountains in full gear and say "See you," and six hours later if you were lucky you'd stagger into a military camp in North Wales armed only with a compass and a bit of cheese. Very useful little things to know in life. And certainly, it prepared me for Python movies . . .

So yes, things were rough, but we fought back. We organized our own nightlife. There was a girls' school under the same roof. We'd see the girls in chapel because church was compulsory twice on Sundays, but they would be on their side of the chancel and we on ours. Of course, being teenagers with rampant hormones, we'd try to slip messages to them during the long and interminably boring psalms while God was being cruel to the Children of Israel. As we said of the Children of Israel, "When will they *ever* grow up?"

I volunteered for the job of School Post Boy. Every afternoon I'd collect the official mail and take it down to the bright red pillar-box on Penn Road. I'd exit through the back gate of the Boys' School, turn left, and walk fifty yards to the back gate of the Girls' School, where there was always a crowd of young females hanging out. I exchanged pleasantries and clandestine billets-doux not intended for the public mailbox. They had cryptic acronyms on them, SWALK (Sealed With A Loving Kiss) and BURMA (Be Undressed Ready My Angel). On my return, there would be hastily scribbled responses. By being both helpful and flirtatious I soon had a girlfriend of my own.

In the Long Dorm, we slept in numerical order. They'd have made us shit in order if they could. My number was 63 and, randomly, next to me was 64, Halls Junior, a wonderfully subversive chap and luckily in my form. We became accustomed to slipping through the back gardens to the off-license to buy bottles of Mitchells & Butlers Old English stout and Caerphilly cheese. These we would consume after lights-out in the comforting warmth of the metal stove in the Scout Hut, where the Boy Scouts met by day and we relaxed by night, smoking Balkan Sobranie in clay pipes or Baby's Bottom tobacco through long-stemmed rosewood churchwarden pipes. At this point Halls Junior and I upped our game. We realized that while the Girls' School was desperately out of bounds, it was terribly close and there were no actual locked doors between the Boys' and Girls' Schools. All we had to do was face the fifty yards of darkness and suddenly we would be there. Fortunately, the Cadet Corps had taught us how to creep about silently in the dark, so we made a recce and it all worked perfectly: no one was around in the early hours of the morning. Thus emboldened, we climbed the stairs up into the girls' dorm, made rendezvous with our respective amours, and led them back to the Scout Hut, where we enjoyed a bottle of sweet martini and some Babycham, a cheap pear champagne.

These midnight encounters continued for some time until finally word got out and other boys began to take advantage of this exciting opportunity. Eventually it was not uncommon to be woken at night by a girl asking where so-and-so's bed was. In the end, the clandestine nightlife of the school became so sophisticated that we stole and copied the key to the swimming pool, a reeky green steamy hellhole, and if you wanted to go swimming with the girls, all you had to do was to put your name down on a list after Prep, and you would be woken and escorted by flashlight through the byzantine corridors down to the pool, where a small group of girls in dressing gowns awaited.

It's amazing we were never busted. The reason of course was that the prefects became involved and thereby utterly subverted. Hard to bust other boys when you have a sweet companion in your own bed. I'm not too sure how much all of this led to full intercourse. I think a lot of it was what was called "heavy petting" in those days, for despite all this opportunity I managed to enter Cambridge a virgin. But unlike Isaac Newton, I did not leave it like that . . .

I got very good at misbehaving and being sneaky and antiauthoritarian at the Ophny. It was like a combination of the army and prison, where you learned to adapt and trust your peers. My form was a highly organized criminal group. We never took a straight exam until O level at sixteen, because we'd always steal the exam papers. Some boys were very adept at picking locks, or they'd unscrew the backs of wardrobes where the teachers stored the tests and then they'd write the answers overnight on stolen exam paper and smuggle those in under their jumpers and substitute them. It was only at O level that I discovered I was comparatively clever when most of the other boys in my class simply didn't return after the summer holidays. They'd all failed. That was the first straight exam they'd ever taken. I think only eight of us returned. There were rumors that some were already in jail . . .

We had very muddy playing fields and I wasn't very good at football, so on a Thursday afternoon, instead of changing for compulsory games, I would put on my school cap and march out the front door and go downtown to Wolverhampton and watch a movie. I did this regularly, walking boldly past the headmaster's study, and nobody ever caught me, because if you've got your bright red school cap on and you're using the front door, you're clearly doing some school business, right? So, I learned very early on that if you're brazen, nobody questions you. If I'd been sneaking out, I would probably have been caught. Well, I finally *was* caught in my penultimate year. I was a senior prefect and taking Prep when the headmaster sent for me and he said, "Ah, Idle, did you enjoy the movie this afternoon?"

"No, not very much, sir, it wasn't very good," I said, annoying him.

I'd been spotted and reported for watching a racy film, *Butterfield 8*, with Elizabeth Taylor. So I was beaten of course, six of the best, and next morning hauled up in front of the entire school and denounced by the headmaster for this dreadful crime. Idle had been caught downtown going to an X-rated movie! Well, I couldn't have given myself a better PR job. Suddenly I was a hero. The whole school loved me! I was publicly sent to the back of the hall and I was no longer a prefect. Kids were slapping me on the back and giving me the thumbs-up. It was brilliant. Then, at the end of the year the headmaster left the school with the surprising recommendation that I be made Head Boy. Maybe he liked me. Maybe he liked Elizabeth Taylor. Maybe he just wanted to screw up his successor . . .

In the first term of my final year, my wonderful ex-RAF history teacher, Mr. Fry, arranged for me to apply to his old Cambridge college, Pembroke. I took a Harry Potter steam train to the Fens and was interviewed to read English by an economist, the Dean, and an Arab scholar. Amazingly, they offered me a place if I could pass O-level Latin in a year. A doddle.

Since I was now suddenly and weirdly Head Boy, the school insisted I must also be the head of the Combined Cadet Force, which I didn't want to be. At the end of six years of military training they had made the mistake of sending us off on a Civil Defence course, which showed precisely what happens when a nuclear bomb goes off, and as a result I had become violently pacifist. During the Easter holidays (1962) I went on the Aldermaston march, the annual CND anti-nuclear rally. We marched from Aldermaston in Hampshire to Hyde Park, a distance of about fifty-four miles, behind banners, singing protest songs. *We shall overcome.* We didn't. Instead we camped overnight in Reading and then marched proudly into London. My friend Alan Sinfield, a dark-haired, saturnine, poetry-reading guitarist from our folk trio, was by then at University College, London, and we were very lefty and very committed and it was great. When I got back to school, the new Padre called me in and said, "You're a hypocrite, Idle. You're the head of the CCF and you went on the Aldermaston march." And I said, "Well, I resign." And he said, "You're not allowed to resign." So, at the Monday Army Parade, I would take the salute from the English master, turn "the wrong way about" to annoy the professional drill sergeants, and slope off and read. I refused to go to military camp in Wales at the end of the year. They couldn't throw me out, because I'd left. I'd been accepted by Cambridge University, I was on the Aldermaston march and I didn't take any of their Combined Cadet Force bollocks seriously.

Then my entire life changed.

What changed me forever was Comedy. My epiphany began at *Be-*

yond the Fringe. In early 1963, I stayed with Alan Sinfield in North London, and we went to every single play we could. It was the time of the playwrights known as "the angry young men," so named after *Look Back in Anger,* John Osborne's groundbreaking play, which we saw at the Royal Court Theatre. For this new sold-out revue at the Fortune Theatre, performed by four men from Oxbridge, we could only get standing-room tickets, which was just as well because I would never have stayed in a seat. I rolled around screaming with laughter. I have never laughed so hard in my life. I had no idea you could be that funny, or that you could laugh at the Prime Minister and the Army and the War and the Royal Family. Everything I secretly hated was being mocked, and they were doing this so wittily. They were young, smart, and dangerously funny. This was anger, but it was being used for laughter. I immediately bought the record and learned everything— Alan Bennett's sermon, Peter Cook's prime minister speech, Jonathan Miller's whimsical monologues—and we would go and watch Dudley Moore playing jazz piano in Oxford Street. *Beyond the Fringe* was an amazing show. From that point on I could not conceive of life without comedy.

3

LUCKY BASTARD

Emerging from twelve years underground as a chrysalis in Wolverhampton to three years as a butterfly in Cambridge, I was a lucky bastard. Didn't Napoleon say it is better to be lucky than funny? (No, he didn't, did he.) Still, I first began to perform comedy at Cambridge University, almost by accident. It was certainly good fortune that I found myself in Pembroke College, for the great Peter Cook had recently been there and people were still quoting him:

"Tragically, I was an only twin."

"I'd like to invent something really important: like fire."

It was fairly extraordinary that a lower-middle-class boy like me from a lowly Midlands charity school was accepted, but Cambridge was changing. My education was paid for by Warwickshire County Council, and my old school generously kicked in a decent scholarship, which meant I was better off than many of the public-school boys who had to try to shake down their parents for cash. Packing for Cambridge, I had included a condom I had been optimistically carrying around in my wallet for two years. But in 1962, Cambridge was still a monastic society. There were no females in the all-male Pembroke. Women had their own colleges. I was still going over the wall to meet girls. In order to increase my chances, I joined the Pembroke Players. At their Christmas party, I wrote and performed a cabaret, which was greeted so well I was told I should try out for the Pembroke Smoker, a three-night comedy revue held in the Old Reader underneath the Wren Library. I found myself auditioning for Tim Brooke-Taylor and Bill Oddie. Isn't it odd that two future Goodies, Tim and Bill, who would soon have their own BBC TV comedy series with Graeme Garden—who would himself spend two years doing Cambridge Cabaret with me—should be casting a future Python? Odder still was that on my debut they gave me a piece to perform written by John Cleese. John wasn't at Pembroke, but he dined there every night. He couldn't appear in the College Smoker because he was not a member of the college, but I could, and he was there at my first-ever public performance, watching me do a sketch he had written for himself. It was called "BBC BC," about the biblical news. I played a weather forecaster.

> Down in the south, well, Egypt has had a pretty nasty spell of it recently. Seventeen or eighteen days ago it was frogs followed by lice, flies, and last Tuesday, locusts, and now moving in from the SSE, boils. Further outlook for Egypt, well, two or three days of thick darkness lying over the face of the whole land, followed by the death of all the first born.
>   Sorry about that, Egypt.

After the show Humphrey Barclay, a highly talented Harrovian Head Boy who could act, direct, and draw cartoons, introduced me to John Cleese, a very tall man with black hair and piercing dark eyes. They were very complimentary and encouraged me to audition for the Footlights. I had never heard of this University Revue Club, founded in 1883 to perform sketches and comedy shows, but it seemed like a fun thing to do, and a month later Jonathan Lynn and I were voted in by the Committee, after performing to a packed crowd of comedy buffs in the Footlights' Club Room. Jonathan, a talented actor, writer, and jazz drummer, would go on to direct *Pass the Butler,* my first play in the West End, and also write and direct *Nuns on the Run,* a movie with me and Robbie Coltrane. The audition sketch I had written for us played surprisingly well and, strange details, in the front row, lounging on a sofa, laughing with some Senior Fellows, was the author Kingsley

Amis, next to the brother of the soon-to-be-infamous Guy Burgess, who would shortly flee the country, outed as perhaps the most flamboyant of all the Cambridge spies—for whenever he was outrageously drunk in Washington, which was every night, he would announce loudly to everybody that he was a KGB spy. Nobody believed him.

I soon adapted to Footlights Club life. We had our own bar, which opened at ten at night and stayed open as long as we wanted. Lunches were provided on the premises and twice a term there were "Smoking Concerts," where you could try out material. I soon learned a very valuable lesson, for one day I picked up a headmaster sketch written by John and read it and didn't find it very amusing. That night he performed it and absolutely killed. He brought the place to a standstill. So much is *how* you do it. That was the most valuable thing about the Footlights, learning the art of writing and performing by watching and doing. That year's Annual Revue, which ran for two weeks at the Cambridge Arts Theatre, was the funniest thing I had seen since *Beyond the Fringe.* It was called *A Clump of Plinths,* a very Cleese kind of title, and John stood out head and shoulders amongst a great cast. Unlike the others, he never ever let on that he was being funny. He was always deadly serious, the deadest of deadpans. I watched in sheer joy. The show toured the U.K. and was then picked up by producer Michael White and put into the West End under the title *Cambridge Circus.* By that time a tall, gangly, pipe-smoking Graham Chapman had joined the cast. He had studied medicine at Cambridge and was now at St. Barts Hospital, where he was learning to become a fully qualified alcoholic. He also became a doctor, something he frequently warned us about. "Always remember doctors are just ex–medical students." He was very funny, and odd in a deeply serious way.

Oh, and finally the condom got used, after a Pembroke Players party where a Belgian wardrobe mistress showed me how to wear it and kindly removed me of the burden of enforced chastity, showing me that so often show business is about sex. This was a double kindness, as I had been fending off an aggressive marital attack from a determined Northern Teachers Training College lass, who grudgingly gave up bases, each base surrendered after more compromising promises on my part. Luckily, I realized her game was to have sex only after marriage and she was planning to take me home to Blackpool to meet her mother. I fled. Overseas.

The previous year, in the summer of 1962, just before going up to Cambridge, I had set off hitchhiking through France and Germany with my friend Alan Sinfield. We carried rucksacks and slept in sleeping bags in fields and half-built houses on building sites, heading optimistically for Vienna. We'd been having pretty good fortune with rides when, on the Autobahn entrance just outside Stuttgart, we were picked up by a young German couple in a black Mercedes.

"Where are you heading?"

"Vienna."

"How about Munich?"

"Wonderful."

It was a great ride, though the man and his young, apple-cheeked girlfriend didn't say very much. We stopped for lunch and he generously paid for everything.

"You're heading for Vienna? Hey, why don't we stay overnight in Munich and I'll take you on to Vienna tomorrow? Tonight, we'll dine at the Hofbrauhaus."

"Sounds amazing. Gee, thanks."

He checked us into a little pensione in Munich. Two twin rooms for the night. One for him and his girl, one for us. Fabulous.

"I'm just going to gas the car and then I'll take you to dinner. Okay?"

"Okay."

Too busy believing in our own good fortune, we hadn't even brought the baggage out of the car yet, but his girlfriend was with us, so what could go wrong?

He didn't return.

Two hours passed. Something was not right.

"Where the hell is he?" we finally demanded of his girlfriend.

She broke down in tears.

She didn't know him. She wasn't his girlfriend. He'd picked her up in Pforzheim just before Stuttgart, where he stopped to pick us up.

"What?"

"Shit."

So, he'd gone, with our rucksacks and everything we owned in the world: passports, traveler's checks, clothing, underwear, sleeping bags, the lot.

Shit, shit, shit.

The girl was in tears. We had no money. We had to go to the local police with the weeping Fräulein. They took notes and shrugged. We must go to the British Embassy. But it was Friday evening; it wouldn't open again until Monday. What were we to do? They shrugged. Farewell to the nice pensione. Alan and I had only the clothes on our backs. We slept rough for three nights in the parks and the Munich train station. Finally, on Monday morning we were issued with temporary visas by the British Embassy and given a little cash to get home. We hitched back the way we came, telling our sad tale. The Germans who stopped were all embarrassed by what had happened to us. They went out of their way to be nice, paying for meals and even inviting us into their homes. Broke and baggageless, we slunk back to England. We never saw Vienna.

Still, *"Schau immer auf die Sonnenseite des Lebens."**

Interestingly, we got our rucksacks back. Turns out the man was a North German criminal on the run from Hamburg, wanted by the police. We were probably good cover for him. Eventually they caught him in Italy.

Undeterred by our first experience, we decided to try hitchhiking to Germany again the following year. This time we set out a little more prepared. Alan had some relatives in Berlin who offered us a room, so we hitched as far as Nuremberg, where we stood on the reviewing stand at the national parade grounds where Hitler had stood and did our Charlie Chaplin impersonations. This was as far as we could go. The only way to get to Berlin was through communist East Germany, so we booked ourselves a bus ride.

We should have wondered what was up when we were immediately

---

* "Always look on the bright side of life."

pulled off the bus and roughly searched by the East German border guards, who interrogated us as to the point of our visit. Two English boys with nothing very much on them; why were they so interested? We had seen no newspapers in three weeks. We found ourselves the only people in Germany totally ignorant of the fact that U.S. president John F. Kennedy was paying a state visit to Berlin the very next day at the height of the Cold War. We were inadvertently at the center of the world.

Alan's relatives greeted us warmly and we even had beds. Next day we lined the streets with thousands of Berliners to watch the cavalcade go by, sixteen limos of Secret Service followed by seventeen limos of press. Finally, they appeared: Konrad Adenauer, the West German chancellor, and Willy Brandt, the legendary mayor of West Berlin, standing up in the back of an open vehicle flanking the smiling JFK. I remember the shock of his hair, and how surprised I was by his very ruddy appearance. The Germans went nuts. We went home and watched the famous *"Ich bin ein Berliner"* speech live on TV. Within an hour, flyers and cards and posters with this slogan appeared on the streets. Turns out he had less than four months to live.

The next day, East German leader Walter Ulbricht visited East Berlin, and the day after that tensions were high as we slipped though Checkpoint Charlie on a closely guarded tour bus to visit the bleak industrial workers' paradise, which did so much to make one grateful for the West, where you could be theoretically left-wing without having to suffer for it. We rode past a series of ugly 1950s flats. At a distance, Hitler's bunker, and at the end of every street, always *die Mauer:* the Wall.

Safely back in West Berlin, we discovered that the Pembroke Players were in town, giving performances of *Macbeth*. We went along to say hello. Oddly, they had a telegram for me. *In Berlin?* It was from the Footlights, from Humphrey Barclay. *Cambridge Circus* was such a success in the West End that they weren't going to be able to make their Edinburgh Festival booking, so Humphrey wanted me to do it with him and Graeme Garden. I was to report immediately to Cambridge for rehearsals!

4

SHOWBIZ!

Summer term in Cambridge. Always the best of times. The colleges were out and there were lots of girls about in their summer frocks. The exquisite couple Gita and Sonny Mehta (he, later a distinguished publisher at Picador in London and Knopf in New York, and she, a respected author) held court in their superior digs, packed with books, while I lived in a tiny room above a smelly restaurant as we rehearsed for three weeks in the Footlights Club.

Edinburgh was a blast. We all dossed in a walk-up sixth-floor cold-water flat, but finally this was showbiz. At the tender age of twenty I made my first television appearance on Scottish TV's *Festival Special,*

Humphrey Barclay and me performing John Cleese's "Secret Service" on *Festival Special.*

with Humphrey Barclay, the director of *Cambridge Circus*. Doing a John Cleese sketch, naturally . . .

Footlights '63 was a sold-out smash, mainly because we had all the best sketches from the Footlights' West End hit. Harold Hobson of *The Sunday Times* said, "They attract admiration as effortlessly as the sun attracts the flowers," which was nice of him because the next night we nearly killed him as all the sets collapsed when the revolving stage utterly failed to revolve in the world premiere of Henry Miller's only play, *Just Wild About Harry,* directed by Stephen Frears. This legendary disaster had brought all the London critics up to Edinburgh.

The Cambridge Amateur Dramatic Club had discovered that Henry Miller once wrote a play that had never been produced. Nothing would prevent them from giving a world premiere to this piece at the Edinburgh Festival. Being Cambridge, they had decided to turn an old Baptist church into a modern theater complete with a revolving stage. For six weeks, heavily bearded men sawed and hammered away, but by opening night it was clear that neither the theater nor the stage was ready, and there was nothing to do but delay. Being Cambridge, they had thought about that too. Holding a press conference, they said that the "very minor changes" demanded by the local Watch Committee (who censored plays and public performances in Scotland) were so egregious that they must first contact Henry Miller to see if he would even permit them.

There was some delay in contacting Henry Miller in California. When he was finally reached, not only did he seem surprised anyone was putting on his play, but he had no objection to whatever they wanted to do with it. So that was alright. For Cambridge, a perfect storm in a teacup. They could go ahead. Headlines were written, tickets were sold, and the play would open on the morrow. Except it didn't. The first scene passed safely enough as I, who had been co-opted into the play amongst the thespians, exchanged a few words with a specially engaged professional little person, while we pretended to paint an apartment in San Francisco. Okay, she was a female acting a male, but it's not that easy to find short people on short notice for amateur productions of unwanted Henry Miller plays. And Cambridge has always been notoriously gender-lax. And a jolly good thing too. Still, so far so good, the audience applauded dutifully. But the theatrical dream ended at the same time as the scene. The revolving stage refused to revolve. Twenty minutes passed. Of pushing, shoving, heaving, and cursing. No matter how many pushers and shovers and heavers and cursers, the stage stayed firmly locked in place. The actors in the next scene remained firmly offstage. Finally, with one last desperate heave, the revolving stage lurched; the heavy flats began to shake and then slowly collapsed into each other like a pile of dominoes. The theater critics fled up the aisle for their lives, leaving poor Harold Hobson alone up front in his wheelchair. Henry Miller's only play was dead. That show lasted only one night, but our revue was a different story. We were a big hit.

We naturally checked out our rivals, the Oxford Revue. Where we appeared bright and frothy onstage, they were cool and sardonic. They also had girls. Bastards. They did something called Rejects Night, where they took sketches that hadn't quite made it, and tried them out on an audience after their main show. This meant we could go along after our own show, and it was here that I first met the lovely, funny Terry Jones. Dark-haired, deadpan, handsome, with the looks of the movie star Anthony Newley, he too brought a tremendous seriousness to everything he did, including singing a song which sounds like an early precursor of "The Lumberjack Song."

> I was Miss World from 1907 to '24 . . .
> I was Miss World, lovely belle amour . . .

Totally ignoring the transgender implications, it lamented the fact that, sadly, age meant:

> No one wants to see me, anymore.

Next summer Terry would go on to star in the West End in the Oxford Revue *Hang Down Your Head and Die,* a bitter polemic against capital punishment. Oxford, as always, was far more serious about everything.

A year later in Edinburgh, in 1964, I met the unforgettable Michael Palin, who had joined Terry Jones in the Oxford cast. I first saw him onstage and he bowled me over. He did an extended character monologue about an old Northern performer who came on to begin his terrible act with an appalling song, only to notice that on the stage beside him was a large gift-wrapped present. He tried to ignore it but couldn't, and stopped his song to take a look at it.

He read the label out loud.

"To Mikey, with love from the audience."

He was overcome.

"Oh, every people. I'm touched. I'm speechless. This is so special for me. I had thought perhaps my act was over, and that people didn't care anymore; that somehow, I was too old and nobody remembered me. But now this. From you. The audience. It means so much to me. Well, there's only one thing I can do to thank you, and that's to sing my song, 'When Love Breaks Your Heart in a Million Tiny Pieces.'"

With tears in his eyes, barely able to restrain himself, he began to sing.

When love, breaks your heart, in a million tiny pieces—

Boom! The present exploded.

The look on his face as he quietly limped offstage was brilliant; and that's Michael Palin, really. He writes real character sketches and acts them with genuine emotion. I became very aware of this writing talent of Michael's when I was adapting *Spamalot* for the stage from *The Holy Grail.* I loved putting in Mike's writing, because it was always character-driven.

"What, ridden on a *horse*? You're using coconuts . . ."

"One day, lad, all this will be yours."

"What, the curtains?"

"*Not* the curtains, lad."

Albeit unknowingly, by September 1964 all the future Pythons (save for the wild-card American animator) had met and admired each other.

5

GATESHEAD REVISITED

With no threatening finals, the second year of Cambridge was fun. After Edinburgh, we were the big stars of the Footlights and it was even profitable. Graeme Garden and I drove around the country every weekend in our dinner jackets with David Gooderson, a man who became famous for doing a one-man show where he outnumbered the audience, and Jim Beach as our pianist, playing cabaret at various Hunt Balls, May Balls, Debutantes' Balls, and Upper Class Social Events. Usually performing two a weekend, we pulled in twenty-five quid a week for four of us, three performers and a pianist. Decent money for those days. How do we know some people will recur throughout our lives? Jim was irresistible. Today he manages Monty Python. And Queen. Jim led the band in our Edinburgh show, *Footlights '63*, and then ran a "debs' delight" band called the Autocrats for many years, which included a Peer of the Realm on drums.

I had realized early in my first year that I didn't have to attend lectures; it was our *opinions* they wanted, and provided I read the books I could supply plenty of them. So, unencumbered by hard work, my social life was glorious and involved fine sherry, pubs and punting, and lots of vinous games of croquet. I used to refer to this life as *Gateshead Revisited*. Jim had a propensity for outrageous suits in bright orange and lime green, which he wore with floppy hats. I remember one spectacular night walking back from his college, Queens, to my digs near Pembroke with Jim wearing an outrageous lavender suit. We had been drinking. Jim had climbed up and was precariously walking along the parapet of the Silver Street Bridge above the River Cam at about four in the morning.

"I want a fuck!" he suddenly yelled at the top of his lungs.

"Shhh, Jim," I said, "it's late."

"You want a fuck too," he bellowed, "you're just quiet about it!"

Then two events changed the world. John F. Kennedy was shot in Dallas, and the Beatles came through Cambridge. In America, a monochrome world of grief gradually slipped into outrage as Vietnam put its fatal grip on America. There were civil rights marches in Selma and Alabama. Back in the U.K. the drab postwar era was passing; black-and-white Britain suddenly turned into color. We were no longer young undergraduates in Harris tweed jackets with elbow patches, we were part of a movement. The Sixties. We bought black collarless Beatle jackets. We were first in line for their singles, we discussed our favorite Beatle, we adored "A Hard Day's Night." Suddenly England started to matter. And swing. A bit.

That summer, my friend Carey Harrison, a tall, handsome fellow English student from Jesus College ("What a friend we have in Jesus," we would say about him), introduced me to the joys of the French countryside when we took a train down to the Dordogne. We sat reading Dickens in the soft June sunshine, attended floodlit cycle races in the streets of a French village, and rode to the local fetes in the ubiquitous Deux Chevaux. We even played cricket in the square at Monpazier. It was heaven. Carey, now an English lecturer, playwright, and novelist, was a polymath. I watched him on the train home in one railway carriage carry on four simultaneous conversations—with a Frenchwoman in French, an Italian businessman in Italian, a German traveler in German, and me in my demotic English—in his deeply rich Harrovian voice not a million miles away from that of his matinee idol papa, Sexy Rexy. I had several older friends too. I particularly liked Aussies and Yanks, usually because they had already done degrees, but also because they were funny. By the time he arrived on his Fulbright scholarship from Yale, my friend Stephen Greenblatt had already published a book:

Three Modern Satirists on Waugh, Orwell, and Huxley. Recently, when I interviewed him for Writers Bloc Presents at Temple Emanuel in Beverly Hills about his book *The Swerve,* the medieval discovery of Lucretius's extraordinary poem "On the Nature of Things," he said that he had known me for many years, but for him the greatest achievement of the evening was finally getting me into a synagogue!

My friend Jim Beach became a lawyer at Harbottle & Lewis, and years later when we won a lawsuit against ABC and the BBC in New York for airing butchered versions of *Monty Python's Flying Circus* without our approval, he advised us *not* to accept the two million pounds on offer but to ask instead for our masters. This brilliant piece of advice earned us everything: ownership and worldwide control over our TV series. It means that, including movies, Python now owns almost everything we ever made. We may be silly but we're not stupid.

In my final year at Cambridge I became president of Footlights. Appointed by the outgoing president (Graeme Garden) and Senior Fellows, I got to wear a faded, tattered pink dinner jacket at Smoking Concerts, appoint my committee, organize our cabarets, and take care of business, ensuring the smooth running of the club.

As if to prove you shouldn't allow lower-class boys into positions of power, I single-handedly altered the rules of this 1883 organization to permit women to join as members, to the unhappiness of several older dons who thought I was ruining the club. I wrote a letter to Harry Porter, the Senior Treasurer, demanding women be admitted to full membership in the Footlights:

> I think it is degrading and fantastically backward looking
> that women should not have the same opportunities at Uni-
> versity as men, and it is rather sad that the Footlights lag even
> behind the union in this.

I am still proud of that. It would be several years before the colleges themselves followed suit. The very first woman admitted to the Footlights was Germaine Greer. It's odd that Germaine should have gone on to write *The Female Eunuch*, as she had the biggest balls of any woman I have ever known. She was hilarious. Her audition piece was a stripping nun that brought the house down. She had come as a mature student from the University of Melbourne, where she told me she performed what she called "virgin duty," sexually liberating first-year students. Soon after she left Cambridge she would become the first lecturer at Warwick University to appear on the cover of *Suck* magazine. I adored her. She was with me in my final Footlights revue, which toured the U.K. for a few weeks. She bet me she could sleep with every single member of our tour. I won. She got stuck on the horn player.

Germaine had come through the Footlights door with Clive James, and we became friends. He introduced me to his poetry and Brett Whiteley drawings, and I observed his unceasing pursuit of the female. His father, too, had not returned from the war. I found I unconsciously bonded with several people like that, including Germaine and Harry Nilsson.

Our puzzlingly titled and not particularly funny revue *My Girl Herbert* limped into London and floundered after three weeks at the Lyric Theatre in Hammersmith. John Cameron, a leather-jacketed rocker who played crazy piano and sang like Ray Charles, joined me in a duo and we were picked up as a musical cabaret act by the Noel Gay Organization. They immediately booked us into the Blue Angel, a nightclub catering to Guards officers, where we triumphed on opening night and then faded quickly throughout the week. Upper-class twits brayed drunkenly during our set, while trying to paw their Kensington girlfriends. As we progressively died each night, John Cameron slid further and further behind his piano until he was finally totally hidden and I was left alone onstage to face the hoorays. It was the end of our less than dynamic duo, and I went off to Leicester Rep to perform in a musical, *Oh, What a Lovely War!*, directed by Richard Eyre, another contemporary. The Phoenix Theatre, Leicester, surprisingly asked me to stay on for their Christmas production, where I learned I was not cut out for acting. I just don't have the patience for it. Their holiday offering was a Ray Cooney farce about a butler called *One for the Pot*, and I became

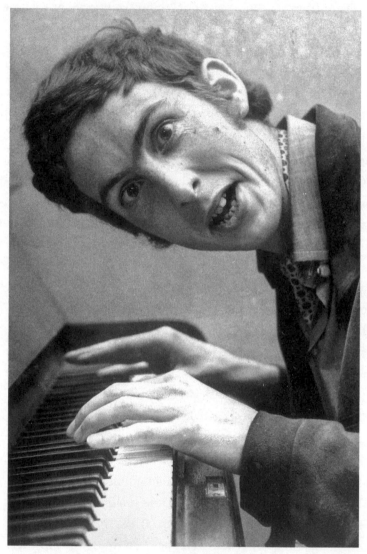

The author pretending to play the piano.
One of the many skills he lacks.

so bored that I began writing scripts backstage in my dressing room for a new BBC Radio comedy series produced by Humphrey Barclay, called *I'm Sorry, I'll Read That Again,* which starred John Cleese, Bill Oddie, Tim Brooke-Taylor, and Graeme Garden, the returning alums from Broadway. One night, engrossed in writing comedy, I noticed that the theater had fallen silent, and Richard Simpson, the very calm leading actor, was looking over my shoulder.

"How's the writing going, Eric?"

"Oh, fine thanks."

"Good. Funny?"

"Not bad."

"Good. Look, I'm sorry to bother you but would you mind joining me onstage?"

Shit! The silence was the empty stage. I was "off." Richard, who could only remember the next scene by who came on, had finally figured out that the absence of anyone entering at all must mean me, and calmly came to find me. Oops. The Leicester audience seemed to enjoy the empty stage as much as the play. I was not asked to stay on. Fortunately, Humphrey Barclay liked my radio scripts, and wanted more. So I set off for London to see what the Sixties were all about. Mainly, I suspected, other people having a far better time than me.

In January 1966, I began life in London with a long-lasting case of mono (glandular fever), which left me debilitated but still able to write. I spent so much time in bed that I started the Micky Baker Complete Course in Jazz Guitar, which taught me all the sneaky funky chords I eventually used in "Bright Side." I liked all the diminisheds and major and minor sixths and sevenths. The chords I could read from the tablature, but I gave up when I got to the dots.

Thanks to Humph, I was now a professional scriptwriter, as *I'm Sorry, I'll Read That Again* paid me three guineas a minute for my material, and we would congregate on Sunday nights at the Playhouse, the BBC's Radio Comedy theater, where the recordings took place before a large and wildly overenthusiastic crowd, after which we'd all hang out with the cast at the Sherlock Holmes Pub.

There were occasional forays into acting. I was chosen by Ken Russell to play the Death Chauffeur in the BBC TV production of *Isadora*, accidentally drowning her children in the Seine in a tragic car accident, and then sitting on top of a hearse with Michael Palin and Terry Jones as a jazz band, while she had sex inside with a wild Russian poet. I was co-opted to play a slow loris in the Pool of Tears in Jonathan Miller's *Alice in Wonderland*, which enabled me to hang out with my heroes—Jonathan, Alan Bennett, Peter Cook, and Dudley Moore—as well as an incredible cast, including Peter Sellers, Wilfrid Lawson, and Michael Redgrave. It was halfway through the Sixties, the birth control pill had begun its work of female sexual liberation, and the party was definitely starting . . .

Ah, the Sixties. A beautiful blonde I was crazy about generously gave me hepatitis wriggling around on a naugahyde sofa, and a sweet hippie girl kindly shared a mild sexual disease which sent me embarrassingly to a clinic. My relentless pursuit of women was perhaps understandable after being locked up for twelve years, but it meant that while I never got to understand the Female outside of the bedroom, at least I was getting a fairly healthy introduction to her anatomy. I was well on my way to becoming the Artful Nudger.

"Is your wife a goer, know what I mean, nudge nudge, know what I mean?"

6

THE ARTFUL NUDGER

David Frost had plucked John Cleese from the shipwreck of the extremely funny *Cambridge Circus* revue, which had foundered on Broadway thanks to a panning in *The New York Times*. David, although a poor performer himself, was always at pains to surround himself with funny men, and he knew the value of having good material. His unexpected call to John Cleese in New York asking him to be on *The Frost Report* secured John's future in television, away from his mother's ambitions to make him manager of a Weston-super-Mare Marks & Spencer. Grocery's loss was comedy's gain.

Frostie gave all of us great jobs as writers on his new BBC TV show, for which we remained highly ungrateful. Suddenly, almost straight out of college, we were all part of a big hit. *The Frost Report* broadcast live once a week from the BBC Television Theatre in Shepherd's Bush. Its hilarious cast of Ronnie Barker, Ronnie Corbett, Sheila Steafel, and John Cleese performed sketches on a weekly theme (education, politics, art) linked by what David rather pretentiously called CDM (Continually Developing Monologue) and which John and Graham contemptuously called OJARIL (Old Jokes And Ridiculously Irrelevant Links). Amazingly, at twenty-three I was a writer on this very funny show. Where I had been paid three guineas a minute to write for BBC Radio, now I wrote gags and sketches for BBC TV at ten guineas a minute. I had money in my pocket, a car, girls, and an agent: Roger Hancock, brother of the legendary British comedian Tony Hancock, who gave me this invaluable advice: *Be available.* And so, I was: for money, sex, and showbiz. I lived in a top-floor flat in Notting Hill Gate and lunched at the Sun in Splendour in the Portobello Road, listening to customers at the bar quoting my jokes from last night's TV. I soon learned the comparative value of writing and writers. On the day of the show a taxi came for my gags; I had to go by Tube.

When *The Frost Report* won the Golden Rose of Montreux, it was my karate joke they showed on BBC TV News. My cup ranneth over.

David Frost now asked me, Graham Chapman, and Barry Cryer to create a TV sitcom for Ronnie Corbett called *No—That's Me Over Here!* Graham had graduated from St. Barts Hospital and he now wrote professionally with John. They had recombined with Tim Brooke-Taylor in an extremely funny late-night comedy show produced by David, called *At Last the 1948 Show,* in which I would play small parts each week. John had asked for Marty Feldman to be in it, but David had balked about casting Marty. "What about his looks?" he asked, but John's will prevailed. And he was right: Marty was an instant star. After two short seasons of this brilliantly funny comedy, Marty went off to the BBC to do his own series. I loved Marty. He and his wife, Lauretta, took me under their wings and, on Sundays, to live recordings of *Round the Horne,* England's most popular radio series, which Marty wrote with Barry Took. I once found him and John Cleese in a street laughing their heads off. They had just come across two very attractive young ladies bent over, searching the pavement.

"What are you doing?" they asked.

"We're looking for a screw," said one of the ladies.

Collapse of hysterical comedians.

Legendary television scriptwriter Barry Cryer had mentored me as a young writer, along with Dick Vosburgh, on *The Frost Report.* He seemed to have an endless supply of gag books. Often, while Barry and I wrote for Ronnie Corbett, Graham would be absent writing the '48 *Show.* One day we called and asked to speak to him because we had a plot problem we needed his thoughts on.

"But he's with you," said a puzzled Tim Brooke-Taylor.

"Er, no, he's with you . . ."

But of course he was with neither, having sneaked off to Hampstead, where he had a boyfriend hidden. He had met David Sherlock in Ibiza, where he and John were writing a movie, and had fallen in love, secretly moved into an apartment with him in Hampstead, and concealed all this for a year. Finally, all was revealed at a coming-out party where the first person I saw was Graham's female "fiancée" in tears.

"This is the man I'm in love with," said Graham, introducing David to me.

Of course. Now it all made sense. *That's where he was!* Unfortunately, Graham misread my thoughts for disapproval and wrote later that I seemed not to know what a homosexual was; hardly likely after twelve years of boarding school, three years of Cambridge, six months in rep, two years at the BBC, and currently living upstairs from *Gay News* in Redcliffe Square. I clearly remember my thoughts at the party. *You bastard! You were up in Hampstead knobbing when you were supposed to be writing with us.* Anyway, David Sherlock is a very nice man and Graham lived happily with him for the rest of his life. Marty called us all next day and said, "Don't stop making the gay jokes."

A few years later I got this letter about Graham:

Liverpool
Merseyside

25/10/74
To Mr. E. Idle

Dear Sir,

On the 18th July 1960, I was in St. Elizabeth's Church, when Our Lord Jesus Christ, appeared to me. He showed me how He created us, with the middle finger of His left hand. He pointed to a white cloud of dust!

There was a man, he wouldn't give his name but he said he was out of Monty Pythons Flying Circus, he was being interviewed on the television, and said he was a homosexual.

In the Holy Bible Leviticus page 102 Paragraph 20 verse 13, God says "If a man lies with a male as with a woman, both of them have committed an abomination; they shall be put to death, their blood is upon them."

"Praise be to thee O Lord"

God bless you.

Mrs. B. Campbell

I wrote back.

To Mrs. B. Campbell
BBC TV Centre
Shepherds Bush
London

24/11/1974

Dear Mrs. Campbell,

Thank you very much for your letter.

We have found out who it was, and have put him to death.

Yours sincerely,

Eric Idle

Another momentous phone call from Humphrey Barclay once again changed my life. Would I like to write and perform in a kids' sketch show on ITV? *Hell, yeah.* I sensibly asked if I could have Michael Palin and Terry Jones. He agreed, they agreed, and suddenly we were starring in our own TV series, with David Jason and Denise Coffey. Sure, it was only for kids, but we decided that we would not talk down to them. We would just do what we found funny. Humph brought in the Bonzo Dog Doo Dah Band, an eccentric group of ex–art school students who performed downright weird songs with Vivian Stanshall as lead singer and Neil Innes on piano. I'm sure Python gained a surreal boost from this encounter with the Bonzos, a bizarre Dadaist orchestra. For two whole seasons, we Oxbridge boys collided with the best of British art schools, as they came in weekly from the rigors of the road to commandeer the hair dryers in the makeup room. Their mad, whimsical, wonderful music meshed perfectly with our straight-faced determination not to talk down to our kids' audience.

Terry Jones, Denise Coffey, Michael Palin, David Jason, and me in
Do Not Adjust Your Set.

One day a strange-looking American with long hair, who looked a bit like singer-songwriter John Denver, wearing a yak-skin Afghan coat, came back after a show to meet us. It was love at first sight. I loved that coat. He brought an exotic girlfriend and some sketches, both written and drawn. He had been sent to Humphrey Barclay by John Cleese, whom he'd met in New York, and he wanted to work on our show. Mike and Terry disliked him at once. What on earth did we need another writer for, and an *American*? Was I nuts? I don't know why, but I was convinced he had something, and it wasn't just his exotic coat. Luckily they listened to me, and Terry Gilliam entered our lives, soon finding his métier making short animations, including the magnificent "Christmas Cards" and a weirder one called "Elephants," whose stream-of-consciousness flow would eventually form the basis for Monty Python.

Do Not Adjust Your Set was a big hit from the start. We began on the Rediffusion channel in black and white, winning the Prix Jeunesse in Munich, and when that company lost its license we were picked up by its successor, Thames Television, for a second series, this time in color. Our time slot of 5:25 p.m. meant that not only did we get kids, we got all the waiters in London, and a decent proportion of adults coming home from work early. Two of those who always stopped work to watch were John Cleese and Graham Chapman. They thought it was the funniest thing on television. One day in 1969 they called and asked if we'd like to join them in a show for the BBC to provide quirky alternative viewing for late-night Sunday audiences after the pubs closed. By then we had a serious offer for our own ninety-minute grown-up prime-time show on ITV, but unfortunately we had to wait eighteen months for a studio, so we decided we might as well fit in the BBC thing with John and Graham while we were waiting for our big break . . .

So began Monty Python.

As you see, when I started Monty Python I had a very small head.

7

AND NOW FOR SOMETHING SLIGHTLY COMPLETELY DIFFERENT

So much has been written about *Monty Python*. There have been memoirs, diaries, books about the Pythons, books by the Pythons about the other Pythons, articles about the books about the Pythons, countless interviews, autobiographies, documentaries ... *so many* documentaries. I honestly think there are more hours of documentary about *Python* than there are hours of *Python*. So, to the mass of mangled memories do I now add my own muddled, prejudiced, and deeply cynical account of what I think might have happened? Of course. But you, dear reader, who have already parted with far too much money on this book, can feel free to skip ahead to the dirty bits.*

George Harrison once said to me, "If we'd known we were going to be the Beatles we would have tried harder." I think the same could be said of *Monty Python*. How on earth could we possibly know we would become *them*? At the time, we were only doing another show, and a fill-in show at that, while we waited for our big break on ITV. Who decides these things? The gods of television, or a little old lady in a cottage near Luton? Well, obviously the latter, but she's very hard to find.

Why was *Monty Python* so successful? Was it *really* so very different? Of course it wasn't. People seem to think that it somehow sprang full-blown from the head of some mad media Medusa, but that's not

---

* Fat chance. There aren't any.

true at all. In the mid-Sixties, there were a host of similar shows all evolving, banging into each other and disintegrating: *The Frost Report; I'm Sorry, I'll Read That Again; Twice a Fortnight; Broaden Your Mind; How to Irritate People; The Complete and Utter History of Britain* . . . All of the eventual Pythons were involved with all of the eventual Goodies in one show or another. *Monty Python* itself was the result of a collision between *Do Not Adjust Your Set* and *At Last the 1948 Show,* when the creators of the former (me, Mike Palin, Terry Jones, and Terry Gilliam) rammed into the remnants of the latter (John Cleese and Graham Chapman).

So, of all the TV shows on air at the end of the Sixties, what made Python so successful? Well, we were young. We were ready. We had done Malcolm Gladwell's recommended ten thousand hours of preparation. (See *Outliers.*) We were digital, and we were in color—only by a few months, but that was vitally important. *Python* began right at the start of the digital era, which meant that fifty years later the show physically still doesn't look as dated as it would had it been shot in black and white and on film. Thanks to new technology we can polish the dots, so that visually the show looks even fresher today than it did when it was first transmitted back in the Stoned Age. Additionally, we were both the writers *and* the performers, though the writers were definitely in charge. Importantly, the show is encyclopedic. *Python* isn't just one type of humor, it is a compendium of styles. While the cast remains the same, the writers are constantly changing, though you never notice which hand is on the tiller. So there is visual humor, verbal humor, clever humor, silliness, rudeness, sophistication, and brazen naughtiness, constantly alternating, which means there is something for everyone. I found that while people said they liked it, not everyone could agree on which particular bits they liked. Also, we were at the BBC, who opened up a new time slot for us late on Sunday nights, when the Queen normally came on-screen sitting on a horse and television closed down. They didn't know it, but there were a whole lot of people who liked to stay up after the pubs closed. I often joke about "executive-free comedy," but the BBC really did leave us alone, especially at the beginning, and by the time they wanted to intrude it was too late. Plus, we could be physically daunting. Six large men, three over six foot, occupying a BBC office were enough to intimidate the bravest program planner, even if we hadn't already established on our show that we considered them foolish, ignorant, hopeless idiots, without degrees . . . The fact is, we scared them. We didn't know what we were doing, and insisted on doing it.

The legendary chaotic Python first meeting with Michael Mills, the head of Light Entertainment, did take place at the BBC on May 23, 1969. We had met previously at John's apartment in Basil Street, so we were not entirely unprepared, but we had reached no agreement on anything. That state would persist till the end. We couldn't agree on the title of the show. We didn't know whether there would be music (er, *perhaps*) or guests (er, *maybe*) or film (*oh yes film,* good idea). In the end, faced with our confident uncertainty about what might be in our show, Michael Mills finally said, "Oh just go away and make thirteen." We could do what we liked, but what would it be? Even we had no idea.

On *Do Not Adjust Your Set,* Terry Gilliam had created highly surreal animations in a free-flowing style that inspired Terry Jones to proclaim that this was how our new BBC show should be. These arresting animations bookmarked the Python show, and added a stylish Victorian framework that provided apparent connections between completely disparate sketch material. No punch lines, everything would just flow. This, and our attempts to link skits by ideas, theme, and content, made *Monty Python* something slightly completely different from the start. Even though we didn't know what we wanted, we knew absolutely what we didn't want. We were determined not to make the usual kind of BBC light entertainment show where someone said, "And now for something completely different" and some prick sang. In fact, so determined were we not to do that, we co-opted their very slogan and used it as a catchphrase. We were the antithesis of the satire boom of the previous generation. Nothing was topical (so it could last) and the comedy was generic: types not individuals. But it was our attitude that came across. Python was in your face, challenging, and very silly. It was not immediately popular, there were complaints, the executives hated it, but it filled a hole in their schedule and the BBC wisely ignored the disapproval. So, *Owl Stretching Time* began. So, *A Horse, a Spoon and a Basin* started. So, *Whither Canada?* commenced. So, *The Toad Elevating Moment* came into being. So, *You Can't Call a Show Cornflakes* appeared. We still had no title for the show. The BBC were going nuts. In their contracts, they called it *Barry Took's Flying Circus,* because he had set up the fatal meeting. But each of our scripts that came in had a different, and to their minds worse, title. Finally, in late July, with the series already filming, they presented us with an ultimatum. They had to print tickets for the audience. They must have a title.

We all liked *Flying Circus,* but we couldn't agree on whose Circus it should be. Michael wanted to surprise a little old lady in Suffolk called Gwen Dibley by naming the show after her, but while that was funny, there were legal issues. In the end John suggested *Python,* and I suggested *Monty* after a chap with a mustache and bow tie in my local pub, the Dog Inn, Mappleborough Green. *Monty* had echoes of the great British general Montgomery, who, at El Alamein, was the first to defeat the Nazis; as well as sounding like a sleazy Soho theatrical agent. So, *Monty Python* it was. But what was the show to be? We still hadn't a clue.

We tried discussing what it should be about, but failed hopelessly. So we just went ahead and wrote what we felt like and then came together at Jonesy's house in Camberwell and read out our sketches. If we laughed it was in, and if we didn't we sold it to *The Two Ronnies.* Fortunately, I had written one sketch for Ronnie Barker that had been turned down. If you read it silently it obviously has no jokes. "Is your wife a goer, know what I mean, nudge nudge, say no more, say no more, say no more, know what I mean, nudge nudge." Where's the comedy in that? But when I read it aloud *in character* they all hooted, and it was almost the first thing accepted by us.

We became fairly good at editing our material. "That sketch was really funny until page three and then it just went on and on." Honesty from people you trust is very useful, and often we would swap sketches around and let someone else have a go at finishing a piece. When it came to voting, I was always outnumbered. Mike and Terry were a team and John and Graham another, and when they read out their sketches they always had a partner to smile and laugh along. I faced five people. But then on the other hand I'm still with me. Terry Gilliam came in and out of the writing sessions and was a very useful free-floating radical. Early on we stopped him reading out his cartoon ideas, which consisted of a lot of *bangs,* and *booms,* and *biffs,* and told him to just go away and make them.

We never cast the shows until we had finished the writing, so we could not be influenced by any acting preferences. It was usually obvious who would play what, and the authors of the piece would get first dibs. John and Graham had settled into a kind of classic sketch form begun in *The Frost Report,* where John would be the aggressive protagonist responding to interruptions from a very silly man. (Marty played these roles in the *'48 Show,* but in *Python* Michael made a superb foil for him.) Graham played authoritarian but hopelessly weak figures responding helplessly to exterior chaotic forces (colonels, King Arthur, Brian, etc.). Terry Jones specialized in aggressively noisy, frumpy women, and Terry Gilliam was given anything that involved long and heavy makeup, so it was no surprise when he married Maggie Weston, our makeup lady. The rest of the characters, often a whole raft of them, were designated Mike or Eric, and then the authorship would decide who played what: Nudge for Eric, Ken Shabby for Mike.

Significantly, *Monty Python* was not released in America until 1974, after we had finished on U.K. TV, so we were not seduced by personal fame. We didn't have to cope with the hot blast of instant celebrity that the *Saturday Night Live* cast faced. With the exception of John Cleese, who was famous from *The Frost Report,* no one had a clue who was who. Looking back, it is amazing that John even wanted to be in another gang show, his fourth since leaving Cambridge—*I'm Sorry, I'll Read That Again; The Frost Report;* the *'48 Show;* and now *Monty Python.* In fact, he soon tired of *Python,* and no wonder: he had been writing and performing sketches on TV and radio since 1965.

In the meantime, I got married. I had fallen in love with a beautiful Australian actress called Lyn Ashley, whose painted breasts I first saw on a poster outside my local cinema advertising the Michael Winner film *I'll Never Forget What's'isname,* in which she starred with Oliver Reed. Some friends had set us up on a blind date for a weekend, in a wincingly cold Elizabethan mansion in Suffolk. The wind howled through it. The kitchen with its Aga stove seemed to be the only warm spot, and the house was infested by kids. We found the hostess was fighting with her husband, had taken to her bed, and refused to emerge from her bedroom. I enticed her out with a bottle of champagne. Some kind of order was restored. Lyn and I found a warm spot in the guest wing and became acquainted, while I fought off the blocking moves of her mother's poodle. We soon moved into my apartment in Redcliffe Square, flew off to Mihas in Spain, where I bought a ring, and one year later, in July 1969, when *Monty Python* commenced filming, I managed to wangle the first week off to get married. We were married in the Kensington and Chelsea Registry Office and my new mother-in-law,

Sixties Wedding Day, July 7, 1969. Matching Ossie Clark outfits.

Madge Ryan, threw a huge party at Adrienne Corri's house in St. John's Wood. (Both actresses had appeared together in Stanley Kubrick's *A Clockwork Orange*.) Then off we all went to the seaside. The Pythons to Devon, me to Nice. While the others took the bus to Torquay, I flew with my new bride to Cap d'Antibes, where Lauretta and Marty Feldman had invited us to join them.

Monty Python's Flying Circus began broadcasting on BBC1 at 10:55 p.m. on Sunday, October 5, 1969, with the second show we had recorded, subtitled *Whither Canada?* The original audience consisted largely of little old ladies who had been bused in to the BBC Television Centre thinking they were going to see some kind of a circus. Neither they nor we had a clue what they were in for. While there were some very funny sketches, there were also some very odd moments, like Terry Gilliam popping up in the middle of a sketch dressed as a Viking with a ferret through his head, saying "However." I think these were attempts by us to flex our muscles and experience the joys of this newfound freedom. We did them because we could. As if to keep us in our place, the BBC would unexpectedly take our show off the air from time to time and replace it with an episode of *The Horse of the Year Show*. Occasionally, different BBC regions put out their own local show instead. This led to some confusion amongst our audience, a confusion we were keen to exploit. We began to shoot false openings, in one case ten minutes of a totally fictitious pirate film before the buccaneers passed John Cleese at a table, who announced blandly, "And now for something completely different." It didn't matter. No one was watching. We could do it to make ourselves happy.

This sense of being apart, in a different TV world from the comforting domain of light entertainment, was very liberating, and oddly we began to attract a following. After the first season the BBC made us do a record, which was a disaster since they recorded it in front of a dead audience live on a Sunday morning in Camden Town Hall. None of us liked it, after which we simply made our own albums. The finest example of this was a three-sided record, *The Monty Python Matching Tie and Handkerchief,* where we ingeniously cut double grooves on Side

Two, to create two shorter, parallel sides. Which track played depended on where the needle dropped. There was no announcement or warning. To further puzzle listeners, we started both of these mini sides with the same bad gag—"And now a massage from the Swedish Prime Minister"—so they couldn't even try to find the side they wanted. Confusion was good.

We were still "outsiders" and rebellious. We took exception to BBC Light Entertainment inviting us to their Christmas party because the invitation said *Black Tie*. The first year we simply didn't attend, but the second year John Cleese and I determined to make a protest. We decided to go overdressed. We turned up at the BBC in top hats, white tie, and tails, complete with gloves and canes. Our arrival at the party caused quite a stir. Eric Morecambe came over to me and said, "John Cleese just bit me on the neck and flew out the window."

We all agreed that our show would never play in America. They just wouldn't understand it. And besides, with its nudity and its naughtiness it would never be allowed on TV there. So when some serious American TV producers approached us, we laughed. It appeared they wanted us to make our show for America. We laughed more. Alright then, could they buy our format? Now we really laughed.

"We don't have a format."

"Then let's *not* sell it to them."

We laughed even harder.

John's friend Victor Lownes, who ran the London Playboy Club, commissioned a movie from us of highlights from the first two seasons, because he felt there was an audience for *Python* in colleges and it should be a film. We shot *And Now for Something Completely Different* in an old dairy in Hendon for eighty thousand pounds. Our TV director, the wild Scotsman Ian MacNaughton, was appointed director. Ian had begun as an actor but had joined the BBC, where he became involved directing shows with Spike Milligan. This is what attracted him to us. He wasn't available for our first four TV recordings, and John Howard Davies had stepped in. As a young boy, Davies had played Oliver in David Lean's classic movie *Oliver Twist*.

"Please, sir, can I have some more?"

He would go on to direct *Fawlty Towers* for John Cleese, and Ian directed all our subsequent *Python* shows. It was Davies who brought Carol Cleveland into our show, when we needed a real woman to play the sex scene in my "Marriage Guidance Counselor" sketch. The gag just didn't work with a guy in drag, and Carol would remain a fixture whenever we wanted a real female. She was a jolly good sport and came on the road with us on our tours. *And Now for Something Completely Different* was the first of the movies she did for us.

MacNaughty, as we called him, was definitely "a Scottish loony" with a penchant for whiskey. John pilloried him mercilessly as a drunken director in "Scott of the Sahara," and then claimed it wasn't him at all but Joseph McGrath, another hard-drinking Scots director. Ian would be fine until lunchtime, when he could never resist going into the pub and then would have to go and lie down afterwards, so usually one of the Terrys took over. We weren't in charge of the final cut, none of us liked it, and it was memorable only for a controversy about a fart, when the American producer said:

"Keep the fart, you'll lose Disneyland."

We kept the fart.

Columbia ended up releasing the movie, and eventually Victor Lownes's boss Hugh Hefner bought it, so it had its uses getting us into the Playboy Mansion in the Eighties, when that seemed like a good idea.

In 1971, we tackled the publishing world when I took on the editing of *Monty Python's Big Red Book,* which naturally was blue, and then *The Brand New Monty Python Papperbok* (1973), whose cover deliberately contained grubby finger marks, so that people kept returning them to the booksellers. Terry Gilliam refused to have anything to do with the first book, snorting disdainfully, "Comic books don't sell." I suppose his experiences with Harvey Kurtzman's *Help* magazine in New York, where he drew cartoons and shot *fumetti,* had clouded his judgment. His assistant Katy Hepburn was helping me design the book and I had to get her to break into his studio and steal bits of his artwork.

Fortunately, Terry was wrong, as that first Python book flew off the shelves, into massive reprints, inventing the Christmas comedy book market.

Books, records, films, TV shows, slowly the Python tentacles wound around the neck of an unsuspecting public. I persuaded the Pythons to do a live stage show for three nights at midnight at the Lanchester Arts Festival in Coventry, selecting the sketches and putting together a show that we briefly rehearsed. The audiences went nuts. I think it was the first time they found that other people liked our show too. The BBC didn't pay us much, but after Coventry, Tony Smith and Harvey Goldsmith offered us a ton of money to tour the U.K., so we set off on the road. It was a fairly disastrous start, thanks to a stoner sound engineer who was in charge of our radio mikes. He hadn't a clue which of us was which, so you could clearly hear Graham in his dressing room but nobody onstage at all. We finally persuaded the management to dispose of him before we were forced to kill him, and the show soon got into a groove.

Graham's drinking, at first a secret, now came to the fore. Often he would be late onstage for his sketches, particularly with poor Mike waiting around to start Ken Shabby. Once, John and I heard the ominous silence from the audience and both leapt onstage at the same time from opposite sides. Then, as if we had rehearsed it, we fell in behind each other and played Graham's part in tandem, to the hilarity of Mike, who giggled helplessly. Finally, Graham came lurching on as the Colonel, seemed not to notice, and launched into the beginning of the sketch again. After the show, he was furious and accused me of upstaging him.

"But Graham," I said, "you weren't *on* stage."

He never said a word of complaint to John. The only time I ever saw him lose it was when John hid his pipe as a prank and Graham went totally berserk. (Yes, we *know*, Dr. Freud.) He was a very mild and patient man but the alcohol turned him into a beast. He would go crawling round the floor at parties, putting his hands up ladies' skirts and barking like a dog. It was great when he finally managed to conquer his alcoholism. John would occasionally bait Jonesy until he exploded in a fit of temper, but on the whole we got on very well for a group of six outsiders. Just look at the work we managed to achieve in the fourteen years between 1969 and 1983. Five movies, forty-five TV shows, five stage shows, five books, and countless records, including a hit single. So yes, we did okay, but fame still beckoned.

8

WHITHER CANADA?

I remember quite clearly the moment I realized Monty Python had become famous. From the British tour, it was evident we had achieved celebrity, but by the Canadian tour this fame had turned into fanaticism. I can pin this instant with precision to the June day in 1973 when we arrived at the Toronto airport for Monty Python's First Farewell Tour of Canada. As we came into the arrivals lobby there was a tremendous scream. Instinctively, every one of us turned around and looked behind to see who was coming. Surely some famous rock group was arriving? Then came the dawning revelation: it was for us. There were screaming fans waiting at the airport. They held banners and signs and went totally crazy. We responded with surprise and a little embarrassment. Terry Gilliam reacted by lying down on the baggage carousel and riding around, to John's evident disgust. To be honest, we were not entirely sober. We had begun the flight quietly enough, scattered throughout the Air Canada first-class lounge, but when a stewardess asked if passenger Cohen would identify himself, Neil Innes began it. He rose to his feet and said, "I'm Passenger Cohen."

"No, I'm Passenger Cohen," I said, raising my hand.

"*I'm* Passenger Cohen," said Gilliam, getting into the Spartacus gag.

"No, I'm Passenger Cohen," said Carol Cleveland.

The stewardess was utterly bewildered as eight different people insisted they were passenger Cohen from all over the first-class lounge. Then the bar opened . . .

So, suddenly we were face-to-face with Canadian adulation. The promoters stuck us on the upper level of an open-top double-decker bus, and we were followed into Toronto by cars honking and people yelling.

Me and Terry on top of a bus at the Toronto airport.

The Canadians were nuts about *Python*. They had been watching the TV show since very early on, and there had been mass protests outside CBC when they tried to take it off the air. These fans were crazy.

"Shut up," John would yell crossly at the screaming audience as we appeared onstage. "We haven't done anything funny yet." But they only laughed more. They had come for a good time and nothing would stop them. At one show in Winnipeg the curtain rose to reveal the entire front row dressed as a caterpillar. You can't really fail with an audience like that.

Graham went off happily visiting bars recommended to him by his useful *Gay Guide to Canada*, suffering only on Sundays when he legally couldn't get a drink anywhere except in his hotel room and then only with food. Nancy Lewis, a U.S. record executive and our number one supporter in the early days, remembers visiting him and finding piles and piles of trays of untouched Caesar salads outside his door that he had ordered with each round.

Tony Smith, our promoter, had never been to Canada and had no idea of the huge distances between cities, so it was essentially a dartboard tour, where we ping-ponged back and forth across the lakes and plains. To make matters worse, Air Canada was on strike and after the first show in Toronto we never saw our set again; we were always one gig ahead. Fortunately, we had the movie reel and the costumes with us, so we needed to find only tables and chairs and a dead duck wherever we went, for a gross sketch about cocktails. "Twist of lemming, sir?" We joyfully sang "The Lumberjack Song" dressed as Mounties in Regina, the home of the Royal Canadian Mounted Police. Of course, Graham found a gay Mountie afterwards. That's rather the point of the song.

We all reacted differently to this newfound fame. John decided to leave. In my case, fame went to my balls. It would have been impossible not to have been affected in some way, especially when we went on down to California, where the Sixties were still raging. The North American Female proved to be very grateful. The Canadian boys assumed that we were all on drugs, and thoughtfully supplied them. I was an English boarding school boy let loose in a candy store. Was I becoming an asshole? I'm afraid so. Back home I had a lovely wife and a newborn baby. What was I thinking? Clearly, I wasn't. Men have a brain and a penis, and only enough blood to supply one at a time. The fact is, until quite late in life men think with their dicks. It's a pity, it's regrettable, it's unfortunate, and I say this with no pride, but it's true. The inevitable fall lay ahead.

The BBC had offered us a fourth season, and John was definitely not keen on the idea. For him, the Canadian tour was the tipping point. He hated it. He took to dining alone at a table in the same restaurant as the rest of us, reading a book and pointedly ignoring us as we got rowdier and rowdier. He had some silly idea for a sitcom he wanted to do, about an angry hotelier, set in a British holiday hotel in Torquay . . . Well, good luck with that. He decided to turn down another *Python* series. Graham broke the news on the flight to our final gig in Vancouver. To those of us who were enjoying the newfound adulation, John's decision seemed crazy. To Graham, who needed the money, it was disastrous. He persuaded us to do a fourth season without John.

Meanwhile, California lay ahead. Nancy Lewis had told LA record executive Neil Bogart that we were the next big thing, and persuaded Buddah Records to put out a Monty Python album. They flew us down to San Francisco to promote it and then on to LA, where we checked into the legendary "Riot House" on the Sunset Strip. This Hyatt House hotel had earned its soubriquet from the destruction wrought in it by visiting English rock stars such as Keith Moon, who threw television sets out of its windows and drove cars into its pool. We were soon leading lives of careless abandon in the California sunshine. Graham legendarily took a limo to a restaurant just across the street. He hadn't realized it was that close. The rest of us enjoyed our first taste of America.

Our promotional appearances were mainly on radio, where we tried to explain to puzzled DJs that we were not a circus, and this culminated in a big television appearance on *The Tonight Show,* though sadly without Johnny Carson. David Brenner was sitting in for him. He gave us a heartwarming intro:

"I've never heard of these guys. People say they're funny. Please welcome *Monty Python*."

We were supposed to do half an hour of our best material. The curtain went up on Graham and Terry J. dressed as Pepperpots, screeching in high-pitched British accents. We called these loud, over-made-up ladies Pepperpots because of their physical resemblance to real pepper pots.

"Oo 'ello dear. How are you?"

"I've been up all night burying the cat."

"Is it dead?"

"No, but it's not at all a well cat, so I thought best to bury it to be on the safe side."

To say the response was underwhelming is an understatement. The audience stared at us openmouthed. This very same material that had just carried us across Canada on gales of laughter was greeted with total silence. Two British men in drag screaming at each other about a dead cat? We were from another planet. It was short, it was fast, and it was fucking hilarious. We did the half hour of material in twenty minutes and then ran outside, where we collapsed on the grass screaming with laughter. It was hysterical. I think it's one of the best laughs I have ever had. There is nothing funnier than nobody laughing.

Terry Jones and I fared slightly better when we performed "Nudge Nudge" on a late-night music show, *The Midnight Special,* for George Schlatter and Ed Friendly, the producers of *Rowan & Martin's Laugh-In.* It repeated happily for many years, so the sketch became very well known in America. Elvis called everybody "Squire" because of it . . .

The semi-legendary "Nudge Nudge" sketch.

Meanwhile we spent our time at the Hollywood Bowl, where we saw Gladys Knight & the Pips, enjoyed Little Richard at the Rainbow Bar & Grill, and were up and down the Strip like yo-yos. Well, more like dildos. At the time, people thought we only made records, like the Firesign Theatre. They had no idea that this material came from TV shows. To them we were simply recording artists.

On our return to London, the BBC were less than keen to find they had lost John Cleese, and they punished us in typical BBC ways. We were relegated to BBC2, and were not allowed to use the words "Flying Circus" in the title. For the fourth season, we would be known simply as *Monty Python*.

"Oh, gee, we are so scared."

There were many funny things in those six shows—"The Most Awful Family in Britain," "Queen Victoria Handicap," "Woody and Tinny Words," "RAF Banter"—but for me, something was missing. John, of course. Not his writing, because he did contribute a lot from all the material we had cut from *The Holy Grail*, and even his performing was not so badly missed, as we had all learned a lot in three seasons; but, importantly, the balance was lost. John had kept Terry J.'s explosive Welsh determination in check, and without him that didn't happen. So, when the BBC offered us a further seven shows, it was me this time who said no, on a long walk with Michael on Hampstead Heath.

This turned out to be a good thing, for while John didn't want to do any more TV, he *was* keen to do movies, and all of us were soon happily engaged on writing a new movie, which we were determined we would control and direct. At the second writing stint for what became *Monty Python and the Holy Grail*, we decided it should be entirely about King Arthur and his knights, without any of the distracting modern stuff set in the Harrods toupee department (which we used in the fourth series). John also appeared onstage with us again in March 1973 at the Theatre Royal, Drury Lane, for four weeks, and this time it was impossible not to notice we had become quite a big deal. Almost every single British rock star filled the boxes, from David Bowie to Elton John to Mick Jagger. Some of these rock stars now generously stepped forward to fund our next movie, which we made on a tiny budget of two hundred thousand pounds, filming for five weeks on location in Scotland. These original investors for *The Holy Grail* were Robert Plant and Jimmy Page of Led Zeppelin, Pink Floyd, Tim Rice, Jethro Tull, Island Records, Chrysalis Records, Charisma Records, and Michael White. Bless them for it. They didn't want to interfere, or control, they just wanted to help us make our movie. I think Tony Stratton-Smith,

Graham's great drinking pal and head of Charisma, our record label, was largely responsible for bringing them all in. He even had a horse named Monty Python.

Carol Cleveland wasn't available for *Monty Python Live at Drury Lane,* so my wife, Lyn Ashley, played her parts. Lyn had appeared in a few Python shows, including one of the two German shows we made. The Germans had come to us and said, "We are German, and we have no sense of humor, so we want you to come over to Germany and make a Python comedy special for Bavaria TV." The clincher was they wanted us to come over for a writing recce so they could show us some of the places we could write sketches for. Nobody had ever heard of a writer's recce and it seemed like a free piss-up to us, so we flew to Munich and were met at the airport by a Bavarian band, huge steins of beer, and a big sign saying WELCOME PYTHONS. Then they put us in cars and took us to Dachau.

What the hell was this?

On our way, we got lost and passersby denied all knowledge of the location of the camp. We finally arrived as it was getting dark, and they said it was closing.

"Tell them we're Jewish," said Graham.

Probably his finest moment. Anyway, they let us in. Luckily, they let us out again.

We puzzled over why they had taken us there. Surely they didn't expect us to write sketches set there. Were we supposed to be filming *Dancing in Dachau*? The grim reality of the camp precluded all humor. In the end, we decided they'd probably just wanted to get the worst over with. After that, things lightened up. Our hosts took us to Salzburg in Austria and to mad King Ludwig's extraordinary Neuschwanstein Castle in Bavaria, where we would film for both shows, once at night with the wolves howling.

The first show we made entirely in German. We wrote the script in English, they translated it into German, and we painstakingly learned the words parrot-fashion. It meant we did a lot of visual humor, including "Silly Olympics" and "Philosophers' Football," filmed on the old Bayern Munich ground. We were billeted in a small but friendly guesthouse, where the proprietress was shocked one morning when Graham appeared at breakfast with four young men. She told him with some embarrassment that there was a special hotel down the street "for your kind" where he would be made welcome, and he moved in there and had a delightful time. It was Oktoberfest and we completely lost Graham for a couple of days of filming because he was having so much fun. When he resurfaced, he flew back to London to accept a Sun Award on behalf of *Monty Python.* He took the statuette from the Chancellor of the Exchequer, Reginald Maudling, put it in his mouth, dropped to his knees, and then crawled off the stage through the audience barking like a dog. It made the front page.

One day, halfway up a mountain, John and I wrote a song called "Eric the Half a Bee," while he was dressed as Little Red Riding Hood, still my favorite performance of his. We had finished shooting a *Fliegender Zirkus* scene and broken for lunch at a typical Bavarian cuckoo-clock restaurant. John wandered into the gents dressed in his full dirndl and skirt, to the shock of a stout German burgher in lederhosen. Since it was cold in the Alps, we ordered a delicious bottle of schnapps, and so we were not entirely sober as I pulled out my guitar and we wrote a very silly song.

> *Half a bee*
> *Philosophically*
> *Must ipso facto half not be.*
> *But half the bee has got to be*
> *Vis-à-vis its entity*
> *D'you see?*
> *But can a bee*
> *Be said to be*
> *Or not to be*
> *An entire bee*
> *When half the bee is not a bee*
> *Due to some ancient injury?*

La di dee
One two three
Eric the half a bee.
A, B, C, D, E, F, G,
Eric the half a bee.

Is this wretched demi-bee
Half asleep upon my knee
Some freak from a menagerie?
No, it's Eric the half a bee.

The rest of the crew moved off to film Michael playing Buzz Aldrin. We finished the bottle. It was a delightful afternoon. What the Germans made of our speaking German on the TV show I have no idea, but they invited us back and this time, instead of painstakingly learning the German words, we sensibly spoke English and they dubbed us.

Terry Jones also had his finest moment in Munich. He and I had flown there one cold February to set up this second show. It was Carnival at the time and Müncheners celebrate this with a festival called the Nockherberg, where they brew *Starkbier,* a special black beer so strong they close the beer kellers at ten to stop them killing each other. The feast has been held since 1891 in a vast hall, the Paulaner, where everyone sits on benches at long tables. It was *so* big that there were *two* German bands, one at each end. The one on the main stage was conducted by a man with a metal claw instead of a hand. For ten marks, anyone could come onstage to borrow the baton and conduct the oompah-pah band. In one corner near the stage, I was shocked to see a table of older men wearing Nazi insignia.

The evening progressed with beer and sausages, and after a couple of hours my attention was drawn to the sight of Terry Jones appearing onstage. He took the baton from the claw of the conductor and advanced on the audience. He had a glint in his eyes I recognized. Oh no. He began performing a strip tease, flapping his jacket back and forth across his body like a stripper, then provocatively removing it and twirling it above his head before flinging it away. He removed his tie, salaciously rubbing it between his legs, before chucking it tantalizingly into the audience. People in the hall were beginning to notice what was going on, half fascinated, half horrified. He began unbuttoning his shirt, bumping and grinding to the beat of the band, and then, turning around, he slowly removed it. He spun back round, arms high, revealing his naked chest, demanding applause, and then put his tongue out and began playing with his nipples. He moved inevitably to his trousers. *Shit, he's going to take his pants off,* I thought. *We're going to get killed.* Slowly and to some encouragement he removed his belt and then began to slide down his zipper. He unbuttoned his trousers and began to slip his pants down when the irate conductor raced onto the stage, grabbed him, and physically dragged him offstage.

"We have to go," I said to our hosts. "Get the car."

I raced to the side of the stage and managed to hustle Terry out of the hall, away from the Nazi table, who were indignantly watching this English boy. Somehow we managed to escape unharmed. It was the bravest and maddest thing I ever saw him do.

9

HERE COMES THE SON

The birth of my son in 1973 was the most emotional experience of my life so far. We called him Carey after Carey Harrison, my friend from Cambridge with whom I'd first traveled to France, and as I drove away from the hospital, the Joni Mitchell song came on the radio:

> *Come on, Carey, get out your cane . . .*

I burst into tears.

It wasn't a normal birth. For a start, I was holding the lights. A gynecologist was filming. Our son was born on camera. Because Lyn was an actress, her obstetrician had asked to film the birth and Lyn had gamely agreed. We had done some preliminary shots as her pregnancy advanced, where I played the rather unrewarding role of Husband. Now the hospital room was a damn movie set. What were we thinking? In the end we threw them out.

A year later, in April 1974, with a one-year-old Carey, Lyn was back on the boards. *Drury Lane* was a sellout, and we extended the run from two to four weeks due to popular demand. Once again, the great and the good, the young and the lovely, the rock and the roll flocked to our show. We couldn't extend any longer, as we were due in Scotland for the soggy filming of *The Holy Grail*. Just before we left, the Department of the Environment for Scotland unexpectedly denied us permission to film in any of their castles, calling the film's script "incompatible with the dignity of the fabric of the buildings." Here, where thousands of Scotsmen had slit each other's throats, we were not to talk about the curtains. It was a disaster. The Terrys had scouted and prepped several castles and now we were left with just two in private hands: Doune Castle, which suddenly starred in the movie as we shot it from every possible angle, and Castle Stalker. What had started as an under-prepared and underfunded movie soon turned into full-blown chaos.

The poor Terrys. We had given them both the job of directing, which was smart for us and hell for them. In the end, one of them would edit by day while the other would change everything by night. Our producer was soon disliked by both directors. His qualifications for the job seemed to be that he had once shared rooms with Terry Gilliam. John detested him and even Michael was rude about him in his diary. Later he would sue us for money from *Spamalot*. Of course. We had broken the Mike Nichols golden rule of production: "No assholes." Fortunately, Michael White had supplied John Goldstone, a young, brilliant, bearded Mancunian, to look after his interests and he was our producer for every Python movie from then on.

Filming *Grail* was uncomfortable, to say the least.

Soggy.

We began shooting in Scotland near Glencoe in May, and it was cold and damp and miserable. One of our two cameras broke on the very first shot, while Graham clung to a ledge shaking with nerves. We thought he was supposed to be a mountaineer. We didn't know he was an alcoholic. The shaking was not nerves but DTs, and someone quickly snuck him up a bottle of gin. Both Graham and John refused to run across the rope bridge that spans "the Gorge of Eternal Peril." To be fair, the Bridge of Death was terrifying. It was erected across a deep gorge by Everest mountaineer Hamish MacInnes and his local mountain rescue crew. I for one certainly would never have crossed it, but fortunately my character Robin was killed before I had to. Since we were all wearing woolen armor, jogging across the wet heather pretending to ride horses, you could tell what time of day it was by how far up your legs the damp had climbed. At the end of each day we had to change out of our soggy tights, so by the time we got to the hotel we shared with the crew, all the hot water was gone. John and I soon had enough of this and found a nearby hotel, a Hydro with plenty of hot water, and amazingly, just as we moved in, twenty-four beautiful young damsels arrived for their scenes as the maidens bathing in Castle Anthrax. We didn't tell the others . . .

Grail wasn't fun. Terry J. directed the comedy scenes and made sure the jokes were on-screen, while Terry G. shot the art scenes like the Dragon Boat and the more mystical shots of castles, which made it look like a real movie. Since both Terrys played multiple roles in the film, it must have been exhausting for them. We were completely unsympathetic and would complain endlessly and badger them to get on with it. Terry Gilliam came in for a lot of this abuse because when we'd done a perfect take he would call for one more.

"What was wrong with that?" John would inquire testily.

"Not enough smoke," he would reply, to John's disgruntlement.

The smoke became quite an issue and eventually Graham would quantify it from 1 Gilliam, which was light mist, to 10 Gilliams, which was smoke so thick no one could see the actors. Of course, it's his genius art direction that gives the film its unexpectedly fine cinematic quality, just as it was Terry Jones's comic brilliance that ensured we shot several really funny scenes in one take. That meant no one could interfere with our timing by inserting close-ups or pauses or reaction shots. The Guards scene is the best example. It's all up there on the screen, one long shot. You can see all three of us clearly, including our legs (feet are funny!), and we played it in real time like a scene from the theater.

"Not to leave the room till you or anybody else . . ."

"*Not* anybody else . . ."

The timing of Graham's hiccups is just wonderful. This was the scene we had the most trouble with in *Spamalot,* and often cut it altogether.

At its first public screening, in a cinema in West London, *Monty Python and the Holy Grail* was a total disaster. It tanked big-time. This is where the Python writers committee really came into its own. We commandeered a room and set to work discussing where it went wrong. The two exhausted Terrys, who had been cutting different versions, could only listen and be grateful for the help. Neil Innes's medieval soundtrack was the first thing to go. It wasn't bad in itself but it killed the comedy stone dead. When it was replaced by cliché music from a film library, the comedy began to come alive. It didn't need sackbuts and tabors, it needed swashbuckling Hollywood movie music. Now it was parody, you knew where you were. We made cuts and changes in the text, too, added voice-overs to clarify the story, and did some small reshoots, like a claw turning over *The Book of the Film* (a prop I oddly came across last February at the Pasadena Antiquarian Book Fair; they wanted fifty thousand dollars for it! I didn't buy it, but I did sign it and verify it as the genuine article). It took thirteen test screenings of *The Holy Grail,* dragging the scenes to where the audience laughed, before we were satisfied. It was worth it.

The Holy Grail opened to a perfect storm in New York in April 1975. Ron Devillier at Dallas PBS had bought a very cheap show the BBC were practically giving away, and when he put *Flying Circus* on late-night on Sundays he was rewarded by amazing figures. Other PBS stations followed suit, and soon New York began to play it too. We were a cult hit. When we opened *The Holy Grail* at Cinema 2 in New York, Don Rugoff advertised it by paying a knight to go up and down Fifth Avenue pretending to ride a horse, followed by a squire clopping coconuts. In a newspaper ad he promised free coconuts to the first thousand people to attend the opening screening, at 11:00 a.m. We were woken at 9:00 and told to get over to the cinema pronto, as there were lines round the block. It was something like Beatlemania. For safety reasons the NYPD were insisting they put on an earlier screening. We arrived to huge cheers and were then trapped in the cinema all day, emerging at the end of each showing to sign coconuts. I don't know if you've ever tried signing a coconut, and why would you, but it's not easy. Plus the crowd was so big they had to send out for more coconuts. To keep us company in the long gaps between emerging audiences, two of our investors, Jimmy Page and Robert Plant, very kindly came by and hung out with us. We'd never met them before and they were modest and sweet and, of course, the fans couldn't believe they were there. I'm happy to think they still get money from *Spamalot*.

The next morning, we cohosted *AM America* live on TV and then

Signing coconuts at the New York opening of *Holy Grail*.

were taken off to be photographed by Richard Avedon for *Vogue* magazine. In the limo, we discussed what we might do.

"Well we certainly won't be naked," said someone.

That did it.

Of course, we *had to be* naked. It was a classic Python photo, and we spent a very silly session with the enchanting Avedon, with us all completely in the buff, a photo marred only by the absence of John. When I later reproduced the photo in *Themontypythonscrapbook,* I got Basil Pao to insert a photo of John on set in Tunisia in just his Y-fronts.

In the magazine article Leo Lerman, the veteran *Vogue* writer, said we were like slightly cracked angels. On our way out of the studio we glanced down at Avedon's typewriter, where he had just started a letter.

Dear Princess Margaret, it began.

We couldn't have been happier, leaving in a squeal of giggles, off to the Bronx Zoo to christen a python "Monty." I avoided the beast like the plague.

The opening party was held at Relaxation Plus, a massage parlor in the basement of the Commodore Hotel on Fifth Avenue. No, I don't know why. Each of the rooms had a different theme. Naval flags, for example. There was a large central Jacuzzi into which a naked Terry Jones was soon inviting guests. He's friendly that way. I was chased round a massage table by a very tall actress from *Li'l Abner* called Julie Newmar, who seemed determined on something, but I managed to escape intact. Andy Warhol was there. Jeff Beck was there. Dick Cavett was there. It was odd. We were a thing.

That May we screened *The Holy Grail* out of competition at the Cannes Film Festival. We had thoughtfully taken along Jeannette Charles, a Queen Elizabeth look-alike, to change the name of a street from the Rue Python to the Rue Monty Python.

At our screening that evening, soon after the movie began, local firemen in brass helmets raced in and evacuated the cinema. The audience thought this was part of the joke and stood happily in the street while the *pompiers* searched the auditorium. It was a hoax, but the audience laughed even harder at the movie when they went back in.

With the "Queen" (Jeanette Charles) at Cannes.

I now had my own TV series on BBC2. *Rutland Weekend Television* began taping in January 1975, and our first six shows aired from May through June. I bought the title from John for a pound. Rutland was the smallest county in England, over a thousand years old, and the new Conservative government had just ruled it out of business, stating it was now part of Leicestershire. If you really want to fuck with the English, then history is a good place to start. Rutland was outraged. As soon as the Leicestershire council took down their signs, they would replace them with their own new ones. I liked the idea of having a tiny television station that broadcast from a place that had just been unmade. Sure, it broadcast only once a week, but it had plays like *Three Men on a Goat,* its own rock band with an "all-dead" singer, light entertainment shows, and sports: "International Wife-Swapping from Redcar." It was a good model for TV satire and I had a lot of fun writing and creating sketches for it. *RWT* was shot on a shoestring in a tiny studio next to the weather studio on the fourth floor at the BBC Televison Centre. Even the shoestring was borrowed. I had a great cast of funny people, and Neil Innes contributed songs, which he would send to me and I would turn into sketches or movie ideas. Not many people saw it. Because it had no live audience, I was never very sure whether it was funny or not, and some people kindly went out of their way to point out that it wasn't. That summer we were all working separately, John on *Fawlty Towers*, Michael and Terry J. on *Tomkinson's Schooldays*, and me on *Rutland*. Still, we had a movie to open.

Sometime in August 1975, Terry Gilliam and I flew out to LA to do promo for the opening of *The Holy Grail* in Westwood. It was stinking hot and we were driven everywhere in a little old beater with no air-conditioning. The movie had yet to open in LA. Our TV show wasn't yet on PBS in California. We were so unknown that Gilliam and I joined the line for the first screening of *The Holy Grail* outside a cinema in Brentwood, listening to the fans chattering away about Python. They were fanatics, but only from our albums.

One afternoon I was invited to a house in Laurel Canyon for a swim. When I arrived, it turned out I was the only guest; the young lady who had invited me was wearing a tiny bikini and proposing we relax and take mescaline. The afternoon was filled with exotic promise, when I got an urgent phone call from Terry Gilliam.

"Eric, can you come and get me?"

"What?"

"Just come and get me please."

"Where are you?"

"I'm in the back of Book Soup on Sunset."

"What's up?"

"Just please . . . come and get me."

He sounded desperate. I did the British thing. I apologized to the young lady and assured her I would be right back, but I must leave immediately on an errand of mercy. Racing down to Book Soup, I found Terry cowering in the back of the store. He seemed to have lost it.

"It's all out there. Everything. Hollywood. Movies. It's all out there."

I understood all was not well in the Gilliam cranium. I know Terry suffers from dark moods. It goes with his genius. I think that having grown up in the San Fernando Valley, and maybe dreaming one day of directing, he was now back, having directed his first movie, and it had all become too much for him. I think all the Pythons are nuts in some way, and together we make one completely insane person. I took him to tea and he soon calmed up. My afternoon was in any case ruined . . .

That evening my life changed anyway, for at the screening of *The Holy Grail* at the old Directors Guild on Sunset, I met George Harrison. I had heard that George wanted to meet me, but I was somewhat shy of meeting him. People said he was an enormous fan of Python and a big fan of me personally because I had written a sketch for *Flying Circus* about an actor being busted by the police. The policeman had thoughtfully brought a package of his own. When the actor opened the brown paper bag, he found sandwiches.

"Sandwiches?" says the policeman. "Blimey, whatever did I give the wife?"

Cut to a stoned wife. "I don't know, baby, but it was better than sandwiches!"

This was the only line cut by the BBC from the first series. George had assumed, probably rightly, that the sketch was based on his own drug bust in Esher, where the police had brought their own cannabis, and was anxious to meet me. I was shy and tried to avoid him, but he snuck up on me in the back of the theater as the credits began to roll. I hadn't yet learned he was unstoppable. We began a conversation that would last about twenty-four hours. Who could resist his opening line?

"We can't talk here. Let's go and have a reefer in the projection booth."

No telling what the startled projectionist felt as a Beatle came in with one of the actors from the movie he had just projected and lit up a joint. He managed eventually to get us to leave, and we went off for dinner with Terry Gilliam and Olivia Harrison.

Lunch at first sight. The night Gilliam and I met George and Olivia.

After dinner George insisted I go with him to A&M Studios, where he introduced me to Joni Mitchell. Joni fucking Mitchell, for Christ's sake. Saxophonist Tom Scott was at work on some overdubs of George's latest album, *Extra Texture,* and we listened to some of the tracks and then went back to the Beverly Wilshire Hotel, where we talked and talked and talked for the rest of the night. What was it like to be a Python? What was it like to be a Beatle? What was John like? What was *your* John like? A thousand questions.

"Did you really smoke a reefer in the Buckingham Palace toilets?"

"It might have been a cigarette, but it felt so naughty even doing that there, that it felt like we had smoked a joint," he replied honestly.

Funny and serious and wise, he changed my life. We played together, partied together, argued together. He was irresistible. It was definitely love at first sight.

Back in England, my marriage was drawing to its sad conclusion, but shortly after I returned in early September 1975, George and Olivia invited me to visit Friar Park, their palatial home in Henley-on-

Thames. I drove up for dinner with Lyn and little Carey in our VW. We came across a huge gate, with an exquisite gnomes' cottage behind it, with twisted chimneys. It was incredible.

"This is beautiful," I said, ringing the bell.

"Oh. This is just the gate cottage," they replied, "the house is further up!"

We drove up a long winding drive between huge dripping trees, through banks of rhododendrons, past manicured gardens, and there ahead of us under a magnificent cedar tree was the most amazing Vic-

Crackerbox Palace.

torian neo-Gothic mansion. It was bigger than my boarding school. Friar Park was built in 1889 by the eccentric lawyer Sir Frank Crisp. It is a dream of a palace, with William Morris tiles, polished wood interiors, a huge carved fireplace, and elaborate dining rooms, bedrooms, and drawing rooms. It features caves, grottoes, underground passages, and all kinds of formal gardens and lakes. Carved stone friars' heads popped out of walls with philosophical quotes, many of which were already lyrics of George's and some of which would soon become them.

> Scan not a friend with microscopic glass
> You know his faults now let the foibles pass
> Life is one long enigma my friend
> So read on, read on, the answer's at the end.

On the grounds was a huge scale model of the Matterhorn covered in snow, scattered with edelweiss and alpine trees, under which ice caves led magically back into the house. Large signs instructed you to stay on the grass. Beyond the lawn with its Shiva fountain lay underlapping lakes and underwater caves, with a little electric boat to take you through twisting tunnels behind the waterfalls into a magnificent blue grotto, from which you emerged into a Japanese garden with an exquisite teahouse perched over a high waterfall. It is still the most unique and incredible house I have ever seen.

Following the disaster of what he called "the Dark Hoarse Tour," George had retreated from the world into gardening. He was obsessive. But he did not neglect his music, for upstairs was a beautifully carved, fully equipped recording studio with every single Beatles guitar from every era hanging on the wall. After dinner, Lyn took Carey home and I stayed on for days, spending hours listening to the tracks he had racked up, playing guitars and eating Kumar's curries, talking, sharing, laughing, emerging onto the lawn at dawn to play Frisbee. George made me welcome, cheered me up, and played his two jukeboxes like a professional, to instruct and delight. Of course he had some Monty Python, but they were heavy with Dylan.

I was swept up into a magical world, complete with his friends, for you had to meet everyone—the extraordinary Derek Taylor, local musician friends Andy Fairweather Low, Jon Lord and Deep Purple, Joe Brown, and Alvin Lee. It was like entering Wonderland, and always there was his running commentary, for I soon learned the Quiet One never stopped talking. He spoke about everything and everyone and was never shy to voice an opinion. The only thing we never agreed on was religion, but we agreed to disagree, for it was so much a part of his being, this ex-Catholic who had embraced Hinduism, sought enlightenment in Rishikesh, learned to play sitar, and single-handedly influenced the culture of the world by introducing Ravi Shankar and Indian art, music, and literature into Sixties Britain. All this from a guitarist in a rock group. Of course, they were the *Beatles,* but imagine all that influence stemming from the enthusiasm of a single Scouse and you get a glimpse of the determination of George.

Extra Texture was released in September 1975. He immediately put me to work recording radio ads for this new album, subtitled *Ohnothimagen,* and even had me add a couple of Pepperpot lines on his single "This Song," which was a riposte to the lawsuit he was fighting with the aid of his manager Denis O'Brien. In exchange for my help, he agreed to star in my *Rutland Weekend Television* Christmas special, which aired on BBC2 on December 26, 1975, singing a song we had written together. George lurched on as a truculent and slightly unstable pirate and demanded to know where the pirate sketch was. As the sleazy compere, I insisted he was only there to sing "My Sweet Lord," and there was no pirate sketch. But he was having none of that.

"No pirate sketch? Well, *up you* then," and off he stormed.

Finally, at the end of the show, the set lit up saying GEORGE HARRISON SINGS and he came down the stairs dressed all in white playing the familiar opening chords of "My Sweet Lord" on his twelve-string. Just as he finished the intro, he beamed and suddenly switched into "The Pirate Song," which we'd written together.

> *I'd like to be a Pirate*
> *A Pirate's life for me*

All my friends are pirates
And sail the BB-sea!
I've got a jolly Roger
It's black and white and vast
So get out of your skull and crossbones
And I'll ram it up your mast!

"The Pirate Song," Rutland Weekend Television.

It was a terrific gag and still one of my favorite moments. It is the only Harrison/Idle song, but certainly up there with the best of Lennon and McCartney. Olivia told me she thought it was the bravest thing George ever did. Afterwards we celebrated for hours, and—here is his amazing luck—on his way home to Henley at four in the morning his car ran out of gas, and he slid onto the forecourt of a country pub, whose landlord he cheerfully woke up to begin serving drinks.

10

THE DIVORCE FAIRY

By Christmas 1975 the divorce fairy was hovering. My marriage was breaking up, and no wonder. Lyn was a lovely woman and a good mother and she certainly deserved better. Not surprisingly, my faithlessness was rewarded by hers and she left me and my two-year-old son in London to spend Christmas in France. I did learn that infidelity is not a good basis for a marriage. Best to disappoint one woman at a time. Sad, but with my lovely blond son for company, I got an unexpected boost. On a snowy Christmas Eve, two men delivered an enormous thing wrapped in brown paper from a lorry. We ripped the paper off to find a fully stacked jukebox filled with all George's favorite records. A note said, *Every home should have one, Happy Christmas, love George and Olivia.*

That Christmas, Carey and I danced away. He could only just reach the buttons. He could punch 123, which was "Money" by Pink Floyd, but his favorite was "Bohemian Rhapsody." He adored that song. When I finally moved out of our house in St. John's Wood to a cold flat in Pimlico, Lyn did an amazing thing. She promised me she would never come between me and my son. I always thought that was really mature, and I have always been grateful to her for that. Now I was miserable and alone, and serve me right. I had been an asshole. Men come in three sizes: small, medium, and extremely fucked up. I know men aren't entirely alone in this. A female friend told me she was looking for a boyfriend.

"What sort of man are you looking for?" I asked.

"Well," she said, "he must be breathing and have a penis."

My postmarital depression began to lift in January 1976 when I was offered three TV commercials in Australia for a "Nudge" chocolate bar. From cold-winter London, I was flown first-class to Sydney, where it was summer, with sun, sea, sand, cricket, and that extraordinary harbor with its bridge, its exciting opera house, and, across the bay, artist Martin Sharp's beckoning mad clown head at Luna Park. I went to Bondi, where I ventured into the sea and experienced the first joys of Australian surf, which was like being popped into a washing machine and turned upside down underwater. I emerged eventually onto the beach with a mouth full of sand, and with as much dignity as I could muster. Pommies!

Before I left London, Richard Neville, one of the editors of OZ magazine, who was arrested and tried for a controversial schoolkids edition, had given me a pile of postcards introducing me to the most interesting people in Sydney. *This pallid masturbating wreck standing in front of you is called Eric Idle. Please look after him.*

I think on the first night, at a party, I met them all. Australians are amazingly kind people, and they invited me to everything, including a trip to the Blue Mountains, where I spent a weekend with "Little Nell" Campbell, long before *Rocky Horror,* the exquisite Gaël McKay and her boyfriend Stephen Maclean, and the English photographer Tim Street-Porter. We drank exotic cocktails and stayed at the Carrington, a delightful old hotel in Katoomba. In Melbourne, I shot my "Nudge" commercials next to the Melbourne Cricket Ground—where Australia was engaged in a titanic struggle with Clive Lloyd's West Indies cricket team—and then returned to Sydney for some more relaxation.

Before I'd left for Australia, George sent me a gift. He had been giving me spiritual advice, such as "Leave your dick alone," which was a bit rich coming from him.

"You're going to Australia?" he said. "So you'll be flying over India."

"I guess so."

"Well, I've got to send you something then."

On the day of my departure a beautifully wrapped package with a peacock feather arrived with the instructions: "Not to be opened until over India." *Wow,* I thought, *spiritual guidance from George Harrison.* Some ten hours into the flight I looked down and asked the air hostess, "Is that India?"

"Yes," she said.

Right, I thought, *time for that spiritual advice.* So, I reverently opened the package and found inside a small box. I removed a little handwritten card from George.

It read: *Shag a Sheila for me!*

I took his advice.

On my return from Oz my actress friend Carinthia West, who had been in my *Rutland Weekend Television* series, offered me her basement flat in Praed Street and then kindly told all her female friends I was gay. One by one they crept downstairs to convert me. It turned out to be surprisingly easy.

We were now setting up for a second season of *Rutland Weekend Television,* though this time we had been relegated to Bristol, a two-hour drive down the M4. It is only very rarely when writing comedy that you actually make yourself laugh. It happened to me just once. I had dragged Neil Innes into the *RWT* project and his job was to provide one or two songs per week and send me rough demos of them. I would then fit them into sketches or link them, or come up with film ideas. One of the songs he sent me for the second season sounded so like the Beatles of the *A Hard Day's Night* era that it came to me in a flash: we should do it as "the Rutles." At the same time, I came up with the visual gag of a TV interviewer walking and talking to the camera, and the camera begins moving away from him, just slightly faster than he is walking, so that he has to hurry, then is forced to break into a run to keep up, and finally ends up galloping after the camera, which eventually leaves him behind. This image made me laugh. I just knew it would be funny.

Flash-forward to later in the year and we are filming somewhere in Shepherd's Bush, in the mean little backstreets behind the BBC. We are set to shoot this gag. I am wearing a silly wig (as usual) to hide my shoulder-length hair. Our cameraman has done lots of documentaries and he knows exactly the way the gag should work. The first take works fine.

The first version of *The Rutles*.

A few days later we are down in Shepperton Studios filming "I Must Be in Love," the song Neil had sent me, only now we are dressed as Sixties Beatles and it has become a song from *A Hard Day's Rut*. It's England, it's freezing, it's intermittently raining, and we are making up sight gags in a field that is now a housing estate. The bit cut together like a dream, and it is one of my favorite pieces from the entire series. In this first iteration, I was playing George.

Meanwhile, I had bought a house in St. John's Wood in North West London to be near my son, and I shared it with my friend Robbie Williams, who worked for Pink Floyd. (No, *not* him.) We put a sign on the door that said NO LUGGAGE to deter young ladies from moving in, a vastly overoptimistic hope, as Australian models flowed through and left their flimsy dresses drying over the Aga. It became quite a party house.

In April 1976, we performed *Monty Python Live!* for four weeks in New York at City Center, where we were a big hit with fabulous reviews. We were all getting along really well and the audiences flocked to see us. On the first few nights we would hang out around the stage door and sign autographs for fans, but after a couple of weeks the crush grew so great and the police so concerned that we had to jump into a limo and drive out in a hurry. Otherwise they would follow us to our hotel. It was an instructive lesson in the swiftness and power of fame. Of course, some people *did* follow us home, and our social lives bloomed.

This time the opening-night party was held at Grand Central Station and we were chased around by Leonard Bernstein, who looked dashing in a cape. We pointed him in Graham's direction. Graham was being particularly naughty. He came to Mike and me and confessed he had slept with a lady. Mike and I said it was alright, we forgave him, but not to make a habit of it.

Oddly, we got the news that *Monty Python* had just become the top-rated TV show in Japan. They had changed the title. The literal translation was now *The Gay Dragon Boys Show,* and afterwards four men in business suits sat on chairs seriously discussing the sketches, including my favorite: "The Number One Deciding Guy Skit" ("The Twit of the Year"). Spike Milligan said that watching John Cleese dubbed into Japanese was the funniest thing he ever saw.

At the Python party, I also met Lorne Michaels, John Belushi, Dan Aykroyd, and Chevy Chase, who were just finishing their first season of *Saturday Night Live.* Lorne Michaels, a writer on *Rowan & Martin's Laugh-In,* had pitched the show to NBC as a cross between *Monty Python* and *60 Minutes.* He even came to London and watched us rehearse and shoot one of our shows, although I don't remember meeting him then. Wisely, NBC bought *Saturday Night Live* and it has been running ever since. One night after our show, Terry Gilliam and I went to visit them as they broadcast live from the NBC studios at 30 Rock. Lorne was very friendly and we stood on the stage floor at 8H, where we were surprised to see they had puppets. John and Dan were very scornful of the puppets and happy that at the end of the season they were leaving for London, where they became *The Muppet Show.*

A few days later I met Paul Simon in the queue for Bette Midler's dressing room after the opening night of *Clams on the Half Shell Revue.* I was a huge fan, and we began chatting as we waited a long time for Elton John to emerge. He was inside giving Bette diamonds. When it was our turn she graciously showed us round what had been Debbie Reynolds's dressing room. "And this is where Debbie pooped," she said, showing us the toilet. Paul would eventually marry Debbie's daughter, Carrie. I took him to see Billy Connolly at Carnegie Hall, where the Manhattan audience struggled to understand Billy's broad Glaswegian accent, while the devoted Scots fans roared their approval of this man in black tights and banana-shaped Wellie boots.

Practice, practice, practice.

That fall I would return to New York to host *Saturday Night Live* for the first time. It was the year of the American Bicentennial.

"What's a Bicentennial?" asked Ronnie Wood.

"It means America is two hundred years old," said an American proudly.

"Oh, the same age as my house," said Ronnie.

Ronnie's house, the Wick, a perfect oval eighteenth-century home, was a gorgeous Georgian mansion set high on a curve of the Thames near Richmond. I would set off with the delightful Ronnie to the Stones concerts at the Earls Court Arena, driving straight backstage in the limo into the encampment where you could eat, dine, play, wash, shower, powder your nose, and generally hang out till showtime. I'd watch the gig and then climb into the limo as everyone went back to Woody's for refreshments and snooker. Several days passed in that haze. I love Ronnie. He had come and stayed with me in France when he was joining the Stones, and Mick had given him two tapes: one of all the Stones songs to learn; and the second, how to get laid in French. What a thoughtful bandmaster.

With Ronnie Wood in Provence.

Amongst the many celebrities who flocked to the Python show in New York were Harry Nilsson and Ed Begley, and after I met them on the street we went for a drink at a bar on Sixth Avenue. I liked a drink in those days but Harry was a professional. Ed told me recently that after we'd had a few we all went up to Graham's suite at the Navarro Hotel on Central Park South. He innocently knocked at the door and was startled to be greeted by Graham with a full plonking kiss on the mouth. He said he felt honored.

A few nights earlier George Harrison had come onstage for "The Lumberjack Song" dressed as a Mountie. He behaved perfectly, stayed in the chorus line, and no one would ever have known it was him.

George Harrison onstage with Monty Python at City Center.

Harry heard about this appearance by George, and there was nothing for it: *he* was going to come on and be a Mountie too. So they dressed him up and he entered on cue with the chorus of Mounties, but Harry's performance was a little different from George's. For a start, he was drunk, and he had no intention of remaining anonymously in any chorus line. He was a star and he wanted the audience to know it was him onstage. So he wore dark glasses and waved his arms around; leaving the chorus line, he lurched about the stage, gesticulating, swaying dangerously, and generally drawing attention away from the focus of the song, which was er, well, me as the Lumberjack. This caused a certain amount of frosty disapproval from John Cleese, who was less than fond of Graham's alcoholic rock-and-roll friends but who had been delightfully enchanted by George and his sweet modesty. When the song ended there was a feeling of "thank God that's over" as we all stepped back to let the curtain drop. All, that is, except for Harry. There was a huge wave of applause and cheers triggered by the end of the song, and Harry wasn't going to miss a minute of this. So as we stepped back, he stepped forward. The curtain fell.

"Where's Harry?" we asked, and then laughed as the curtain went back up and he was nowhere to be seen. Ignoring all instructions, he had stepped forward into the dark to acknowledge the cheers and fallen into the orchestra pit. So we all had a good laugh at his expense, and even when it was revealed that he had broken his wrist, some of the more cynical members of the comedy fraternity expressed less than halfhearted murmurs of sympathy, and considered comic karma to have triumphed.

Immediately after the run at City Center, I joined George and Olivia on holiday at the Rockefeller resort at Caneel Bay on St. John in the Virgin Isles.

George had just finished recording *Thirty-Three and ⅓*, the age we both had now reached, and we played happily on the beach as if we were still seven. It was a fabulous time.

One night we met a couple at dinner.

"What do you do?" said George.

"Import-export," they said.

"Oh," said George, "have you got any?"

They had.

Another afternoon, playing acoustic guitar in his room, we were

Spot the looney.

interrupted by a banging at the door. A young lady was complaining that Norman Lear, the legendary American sitcom creator, was trying to write downstairs and our music was disturbing him.

"Oh, sorry, love," said George politely, "we'll stop."

A few hours later a very shamefaced Norman Lear came to the door, utterly embarrassed that he had told a Beatle to stop playing guitar!

Back in England, George asked me to direct a couple of short promo films for his wonderful new record, though this was well before MTV, when music videos became common. I shot "Crackerbox Palace" and "True Love" in the house and gardens of Friar Park.

Son Carey helping direct "Crackerbox Palace."

That fall, Lorne Michaels invited me to host the second show of the second season of *Saturday Night Live* on October 2, 1976, and in my opening monologue I did a very bad version of "Here Comes the Sun." I also made a short film with Gary Weis, called *Drag Racing*, where Dan Aykroyd and I raced in full drag along a tiny landing strip in Flushing, Queens. Lorne asked me to play a clip from my current TV series. I showed him the Rutles gag and a parody of the Who's *Tommy* called *Pommy*, about a deaf, dumb, and blind man stuck in a Ken Russell film and his struggle to get out of the cinema. Lorne selected the Rutles piece. On the live show the runaway camera gag got a huge laugh and there was a great audience reaction to the song and the sight of the Rutles. After the show, there was a surprisingly strong response, many fans writing in, sending letters to the Rutles and begging for more. I was gratified to hear this because, encouraged by George, I had been thinking that this could make a very nice documentary. On the phone, I mentioned to Lorne that I was thinking of doing this for BBC2.

"Don't do that," he said. "Do it for me through my deal with NBC. You'll have a much bigger budget."

If I came to the West Indies for Christmas, he added, we could talk about it and he would go back and pitch it to the network as a special.

It seemed like a no-brainer. A model was making unmistakable signs of moving in, buying HIS and HER pillows and showing disquieting signs of nesting. I wasn't ready for a nest. It was time to move on. Lorne's invitation couldn't have been timelier. So, it was Barbados for me, tra-la-lee. Fortunately, my life was to change again unexpectedly and I finally began to grow up.

11

LOVE LIFE

I was thirty-three before I realized I couldn't shag every woman in the world. Some of them were going to have to remain disappointed. There was no reason to make love to women just because they would let you. I have since learned to love women for being women and not for just what I was trying to do with them. Easy for me to say now that I am no longer a danger to shipping, but most men are completely enslaved by their balls until long after thirty. My epiphany began in Barbados, where I woke up one morning on a beach with sandy knees and no knowledge at all of the young lady underneath me. *This has got to stop,* I said to myself. *You are no longer even enjoying it. It's just a desperate itch. Pull yourself together and stop all this serial shagging.* And stop it I did. At the same time, I ceased to eat meat. Perhaps they were connected. Who knows? On January 30, 1977, after a decent interval of abstinence, I met my wife on my first night in New York and fell in love with her at first sight and told her I would never leave her. I never have. Everything about meeting Tania Kosevich was incurably romantic.

Put simply, I was an asshole in my first marriage and bear much responsibility for its early end. I have no regrets, since I have a wonderful son, Carey, from it. Men are jerks until quite late in life. I was fortunate to get to that tipping point at thirty-three. I had flown to Barbados to spend Christmas at the Coral Reef Club with Lorne Michaels and Susan Forristal, Paul Simon and Shelley Duvall. Unfortunately, Shelley was trying to give up smoking and cried a lot. She was so miserable we

With Tania in Mexico.

begged her to smoke again. Christmas Day was illuminated by an extraordinary performance from a waiter who, slightly inebriated, managed to pour flaming brandy all over himself instead of the Christmas pudding. Luckily only the brandy burned, but it was a startling effect to be served by a burning waiter. It felt like a Pink Floyd cover.

After Christmas, the others left and I stayed on to await a call from Lorne. I had met the South African musician Ricky Fataar on the beach outside Heron Bay, and the friendly man who was renting the Palladian villa where Ricky was staying suggested I move in. Ricky and I spent all day on the beach playing guitar and drinking exquisite rum punches served by Mr. Brown. Ricky was falling in love with the beautiful David Bailey model Penelope Tree, whose father had built, and whose mother now owned, the incredible coral stone villa. We didn't really talk about the strange helicopter pilots who came in at night and met with our host privately. Of course, they were in the drug trade but Ricky and I innocently partied on. I had already changed my diet. No meat was served at Heron Bay, only fish. Now I changed my sexual life. I became a born-again virgin. Finally, after about six weeks of paradise, Lorne called and said to come to New York to meet NBC. That was the day that changed my life.

I fell in love at first sight. It really happened to me. Unexpectedly, surprisingly, and totally. I had flown bronzed and chaste from the beaches of Barbados (86 degrees) to freezing New York (6 degrees),

With Sabrina Guinness and Ricky, just leaving Heron Bay, Barbados.

where Lorne thoughtfully sent a limousine to meet me with an over-coat. I was driven to the Osborne on Fifty-Seventh Street, by Car-negie Hall, where Lorne was lending me his apartment, and then on to Rockefeller Plaza for *Saturday Night Live* with Fran Tarkenton as the host. After the show Paul Simon and Lorne took me to a trendy recep-tion filled with beautiful models. *I'm so over this,* I thought smugly. We didn't stay long and then Paul took us downtown in a white limo to an *SNL* after-party at Dan Aykroyd's loft in the Bowery. It was a large in-dustrial loft with an old, creaking delivery elevator in the bleakest and grimmest district of the Bowery, on Bond Street just by CBGB. Most of our group didn't want to stay long, but I wasn't tired and I knew Danny and many of the people from the show, so I thought I'd hang out a bit longer. Paul kindly offered to send the limo back for me later.

I was standing contentedly by the sink when a tall, beautiful, dark-haired young woman asked me to dance. She said her name was Tania and she lived in the loft too. As we danced I became overwhelmed. I knew I never wanted to leave her side. And not just her side. I kissed her and we necked on the stairs outside her party for two hours until finally I said,

"I'm never going to leave you."

I never have. Forty-one years ago, now. Strangely and wonderfully, and at least for a minute, she believed me. I knew then with the cer-tainty of anything I have ever known that I must not let this lovely lady get away. Paul's white limo drove us in the early dawn up to the Osborne. Discreet veils were undrawn. As I fell into her arms I thought, *I'm home.* It was January 30, 1977. We've been together ever since.

A few days later when I managed to resurface, with a smile on my face and the lovely Tania on my arm, Lorne commissioned me to write a fifteen-page treatment of the Rutles story. I bought every picture book I could find of the Beatles, cut them up and pasted them into a rough shape. I then bashed out a treatment in a white-hot fury and sent it in liberally illustrated. To our delight NBC immediately okayed it. I was commissioned by them to write a full screenplay. I moved into the loft on Bond Street, which Tania shared with Danny Aykroyd, Mike Pahios (a graphic artist for NBC), and an enormous German shepherd called Snark, who scared the bejesus out of me but happily let me walk him in the terrifying streets of the Bowery at night. It was freezing outside but the sauna was on day and night and, since it had no door, the heat escaping from it stoked the loft as warm as Barbados. When I queried the expense, they told me a previous tenant had "accidentally" hooked up the loft's electricity to the Budget Rent a Car downstairs, so they never had any electricity bills.

Tania went off to work in the Garment District every morning, leaving me happy, warm, and in love, writing *The Rutles* with Snark for company. I plundered the bookshops for Beatle photographs, read every memoir I could lay my hands on, cut and pasted and wrote, and after a few weeks I finally had a script I felt worked. A big advantage was that George had shown me *The Long and Winding Road,* an assemblage of Beatle footage that Neil Aspinall, their manager, had put together for Apple to release as a movie. Unfortunately, none of the Fabs could agree on the cut. They all objected to something. The story was indeed a sad one, as it ends up with a lot of bickering on *Let It Be,* when George walked out and John brought Yoko in every day and Paul was clearly unhappy. *All You Need Is Cash,* my subtitle for the Rutles story, is essentially a parody of a movie that never got released. I took some great comic inspiration from it, particularly for the Rutles' manager, Leggy's mum, played brilliantly by Gwen Taylor.

"What made the Rutles so successful?"

"Well, I think it was the trousers?"

"The trousers?"

"Yes. They were very . . . tight."

"Tight?"

"Yes. You could see everything. Clearly. Outlines, the lot."

"Oh, I see."

The Rutles story flowed out of me. It was the happiest I had ever been. Snark kept me company, the sauna kept me comfy, and the lovely Tania returned at night to feed and delight me. In fact, I married her eventually for her sandwiches. The only slight drawback for a writer was the Carol Conway Dance Studio directly overhead; the ceiling would bounce all day to the sounds of "AND one, and two, and three and four . . ."

NBC loved the script and suddenly we were a go. Gary Weis was set to co-direct with me, which was great because we had already made two short films together for *SNL*. The first one I wrote was *Drag Racing,* and the second, *Body Language,* was one of the funniest things I ever wrote. Lorne had carefully explained to me that sadly, because I was British and owing to legal reasons to do with budgets and Writers Guild requirements and the weather and so on, he couldn't actually pay me or credit me for writing them (nor for "Frost Nixon," the sketch I wrote and performed with Dan Aykroyd on the eve of the famous interview's broadcast), but I guess he made up for it in dinners. Well, not just dinners; Tania and I were married in his apartment in NYC. So thanks, Lorne.

It was time for me to go back to London and budget the movie. Tania and I spent a farewell honeymoon in New Orleans, where Lorne had had the crazy idea of shooting *SNL* live from the streets of Mardi Gras. It was total chaos, trying to do a TV show from the middle of a mass of drunks, and we could only get anywhere on the back of Harley-Davidson police motorcycles. The whole show revolved around Buck Henry and Jane Curtin commentating live on a two-mile-long parade. But, sadly, owing to a fatal traffic accident, the parade never appeared during the entire two-hour show and the broadcast swiftly descended into bedlam.

Only Randy Newman and I survived. He because he was onstage, and I because I had written a piece for myself set in a totally deserted street, with just one passed-out drunk, saying, "Only seconds ago this whole place was jumping. Right here. Only minutes ago . . ." to the sound of the live audience laughing in my earpiece.

At our luxury hotel on Bourbon Street, I sadly said goodbye to Tania as she returned to New York. However, the minute I landed in London I couldn't stand being without her and immediately sent her a ticket, and within two weeks she was flying into my arms at Heathrow.

From now on, life would no longer be possible without her, and Robbie discreetly moved out, while the NO LUGGAGE sign went into the trash. When she first arrived, I drove her around London pointing out all the wrong places. "That's Buckingham Palace," I would say, pointing to the Houses of Parliament. "Over there is the Post Office Tower," as I pointed to Big Ben, "and that's the Houses of Parliament," as we drove through Trafalgar Square. She was so jet-lagged she's been confused ever since.

A budget was approved, NBC said yes, filming dates were set, and I commissioned Neil Innes to compose and record a dozen new Rutles tracks, which he did brilliantly as well as play Ron Nasty, his spot-on version of the John Lennon character. He performed this role, singing "Cheese and Onions," on *Saturday Night Live* when I hosted the show again on April 23, 1977. People still think it was really John Lennon.

While in New York I interviewed Paul Simon in his elegant Central Park West apartment about the influence of the Rutles on his life. He played along beautifully, ad-libbing about the Rutles' influence and his memories of them at the time. I then interviewed Mick Jagger at his house.

"How shall I play it?" asked Mick, somewhat nervously.

"Just play Mick Jagger," I said.

"Oh right, okay," he said, and popped straight into character, where, as Mick, he revealed perhaps more than was discreet of his actual memories, a Stones-eye view of the Beatles. Confident we had some usable footage in the can, I returned to London, where Neil was back at work recording mock–Beatles songs with my friend Ricky Fataar, from the beach in Barbados, whom I now cast as the George character. The producer Craig Kellum and I began seeing just how much we could squeeze out of our budget until rather reluctantly I went into hospital for an emergency appendix removal. Ten days later, after a very jolly visit with George Harrison at Friar Park celebrating my new appendix-free life with champagne and curry, I was rushed back into intensive care green in the face. Craig Kellem's face was a mask of panic as I got him to witness my will before the ambulance took me off to the emergency unit at the Wellington Hospital. An unpleasant night or two later and I was feeling much better. Paul Simon called me as I was recovering, and I told him I was like a big gas balloon waiting to explode. I said, "If only I could pass wind I might begin to come back to life."

"Helping people fart is a service I happen to provide," said Paul, and that did it. I started to laugh. I laughed so hard I began to fart. It was loud, long, and deep, like a huge balloon emptying. It lasted for almost two minutes. It was so loud that Tania became hysterical. People popped their heads in to see what was wrong. They saw a loudly farting Brit and Tania in total stitches. When it was over I thanked Paul profusely.

"I have had many thanks in my life, but that's a first for me. Glad to be of use," he said.

I had lost a lot of weight in the hospital but it would prove useful for playing the young Dirk McQuickly. We had a very happy time shooting in London and Liverpool. It was great fun dressing up as the Beatles being chased around by young fans. Gary and I slipped into a comfortable codirecting relationship—he operated the camera while I stood in front of it yammering away as the incompetent BBC interviewer—and it all worked remarkably well. I cast Tania in four different roles: a hooker outside the Ratskeller in the Reeperbahn, the bikini girl lying beside Stanley J. Krammerhead III (the airhead professor from the University of Please Yourself, California), a Rutles merchandise model, and a fetching Gypsy hippie in "Love Life."

We filmed "Ouch!" on the sand dunes of Southport, where I had played as a kid, faking the West Indies with a cardboard-cutout coconut tree. The then Mrs. Jagger (Bianca) came up to play Dirk's wife, "Martini" (my first screen kiss), and we improvised happily. Ronnie Wood played a Hells Angel, Roger McGough played Roger McGough, and George Harrison played a TV reporter interviewing Michael Palin playing Derek Taylor. One day, when we were dressed as Beatles standing by the legendary crossing outside Abbey Road Studios, me as Paul and Neil as the full Lennon in beard and white outfit from ten years earlier, George was talking to us when he was roughly pushed aside by a breathless American tourist, who asked Neil and me if we were *really* the Beatles. He totally ignored the real Beatle.

It was a time of fun, magical madness, and great music, and all too soon the five weeks were over and Gary and I began cutting the movie. I felt it still lacked something. It needed a big performance, so we flew to New York, where I hastily wrote a scene for John Belushi as Ron Decline (Allen Klein), with Al Franken (future congressman) and Tom Davis as his henchmen. I sketched in a nice scene for the totally adorable Gilda Radner (who would go on to marry Gene Wilder), which we shot in the Village, and *SNL* newcomer Bill Murray improvised wonderfully as Bill Murray the K, a very silly DJ from Flushing. Finally, we shot Dan Aykroyd in the Bowery loft where I had lived with Tania and written the screenplay. He played the unfortunate record executive who had "passed" on the Rutles.

"What's it like to be such an asshole?" I asked him.

This was the only line NBC cut.

We flew to New Orleans, where we were fortunate to find some very talented local actors to film a very bad pun, "by the *banks* of the Mississippi" (the First National, the Chase Manhattan . . .), and some interviews about the black roots of Rutles music.

"Yes sir, those four guys from Liverpool came here and stole all my music."

"He's lyin' . . . he's always lyin'."

I flew out to California to stay with George and Olivia in LA, showing a rough cut to them and Derek Taylor, who had been the press agent for the Beatles and was now a VP at Warner Brothers Records. Derek was an enormous supporter of the project and encouraged his boss, Mo Ostin, to pick up the Rutles album from Clive Davis at Arista Records. Derek got us a huge artwork budget for the album cover, which became a ten-page pictorial spread that I helped art director Basil Pao assemble in a creative frenzy in ten days in New York. Michael Palin would co-opt Basil for his Passepartout on his various travel series, but not before we put together a *Life of Brian Scrapbook,* built out of scraps in an apartment on Hollywood Boulevard in only six weeks, start to finished copy! Derek produced an endless stream of promotional postcards, one with genuine pants material stuck on the back, saying, *I think it was the trousers.*

The first preview was in a crammed cutting room high above Times Square. We invited a small crowd, including our executive producer Lorne Michaels and various other friends, who all stared at the tiny screen on the Steenbeck and seemed to have a good time. At the end of the screening we got them to turn around and look out the window at the huge color TV screen in Times Square. They turned in amazement to see it lit up with the words THE RUTLES ARE COMING! Good timing, that, and worth the last of our precious budget.

In the end, we decided to do two cuts. The British version ran longer by about ten minutes and contained the "asshole" joke, and also included a film called "You Need Feet," a parody of Yoko's "Bottoms" film. NBC scheduled us in prime time opposite the enormously popular *Charlie's Angels,* so we were absolutely buried in the ratings, but the late-night repeat a few months later fared a lot better and when the show went to England on BBC2, it was such a smash hit at Easter that they repeated it on BBC1 a month later.

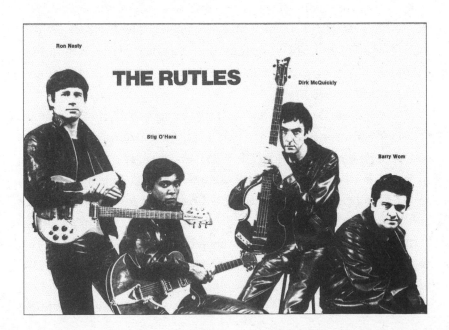

People always ask, "How did the Beatles react?" Well, George was behind it all the way, but the first time I played him Neil Innes's music he got slightly upset and began to sing "Instant Karma's gonna get you!" in a very loud voice. It certainly did, since ATV Music grabbed all the copyright to Neil's songs, but after this slight hiccup George loved the show and was very proud of it. He had supported me throughout, encouraging me to do it, appearing in it, telling me endless Beatles stories and showing me *The Long and Winding Road,* which eventually became the basis for the ten-part documentary *The Beatles Anthology.* Ringo liked the Rutles—"after 1968," he added mysteriously. We bumped into Paul and Linda in Regent's Park one foggy morning and smiled and said hello. Then Linda said, "We don't know if we're talking to you." Paul was a little guarded until Linda revealed she really loved it and went on about it. Paul seemed to approve only when he learned that I had grown up in Wallasey, opposite Liverpool.

"Hey, Linda, it's okay, he's a Scouse, he's one of us!"

I was told John and Yoko loved it, which I thought was very sporting of them since Yoko is portrayed as Hitler's daughter, but then she has a great sense of humor, as I found out when I made a speech at David Bowie's wedding many years later. I was completely inappropriate at the wedding, which of course went down big with the audience. When I looked up at the end, Yoko was standing on a table with both thumbs in the air. And of course, how could she not have a great sense of humor, living with John Lennon?

The Rutles was probably the most fun I ever had filming. It remains the world's first mockumentary, before *Zelig* and before *Spinal Tap.* I'm glad to see it has a continuing life, and I am proud of it. As George said in his book *I, Me, Mine,* "What should have happened is that the Bonzos and the Beatles should have turned into one great Rutle band with all the Pythons and had a laugh . . . *The Rutles* told the story so much better than the usual boring documentary. Try and see that film. That is a recommendation rather like saying: 'Don't bother me—see my lawyer. He will explain everything.' "

Many years later I made a very inexpensive sequel called *The Rutles*

2: Can't Buy Me Lunch, where I interviewed celebrities about the effects of the Rutles on them: James Taylor, Clint Black, Graham Nash, David Bowie, Salman Rushdie, and the wonderful Garry Shandling, who made me laugh so much when he said, *"Hard Day's Rut?* I loved *Hard Day's Rut.* I *loved Hard Day's Rut.* That scene when they came off the train, and the Nazis were there . . . and they . . . wait, they came off the train and . . . I'm sorry, I'm think I'm confusing *Hard Day's Rut* a little bit with *Schindler's List."*

He was a brilliant man and I miss him. For sheer cheek, though, Tom Hanks took the prize for beginning to cry as he remembered the Rutles breaking up. He had been mocked for weeping when he won an Oscar, and this self-parody was just too delicious.

The legendary Rutles *Triangular Album.*

12

THE MIRACLE OF BRIAN

The miracle of *Brian* is that it got made at all, which was entirely due to the generosity of George Harrison. Asked why he mortgaged his Henley home to pay for the entire $4.5 million budget of *Monty Python's Life of Brian*, he said, "Because I wanted to see the movie."

It's still the most anyone has ever paid for a cinema ticket.

The idea for *Brian* had sprung from an ad-lib I made at the opening of *The Holy Grail* in New York in April 1975.

JOURNALIST: Mr. Idle, what is your next film going to be?
ME: *Jesus Christ, Lust for Glory.*

Interestingly, the Pythons began to take my gag seriously. Gilliam and I improvised disgracefully on the theme one drunken evening in Amsterdam, using highly blasphemous jokes, for which I blame the beer, but it was John Cleese who really liked the idea of doing something about religion. Nobody had ever done anything on the subject. It was a big blank space for comedy. We began by doing research, reading biblical history, the Dead Sea Scrolls, and the Apocrypha, some of the weirder books that never made it into the Bible. We screened some of the hilarious Hollywood movies made about Christianity: *The Robe, The Shoe, Ben-Him, Ben-Her,* you know the sort of thing. They were magnificent mainly for the appalling acting of major Hollywood stars that made us laugh a lot.

JOHN WAYNE: Shirley this man was the son of Gawd.

We agreed early on, you couldn't knock Christ. How can you attack a man who professes peace to all people, speaks out for the meek, heals the poor, and cures the sick? You can't. Comedy's business is some kind of search for truth. Clearly this was a very great man, leaving aside for a minute his potential divinity. No, the problem with Christianity was the followers, who would happily put each other to death at the drop of a dogma. You could be burned alive if you didn't believe Christ was actually in the Communion wafer (what, *cannibalism?*), and they are still bickering about whether gluten-free bread constitutes the real Christ or not. I mean, it's nuts. Christ admired, saved, and protected women. The followers denied them, locked them up, and insisted in about the twelfth century that the clergy become celibate, with highly predictable results, from popes shagging their daughters to pedophilia.

What we needed for our purposes was a surrogate for Christ. So Brian was born. For a while he was just one of the followers. He was given the job of trying to book a table for the Last Supper:

"Sorry, mate, it's Seder; we're fully booked."

"No, we can't do a table for thirteen. I can give you one of six, and then another for seven over by the window."

"Why don't you want to use *both* sides of the table?"

At this stage Brian was just a writer, like the other followers who gave the Messiah tips on his speeches: "Lose the bit about the meek, they'll be too timid to turn up anyway, hit 'em with a couple of beatitudes, the parable about the Samaritans plays good, render a bit unto Caesar so as not to offend the Romans, and then end with the trick of changing the water into wine. That's always very popular, everybody has a good drink and you're home and dry."

People say, "Oh, you'd never make fun of Mohammedans," and of course not. We're not Muslims. We were brought up as Christians. I was sent to church twice every Sunday from the age of seven to nineteen, and I loved the language of the King James Bible. I must have heard it read aloud at least three times in chapel. At the age of fourteen I was confirmed by the Bishop of Something, and I even for a while was a believer, but when a boy asked our Padre at school whether he thought Jesus was the son of God, he surprisingly answered: "Well no, old bean." That from the Padre. So, we had earned the right to examine Christianity, and we treated it seriously. People who thought we were attacking Jesus clearly never saw the movie. He is *in* the film twice: once at his birth, where it is made very clear that Brian is born next-door and the Three Wise Men have come to the wrong stable, and once at the Sermon on the Mount, where the crowd at the back, quite reasonably, can't hear very well.

"I think he said, 'Blessed are the Greek.'"

Our movie became about the followers, the interpreters, the exploiters, and the profiteers, the people who seek to control those who wish to believe. A perfectly legitimate target for satire, and one appreciated by many people in the Church, who understood the joke is not about Christ, but about man.

"Or *woman*."

Yes, alright, Stan.

To avoid cheap blasphemy gags, and really examine the subject, Brian became a man who suffers the awful fate of being mistaken for the Messiah. A terrible nightmare. No matter what he does or says, he cannot refute it.

"I'm *not* the Messiah."

"Only a true Messiah would deny his divinity."

"Well, what chance does that give me? Fuck off."

"*How* shall we fuck off, O Lord?"

Brian, of course, is a tragedy. Pursued by his followers and wanted by the Romans, he is captured and sentenced to death by crucifixion, then the major form of execution used throughout the Roman Empire.

"What will they do to me?"

"Oh, you'll probably get away with crucifixion."

"*Get away* with crucifixion?"

"Yeah, first offense."

Mass crucifixions were common. Two thousand of Spartacus's followers were crucified along the Appian Way. Some were even set alight. (An early form of street lighting.) There is nothing special about crucifixion. In a different century Christ would have been hanged and his followers would all now wear nooses. But in March 1976 it gave us a big problem with the script. With Brian and many of his followers headed for death, how on earth were we going to end the film?

I had a lightbulb moment.

"Well, it has to be with a song," I said.

"What?"

"A song. Sung from the crosses. A ridiculously cheery song about looking on the bright side. Like a Disney song. Maybe even with a little whistle."

And they laughed.

"Like a sort of Spartacus musical," said someone.

"They can dance, too," said Gilliam with a gleam in his eye.

And they laughed at the idea that it could become a big production number.

And then everybody said, "That's it! We've got our ending. Hooray, let's go home for the day!"

So, it went into the script as "I'm Looking on the Bright Side," and I said, "I'll write it up," and I took home some notes I'd scribbled on the back of the script, got my guitar out, and it didn't take very long at all. The first thing I wrote was the whistle (G/Dm7/Am7/E7) using jazz chords that I had learned from the Mickey Baker guitar course. It took me maybe twenty minutes to sort out the basic shape of the song using major sixths and minor sevenths and the very useful diminished chord, which George Harrison told me the Beatles called "the sneaky chord." The verse also appeared very quickly: Am7/# (*sneaky*)/G/Gmaj6 / Am7/# (*sneaky*)/G and the words flowed quite simply. After about an hour I had to stop and collect Carey, who was now three years old, from nursery school, and I remember driving home in a hurry so I could play him what I'd written. He really liked the song with its whistling chorus. I had changed the lyric to "Always Look on the Bright Side of Life" to fit my tune, and I recorded it then and there on a little Sony tape recorder, which I still have, and played it the next day to the rest of the chaps. They seemed to like it.

I had been trying to persuade the Pythons to go out to the West

Indies in January 1978 for our writing fortnight instead of staying in freezing London. John Cleese was in favor of it, but Michael was all Alan Bennetty: "Oo, I don't think I can do that. Oo, I don't want to go abroad. Oo, it's so far. Oo, it's a waste of money . . ." And neither of the Terrys was keen. I wanted to show Tania Barbados and we had been invited to spend Christmas in Heron Bay at American U.N. Ambassador Marietta Tree's villa with Ricky Fataar and Penelope Tree. We were being offered the Pink Cottage, the most beautiful coral stone guesthouse, right on the beach. A total dream. No way I wasn't going.

Shortly before we left, Mick Jagger rang me. Was I going to Barbados for Christmas?

"Yes."

Did I know Bryan Ferry?

"Yes. A bit."

Would I take Bryan with me?

"What? No."

Oh. Well then could *he* come?

"Why?"

"I've just run off with Jerry, Bryan's girlfriend, and I need to hide from the papers."

"Oh, alright then."

We arranged to hide him and Jerry Hall on the other side of the island in a little village appropriately named Bathsheba. There they hid away happily in Matilda, a tiny cottage, though the owner said they broke the bed. I would have expected nothing less.

Jerry was a very friendly Texan lass, and when they came over to Heron Bay she climbed on the back of a cow in a field behind the house.

"Careful, Jerry," I said.

"Ah, no need to worry, we ride 'em all the time in Texas."

At which the cow took off at high speed with Jerry on top.

Unfortunately the cow was tethered, so at the end of its rope it came to an abrupt halt. Jerry didn't. She wasn't hurt. Except by our laughing so much.

Christmas in Barbados was wonderful with all the Santas in the

Matilda, where we hid Mick and Jerry from the newspapers. Photo by Richard Avedon. Me, Tania, Penelope Tree, Carey, Max, Ricky, Mike Nichols, and Annabel.

sun, and the wispy cotton wool snow, which is as near to the real thing as I ever like to come. With January approaching and the appeal of winter London paling, I tried one more plea to the Pythons to come out. We could all stay at Heron Bay. It would be brilliant. It would be productive. It would be warm. Amazingly, they agreed. Graham had spent Christmas in detox, fighting off alcohol. The sun would do him good. John was doing some kind of tax year abroad. So out they came. It actually made a lot of sense for everybody to get away and stay together in one house for two weeks. We could concentrate on the script, and talk about it while we dined and swam and relaxed. So it indeed proved. We had a very efficient and very pleasant time staying at the Palladian villa right on the beach in St. James. It was great to think that Ronald Tree's friend Winston Churchill had sat writing in the same splendid drawing room open to the sea breezes; and that Mr. Brown, who served us all cocktails, had also served the great man.

Keith Moon, the Who's drummer, followed us to Barbados. Like Graham, he was on Heminevrin, a dangerous drug used to combat the effects of alcohol withdrawal. Graham had wanted Keith to play the lead in his movie *The Odd Job*, but the producers wouldn't let him and instead we had offered him a part in *Brian*. I had met Keith on a very improbable night in London, where I hung out with him and Lionel Bart, the writer of the musical *Oliver!* They were great pals and quite an act, and Keith was inspiringly generous, once setting off from his home in his dressing gown driving his lawn mower to the nearest old people's home, holding aloft two bottles of champagne, then sitting and playing the piano with them for hours, singing old favorites. Now he would wait patiently for us to play on the beach at lunchtime. Even in the West Indies we worked office hours, and it was sweet to see him in the evening playing Scrabble with Cleese and Chapman, adding the word CAT to their very long words. Mick Jagger also came to dinner with Jerry, and we played charades, at which he was terrific. It was a wonderful time, and very productive. We finished writing the final draft of *Life of Brian* in January 1978.

Writing *Life of Brian*, Heron Bay, January 1978.

One man who was extremely interested in what we were up to was Barry Spikings, a movie executive from EMI, who had a house nearby, and he kept on at me to show him the script, which I did as soon as they all left. He called me the next day and said he had fallen out of bed laughing, and he wanted to make it. So, immediately EMI bought it and everything was hunky-dory. We were scheduled to shoot the film in the autumn in Tunisia. Sets were being built, costumes designed, locations scouted, all the millions of tiny things that need doing on a movie before the actors swan in and complain about everything, when we got the shocking news that EMI had pulled out. Lord Bernard Delfont had read the script, and he and his brother Lew Grade were adamant that EMI should make no such film, which he said was "obscene and sacrilegious." We were totally in the hole for a lot of money, as we had blithely used our own to get the production started, confident in the knowledge that EMI would pay us back. Now they denied all such responsibility. We had no choice but to sue them to recover our costs. It was a simple case and didn't take long, but one of the clauses of the settlement is that I am not allowed to tell you who had to pay for everything. So, I won't. Let's just say that it wasn't us, and I rather cheekily stuck a reference to Lord Delfont into the playout of "Bright Side":

"I told them, Bernie I said, they'll never make their money back . . ."

Now all we had to do was find another backer. John Goldstone and I set off optimistically for New York, where we met several financial people who looked at us as if we were trying to sell them *Springtime for Hitler*. We got nowhere. Not even a tickle of interest. The same in Hollywood. No one was prepared to pay for a movie "sending up religion." It was quite depressing as the clock was ticking in Tunisia, where everything was on hold. From time to time I called George back in England and he would say, "I'm getting the money. I'm going to find the money," but I never really believed him because I didn't think anyone, not even a Beatle, could come up with four million dollars privately. When I had showed it to our old producer friend Michael White, he practically passed out at the figure. It was ten times the amount we had raised for *The Holy Grail*. Still we persisted in Hollywood, but to no effect; it was a total no. What could we do? What were we going to tell the others?

Ring. Ring.

It was George. "I've got the money," he said. "We're making the film!"

Incredibly, he had mortgaged Friar Park, his home in Henley, to pay for the entire budget. A quite extraordinary act of generosity. Denis O'Brien, his wily Bialystok, arranged for the film to become a tax loss, they formed a new company, Handmade Films, and we were on. A miracle indeed, for without George, *Life of Brian* would never have been made. He visited us on the set in Tunisia and when he asked me how it was going, I grumpily muttered something about how between John and Michael it was difficult getting onscreen. He said, "Imagine what it was like with Lennon and McCartney trying to get studio time." Say no more.

John had really wanted to play Brian, and Michael too had been dropping hints about the role, but it was clear to anyone (i.e., me) that Graham was far and away the best choice. He had conquered alcohol unlike poor Keith Moon, who had succumbed to the effects of Heminevrin and alcohol (which are lethal) and died in Harry Nilsson's flat in Mayfair on September 7, 1978. Keith was supposed to be in our movie, and I hugged him the night he died. We were both attending Paul McCartney's opening of *The Buddy Holly Story* and he came racing across and began spouting his lines from *Brian* as a mad prophet:

"And there shall at that time be monstrous things . . ."

He was terrific in his Robert Newton voice and I said, "Yes, yes, Keith, that's great, save it for next week."

Sadly, after the movie that night he took a glass of champagne, and with alcohol and a little bit of food, that was that. He choked to death in the same bed where Mama Cass had died.

The very next day, September 8, a few days before we left for location in Tunisia, I recorded "Bright Side" at Chappell of Bond Street. John Altman had arranged it for a small orchestra with a nice swing jazz feel, and the Fred Tomlinson Singers stood in for the absent Pythons. At the end, I put on a vocal but wasn't happy with it. It was too straight and it bothered me. In Tunisia, we played the track for the crew during a break, and I suddenly realized what was missing: it needed Mr.

Cheeky to sing it. He was a cheery Cockney character I was playing, loosely based on our sparks. We loved these Lee Electric Lighting guys, who would do anything for us and remained ridiculously optimistic in all sorts of distressing circumstances. They were also famous for their practical jokes. Once, on location with us in Devon, they had taken one of their crew, who had passed out from too much beer, and put him in his hotel bed on the hotel lawn with all the hotel room furniture around him, so when he woke up in the morning he was in his room but outside. They were great, and they clearly influenced us.

> CENTURION: Crucifixion?
> MR. CHEEKY: No, freedom for me. They said I could go free
> and live on an island somewhere.
> CENTURION: Oh, right, well that's jolly good, off you go then.
> MR. CHEEKY: Nah. I'm only pulling your leg, it's crucifixion
> really!

With John Goldstone on set, listening to the new vocal.

Now that I knew Mr. Cheeky should be singing the song, I asked Garth, the sound recordist, if we could get a new vocal onto the track. That night I took a bottle of Boukha, a high-octane local spirit of figs, containing between 36 and 40 degrees of alcohol, into his tiny bedroom at the unit hotel in Monastir. We stuck mattresses round the walls and, with him lying on the floor with a boom mike, John Goldstone giggling in a corner, and me swigging on the Boukha, I really let rip with the Cheeky character and the song suddenly came to life. The single is still just a take of me singing live in a hotel bedroom in Tunisia.

13

THE BRITISH EMPIRE STRIKES BACK

Strange things kept happening to me in the Seventies. At some point Python had become not so much hot as cool. Because of that, I met a lot of very interesting people. I didn't seek them out. They found me. What am I supposed to say?

"Fuck off, Keith Richards, I am not coming upstairs with you to sing till dawn in Rome"?

"No, Mick Jagger, I will not come with you to the Monte Carlo Grand Prix"?

"Bugger off, Bowie, who wants to join you on a yacht in the Caribbean"?

Heroes had become friends. Once you're in the circus you're all in the circus, and of course it turns out that they are real people too, and have a sense of humor, which we had effectively tickled. Celebrity fans became even more noticeable after I became friends with George Harrison. A Beatle and a Python is a fairly unbeatable combination. I mean, look at the picture on the next page.

It's my kitchen door in St. John's Wood. Through this same door, George had brought Eric Clapton to meet me. Eric kindly gave me a rock fossil. I hope I refrained from making the obvious joke. We all then went to the Hammersmith Odeon to watch Bob Marley, where we sat *on the stage,* next to the singers. Does *wow* hack it? They were smoking the most enormous spliffs backstage, so I think the concert started two years late.

"And the winner is . . ."

But what is this picture telling us except that Harrison Ford is obviously completely happy, and even the young, sweet, and slightly insecure Mark Hamill is having a good time? I am coming through the door with a beard and a Silver Disc award for a Python album—but which, and when, and why? I found the photograph ping-ponging around the Internet. Somebody sends it to me on Twitter every three months or so. It was taken by the legendary rock-and-roll photographer Lynn Goldsmith, who was staying with the cast's costar Carrie Fisher in our house off Abbey Road. But what the hell is going on? Champagne has already been poured and the evening promises to get rowdy. Rarely did such promises go unfulfilled. The most memorable was an impromptu party that featured the return of the Boukha. In fact, not only did it help *make* one scene in a movie, now it helped *mar* one scene in another.

I had brought back a bottle of this lethal brew from Tunisia for a rainy day, and this particular day it was pissing down. I'd met the delightful Carrie Fisher in New York while doing *Saturday Night Live*. She was utterly adorable, smart as a whip, funny and beautiful, and all the guys were crazy about her. She gave me a ride up Fifth Avenue in her little silver Mercedes, flipped on the stereo, and began improvising scenes from Noël Coward. She rented our house in St. John's Wood while she was filming *The Empire Strikes Back,* and one day I found both her and Harrison Ford very despondent. They were filming at Elstree, which is not the end of the world, but you can see it from there. Shooting long days on a special effects movie can be tedious for an actor, as I found out for myself on *The Adventures of Baron Munchausen,* where I chewed my own foot off. (I got better.) This day they were so down that I said, "You need my special remedy," and I brought out the Boukha rocket fuel, which I had used to sing my vocal to "Bright Side" in the hotel room in Monastir.

"This will definitely cheer you up," I said.

It did. A party broke out and, if you can believe this, all of the Rolling Stones turned up. I of course pretended to the *Star Wars* folk that this was no big deal and happened all the time, but it began an epic night which ended only at 6:00 a.m. when the cars came to pick up the actors for work and the Stones sloped off to hang upside down in their caves. When I saw *The Empire Strikes Back,* I was so proud. The scene they shot that morning bears the scars of the evening. Carrie lurches out of a spaceship to meet Billy Dee Williams and says, "Hi!" Harrison is still clearly drunk. I remain inordinately proud of the scene I spoiled and hope that one day George Lucas will forgive me.

My time in the early Seventies was often pure rock and roll. Sitting with Ronnie Wood in his Malibu Colony rental, we would be suddenly swept up by Neil Young and taken for a ride in his enormous customized tour bus with its exquisite hand-carved wooden interior. There were glimpses of the California governor, Jerry Brown, quietly dating Linda Ronstadt. What a strange world it was—Ronnie Wood naughty and always beaming, Keith laconic, Mick whirling like a dervish. Mick was always very funny about me and would send me up in an impeccable Northern accent by saying, "And now, ladies and gentlemen, a man who has spent the last few years entertaining the British public in a short wig and a funny mustache."

The party went on everywhere; one minute we were at Studio 54 in New York, the next on Dodi Fayed's yacht in Monte Carlo. Mick had driven me, Tania, and Jerry to the Monaco Grand Prix from Bill Wyman's house in St. Paul de Vence, where we were all staying. It was only an hour or two before the race, and I wondered where on earth he was going to park.

"*Parking!*" he said contemptuously. "Don't worry about that."

We drove right to the heart of the race by the Monte Carlo Casino. Police were everywhere.

"Ready, everyone," said Mick. "One, two, three" and we simply got out of the car.

"Good job it's rented," said Mick with a naughty smile, as the Monégasque police towed away his car. *Parking* indeed.

He was instantly grabbed by Régine the New York Nightclub Queen, and within seconds we were sipping champagne at the Moët et Chandon top table at the Hôtel de Paris, while French executives looked at us, puzzled.

The Grand Prix was deafening, the cars racing through the canyons below, shifting gears noisily. We leaned over them on balconies.

"Who's winning?" Andy Warhol asked me, and I was very proud of my reply:

"The red car, Andy."

At the Cannes Film Festival that followed, we had a loud and pissy lunch at the Hotel du Cap with George and Olivia and Ringo. The terrace was packed with celebrities.

"Look," someone said, "there's David Begelman." Begelman was a top studio executive who had been an agent and was currently in the middle of a big scandal for forging his client Cliff Robertson's signature on his paychecks.

I approached his table with a pen.

"Excuse me, Mr. Begelman," I said. "Big fan. May I have Cliff Robertson's autograph?"

On this trip with George and Olivia, we followed their friend Barry Sheene, the British motorbike champion, down to the French Grand Prix at the Paul Ricard Circuit, where he duly won the 750cc motorcycle race going impossibly fast and low around corners.

"I saw you guys," he said, "and I wanted to wave but I didn't have time to take my hand off the accelerator."

He saw us? In the crowd. Jesus.

You met all sorts at George's. I met a strange Peter Sellers, who kept disappearing upstairs with a Swedish model. I think amyl nitrate was the cause of his dangerous complexion, and he would soon die for four minutes in LA, though mercifully he was brought back to life, at least for the time being. Terry Southern, a Texan writer who wrote *The Magic Christian, Candy,* and *Easy Rider,* was a friend of Mick's, and he always carried around a shoebox of little vials and random loose pills that he would casually offer.

"I don't think so, thanks, Terry," said Mick as we stood in a light snowfall somewhere in Greenwich Village.

"What are they?" asked Tania.

"I don't know. Take one," Terry said.

"No thanks," she said wisely.

We went to smart opening-night parties, Dolly Parton's first performance in New York at the Bottom Line on May 14, 1977, and lots of *Saturday Night Live* parties. I hosted the show four times in the Seventies and marveled that they could write anything, so fucked up did they get. Python always wrote office hours. The idea that you would try to write comedy while under the influence of anything was anathema to us. On Tuesday nights on *SNL,* they would write all night, the offices reeking with the scent of marijuana. The host was expected to stay up and hang with them as they got more stupefied and less and less inspired. Rewrites were unheard of. They went straight from pitch to set design. I loved the cast, particularly Dan Aykroyd and Gilda Radner, though they were all sweet and friendly. Belushi was very protective of Tania and gave me warnings not to leave her. As if.

I hosted the classic *SNL* show where Belushi did dueling Joe Cockers, and that was some party afterwards. I remember writing *Good night Joe* on his arm with a Sharpie as he lay peacefully passed out on the floor of a New York apartment. The last time I hosted *SNL,* on October 10, 1979, Bob Dylan was the musical guest, and he was going through his Christian phase with a brilliant album, *Slow Train Coming,* but he seemed very paranoid. He'd get off the elevator at the Essex House hotel on our floor, and then stay with me while he asked Tania to go up one flight of stairs and make sure there was no one outside his door. There never was. I tried a joke.

"We can arrange for someone if you like . . ."

But nothing.

He was highly aware of all that went on around him. John Candy and I were once guest appearing in the "Wilbury Twist" promo video, and I was placed by the director behind Bob Dylan. It's normal in these circumstances, when filming, to lean slightly left or right to find the camera. I leaned right; Dylan leaned right. I leaned left; he leaned left. He was preternaturally aware of where I was behind him and determined to stay in front. He seemed to have extrasensory vision. I was impressed and gave up. Hey, it was their video.

One other guest on my last *SNL* show was the strangely weird and wonderful Andy Kaufman. I had met him a couple of times and went to see his show in New York, where I had very much enjoyed him. During the intermission, he went offstage and left his mike on and you could hear him throughout the interval trying to persuade this poor girl backstage to give him a blow job. I loved his Mighty Mouse bit, and no one ever did a better or more unexpected Elvis. On *SNL*, he arrived with Bob Zmuda, and this was the first time he did his notorious wrestling-women act on TV. They brought on an entire wrestling ring and Zmuda was the referee. Andy baited the women in the audience, boasting he could beat any woman there, saying horrible sexist things about their role and place in society: "God, man, woman, dog . . ." Not surprisingly, he had several angry women takers from the audience keen to wrestle with him. I was on set, racing to change costumes for my next sketch, when I saw one woman Andy was heading toward. He was going to choose her. I ran forward to the stage manager.

"Joe," I said, "you can't let him take her."

"Why not?"

"She's *pregnant*."

My mother in me, the outraged health visitor, had intervened. I'm glad to say they stopped her. We took my mother to see Andy Kaufman when we met her in San Francisco. She was on a world cruise. It was her third time. She said to me: "I wish there was somewhere else to go." She had already been to Egypt, where, she said, "I saw the tomb of Carmen Tutu." My favorite of hers was when she said, "I don't want to come and stay if it's not inconvenient." But apart from world-class malapropisms, she could be good fun, and we met her off the boat and took her to see Rodney Dangerfield, who had Andy opening for him. Unfortunately, Andy sent on his alter ego, Tony Clifton, which was a character he played, an appallingly lush and offensive lounge singer. That night he was particularly vile, and incensed the audience, and then refused to leave the stage. I seriously thought there was going to be a riot. I have never experienced such anger from an audience. They yelled and screamed abuse, and he would only taunt them further. Poor Rodney Dangerfield. When they finally dragged Tony Clifton off, he came on to a cold and angry audience. I went backstage to say hello afterwards and he was shaken and furious. "Never again," he said.

I'm sort of with him on that. My kind of insult comedian was Don Rickles, and he and I played separate heads of a two-headed dragon in an animated film called *Quest for Camelot.* We improvised happily for days in a recording studio and they used not one single word. The movie tanked.

The strange things kept happening. Pink Floyd record producer Bob Ezrin invited Tania and me to visit him in a studio in Provence the very evening Roger Waters was recording his lead vocal for "Another Brick in the Wall." Just him. Just us. Timing.

We don't need no education . . .

Well, actually you clearly do, or you'd say "*any* education."

We hung out a bit with Roger in France. I thought his idea for the *Wall* tour, where they literally built a wall between the performers and the audience, was one of the most brilliant theatrical ideas of all time. I still do, even though Trump has tried to steal it.

More strange things: I stood in an elevator at Madison Square Garden after the Ali vs. Quarry world heavyweight fight, face-to-face with Henry Kissinger. Next to me stood his burly security guard. Behind Kissinger stood Ronnie Wood, putting his tongue out and making silly faces all the way down, trying to make me giggle. Kissinger's security guard hadn't a clue what to do. Had anyone threatened his charge physically his reaction would have been swift and lethal, but he wasn't trained to deal with a Rolling Stone mocking his client behind his back. We both stood side by side, desperately trying not to grin, pretending it wasn't happening.

More strange things. Why was it me standing on a table at Tramp at four in the morning with Harry Nilsson, George, and Ringo, bawling out "Volare" at the top of our lungs, trying to drown out the next table of loudly singing Italian waiters? Someone had to do it, I guess. People seem amazed these days that we all knew each other, but we were all part of the same generation of postwar kids who grew up with the rationing and shortages of the Fifties and conquered the world in every field in the Sixties—writing, art, poetry, painting, photography, couture, rock, and in our case comedy. It was an amazing Renaissance, as this brave new world was created out of the ashes and bomb sites of a world war that had just slaughtered sixty million.

The strangest thing of all was that Elvis turned out to be a big Python fan. That was mind-blowing. He had meant so much to me, and had saved our lives in the Ophny. I now learned he took his guys to private screenings of *The Holy Grail* late at night in Memphis. Not only that, but he had all the tapes of our TV show on his plane. That Elvis should love something I did was the world turned upside down. I knew Elvis had a sense of humor. His Vegas recording of "Are You Lonesome Tonight" where he cracks up after he changes a line to "Do you gaze at your bald head and wish you had hair" went to number one in the U.K. It's not so much the line as the lack of response from the Vegas audience that makes him unable to continue singing the song. He laughs helplessly throughout. It's still on my jukebox.

What finally blew my mind, and I had trouble believing it, was when

I met the delightful Linda Thompson and she told me that Elvis would make her sit up in bed at night and do Python Pepperpot voices with him. They would screech loudly in middle-aged English female voices:

"Oo, hello, Mrs. Thing!"

"Hello, Mrs. Entity. How are you then?"

"I need a new brain."

"Well, why don't you get a new Curry's brain then."

He didn't. I refused to believe it. I made her tell me three times before she finally convinced me, and then only because she knew the phrase "Curry's brain." No American would know that reference. It still amazes me.

"If Elvis had been alive today he would be your stalker. He loved you guys so much. He particularly loved the 'Nudge Nudge' sketch. He called everybody 'Squire' from it. There were only three TV channels, ABC, NBC, and CBS, and when they went off the air late-night he would make me sit up in bed and do Python sketches with him."

I still can't really believe that Elvis, the one who saved our lives at school, was such a fan.

14

A VERY NAUGHTY BOY

From the moment *Monty Python's Life of Brian* opened in the summer of 1979, "Always Look on the Bright Side of Life" began to take on a life of its own. To help promote the movie, it was released as a double-sided single, paired rather oddly with another of my songs, "All Things Dull and Ugly," a parody of the rather bland Victorian hymn "All Things Bright and Beautiful":

> *All things dull and ugly*
> *All creatures short and squat*
> *All things rude and nasty*
> *The Lord God made the lot.*

It got nowhere, of course, but then our singles never did. (Though the evolutionary biologist and author Richard Dawkins reprinted the lyrics in his book *The Greatest Show on Earth*.) When the film opened in California, Harry Nilsson and Timothy Leary were going mad for "Bright Side," and Harry told me he was going to record it for his new album. The recording sessions went on for days, culminating in an all-star celebrity chorus. I have never been one for spending hours in the studio, so I was less than happy to sit around listening to someone doing overdubs on my song, even if it was Donald "Duck" Dunn. In fact, I wrote a waspish little song of my own, called "Harry":

He's a pretty nifty guy
Always looks you in the eye
Everybody passing by will sigh for Harry,

which includes the little stinger:

Here's a little gentle song
A sorta sentimental song
At least it didn't take us very long, Harry!

We recorded it at Redwood Studios in a single day with John Du Prez producing and my lovely singer-songwriter friend Charlie Dore singing along with me. John and I had begun working on "The Life of Brian" with the Otto song, and we would spend the next forty years working together. We did many Python songs for the *Contractual Obligation Album,* recorded about six for *The Meaning of Life,* produced *Monty Python Sings,* and wrote several musicals before eventually having a Broadway hit with *Spamalot.* John was the most perfect partner you could ever wish for. He did everything I couldn't. Effortlessly. Once we were recording "I Like Chinese."

"Damn," I said.

"What?" asked John.

"If we'd thought ahead we could have had it translated and sung a verse in Chinese."

"Well," said John, "I only speak Mandarin . . ."

While he filmed *Popeye* with Robin Williams and Shelley Duvall, Robert Altman had had the insane idea of taking rock musicians with him to Malta to work on the movie's soundtrack. This led to legendary drug excesses and predictable madness on that Mediterranean island. Amongst the ringleaders was Harry. Now we sent Derek Taylor off to hand-deliver our new song, "Harry," to its eponymous subject. The gift took him completely by surprise. Harry responded like a child at Christmas. No one had ever given him such a present. A song about him! He played it to everyone on the movie and then for everyone on the island. He couldn't get enough of it. So fond was he of this little song that not only does his version of "Bright Side" close his final album, he actually opens *Flash Harry* with me singing my song "Harry." That's right, *I open a Harry Nilsson album.* Sadly, *Flash Harry* was only released in the U.K. at the time; it would be another thirty years before it was released in the States, along with a fine documentary film, *Who Is Harry Nilsson (and Why Is Everybody Talkin' About Him?)* which features my little ditty.

There were many nights of madness with Harry in Hollywood, because he liked a good argument and a good drink, and when Harry turned up on your doorstep people often disappeared for days. Not me, I hasten to add, for I had my own Bright Side by my side. In fact, Tania says Harry offered her a huge plate of cocaine at a party at Timothy Leary's house when she was eight months pregnant. She pointedly gestured at her enormous stomach.

Harry said, "Oh sorry, love."

On another occasion, he accidentally knocked his own toddler into the pool. Oops. Harry never really recovered from the Beatle praise from John Lennon: "Harry Nilsson is our favorite group," but he certainly wrote and sang like an angel until all this boozing and schmoozing and smoking and snorting finally put paid to his golden voice, and in the end, far too soon, it put paid to him. He died on the eve of the 1994 Northridge earthquake, which struck in the middle of the night while he was lying in his casket in an Agoura Hills funeral parlor. When the 6.7 tremblor hit, he was thrown clean out of his coffin. A perfect Harry thing to do. Still falling off the stage.

Brian opened to huge controversy. Tania and I were supposed to fly Concorde from Paris for the opening of the movie, but the night before we were due to leave, a thousand rabbis suddenly appeared on the streets of New York protesting the movie. A thousand *what,* now? Everyone seemed puzzled. Didn't they get the memo? The rabbis went away as quickly as they had appeared and were replaced by angry Christians, who picketed the Burbank Studios in LA, claiming that Warner Brothers were the agents of the devil, though everyone knows that's CAA's job. Bob Daley and Terry Semel stood firm. In fact, for them it was a blessing. These controversies were on the TV news. We were making headlines round America every night. There was no need for us to fly to the States and do publicity. There's only one thing you can't do, and that is stop Americans watching what they want. Hey, even pornography is called Freedom of Speech. So, while the movie was being pulled from cinemas across America, people would simply drive across state lines. This pattern repeated itself everywhere. Half of the U.K. banned it and the other half flocked to it. Sweden advertised it as the movie so funny that Norwegians weren't allowed to see it.

One nice footnote to the *Brian* controversy: in our movie, Sue Jones-Davies, a Welsh actress, played Brian's revolutionary girlfriend Judith. She was fiercely naked in one of the scenes. When the movie was first released in her hometown of Aberystwyth in North Wales, the local council banned the film from public screening. Thirty years later she became the mayor of Aberystwyth and overthrew the ban. Isn't that great?

Thanks to all the fuss and protests, the movie did extremely well at the box office, but after this madness I ran away for a while with the lovely Tania. I was tired of fame, and sick of being recognized as Monty Python. *Hey Monty!* Thank heavens we didn't call it *Whither Canada?* or people would be yelling *Hey Whither!* at me. We fled to France, where for many years I remained anonymous, just this whacko Brit who lived on a hill in the middle of nowhere. I had bought a little property with Lyn in 1971, thinking I could write just as badly in France as I did in London, and now I bought her half from her. It was really only a glorified cowshed, with a bedroom, bathroom, and tiny kitchen, but it had beautiful terraced views over the Var, with ancient olive trees and a pine forest at the top and bottom of the hill. We'd had the place for eight years with no electricity, and had even had to find water, hitting a crystal-clear source eighty meters below the ground. Tania and I now decided to build on, behind our little shackeau. We called it the House of Brian.

Who could fail to love Provence? Lavender, rosemary, fennel, thyme, and a wind so furious it has its own name, Le Mistral, which sweeps the sky clean of clouds, taking all meteorological depression away and lifting the spirits and filling you with energy, but then stays for days, banging away like an old quarrel, grating on your nerves, making you irritable and cranky. But then, one beautiful morning, it stops and the sun shines and the countryside twinkles. It's like magic.

When I first discovered the Var, it was officially the most underpopulated Department in France. There were hardly any French, it was mainly Spanish and Italians, and a few *pieds-noir* (Algerian colonists) who had fled from Algeria. Of course, I didn't make it easy on myself by buying a property with no road, no water, and no electricity. Sometimes I feel I experienced all stages of civilization, and that was a good thing. *No water?* A forage. *No electricity?* Oil lamps. *Music?* Cassette batteries. *No cooker?* Gas bottles. *No fridge?* Camping gas. *No road?* I'll hump the gas bottles in a wheelbarrow over the terraces. *No shade?* I'll plant trees. *And fires?* You bet. We were burned twice in forest fires, once in 1979 and again in 1999. Shortly before Électricité de France came bringing electricity, poet Stephen Spender had given me his magic lamp, a superior pumped-up oil lamp from his home in the Alpilles, on the day he got electricity. Now we too were being connected and I no longer had to hump up the hill in the cold dark night and attempt to start an outboard motor to fill the cistern. Of course, the water always ran out at night. Sod's Law is written in French. Everything stops, everything breaks. I used to call it "Fuck Provence" to the intense delight of my fellow-suffering, equally obsessive neighbor, Richard E. Grant. Another acquaintance was a very tall blond-haired man who could often be seen pushing around one of his first inventions—a wheelbarrow with a ball instead of a wheel. He and his lovely wife, Deirdre, and their delightful children were poor and very thin. She taught art and even sold some jewelry to help him build an improbable vacuum cleaner that no one wanted. He was, of course, James Dyson. You have to be completely obsessive to have a house in Provence . . .

After *Brian,* I took a long sabbatical, immersing myself in astronomy, learning about the immensity of our Universe, and generally

self-educating myself in cosmology. I spent the nights gazing at the unbelievable numbers of stars wheeling overhead in the Milky Way, and
wrote a lyric about it. I also read life science books, trying to understand
evolution and the extraordinary appearance of life in the Universe. I
could understand the physical Universe expanding and banging away,
but why does life evolve over billions of years to become you and me?
This opened my mind to the central question of the Universe: *What is
life?* To my mind, nobody has yet answered this question adequately.
Well, alright, Professor Brian Cox did, but we were both pissed at the
time, and we have completely forgotten what he said. Steve Martin, a
philosophy graduate, said that life exists so the Universe can experience itself.

In France, friends came to stay, I played guitar and read, and now
and again the odd Python would drop in. George and Liv visited, Paul
Simon and Carrie Fisher came to stay, Paul sitting in the garden writing lyrics.

One day Art Garfunkel drove up on a motorbike with Penny Mar-
shall and gave me a long ride down to the coast through the Gorges
du Verdon. My first time on a motorbike. David Bowie came to visit.
People loved the rustic simplicity of Provence.

I also wrote a play. I had built a dirt-floor shack in a pine wood up
the hill, and every morning at dawn I would walk up with a thermos
of tea. I had finished the play, and we were going back to the U.K. for
a couple of weeks, when Tania asked me to read it to her, so I went up
and brought it back down. Just as well, because while we were away the
whole forest burned down in a devastating fire. When we returned,
nothing remained of the forest. The shack was gone. Paradise looked
like the Somme. The smell of burnt wood was everywhere. But Tania
had saved my play. In 1982, *Pass the Butler,* directed by Jonathan Lynn,
toured the U.K., and then Michael White brought it into the West End
in 1983. On opening night, a lady said to me just before the curtain
went up: "Well, now let's see whether Tania did right to save the play
from the fire." Nice. With friends like that . . .

Pass the Butler ran at the Globe Theatre on Shaftesbury Avenue for

The Rutland Weekend Television Center. Before and after.

six months to howls of laughter, and only closed late in the Falklands War when people stopped going to the theater entirely. Early on in that war, "Always Look on the Bright Side of Life" was sung by the crew of the destroyer HMS *Sheffield* while they sat on the deck for three hours awaiting rescue from their sinking ship, after being hit by an Exocet missile. It was also sung by the crew of the stricken HMS *Coventry,* and they particularly enjoyed the ironic line "worse things happen at sea, you know . . . ," an ad-lib of mine from the playout. I found this very moving; and also, when it was sung by RAF Tornado Pilots as they suited up to fly dangerous low-level missions during Operation Desert Storm in the first Gulf War. What had started off as a caricature of a wartime song was now a real war song.

One odd footnote from the Falklands. Michael White, the producer of my play, had a dinner party at his Egerton Crescent home, and Koo Stark entered to a flash of paparazzi. Meanwhile her boyfriend, Prince Andrew, slipped over the back wall, aided by his protection detail. I was seated next to him and found him to be quite charming. When I asked him what he was doing, he said he was in the Falklands flying helicopters.

"Jeez," I said, "what exactly do you do?"

"Well," he said, "it's my job to fly around dropping chaff to lure the Exocet missiles away from our ships."

"Let me get this straight," I said. "The Queen is your mother and you've got the job of being a decoy for French missiles?"

"That's right," he said.

"Thank Christ I'm working-class," I said.

Michael White was always funny, and at one Cannes Film Festival, Tania and I played a little trick on him. He was employed by *Vanity Fair* to go to all the parties and take pictures of the stars. We watched him going from table to table clicking away. This was pre-digital time and cameras had real film in them, and because they were on a tight deadline Michael's unprocessed film was rushed to New York at the end of each day. During the party, I noticed that Michael had for once left his camera on the table while he went off and schmoozed. I looked at Tania.

"Come on," I said, seizing his camera and setting off for the gents. Giggling naughtily, we took a series of semi-pornographic selfies of a couple apparently having sex in a stall, without of course showing our faces. We then returned to the table and put his camera back. We tried hard to keep a straight face when Michael returned to collect it, but he didn't seem to suspect anything, picked it up, and went off in search of more celebrities. We could hear him going: "Nicole. Tom. Over here." *Click click click.*

Safely back in our hotel room, we laughed and laughed at the thought of *Vanity Fair* processing and reviewing the footage. In the middle of all those glittering stars they would suddenly come across our porny pictures taken in the toilets. We laughed at this for many years, though without ever telling Michael. It still makes me laugh. Michael "Chalky" White was for many years a fixture at Cannes, where he would play tennis in carefully torn shorts. Once he served a double fault and said unforgettably, "Sorry, I wasn't ready."

15

THE BOLLYWOOD HOLE

In September 1980, Monty Python ran for four nights at the legendary Hollywood Bowl, where we played to eight thousand screaming fans a night, a wild and crazy crowd best summed up by my line in the Bruces sketch:

"It's a typical Hollywood audience. All the kids are on drugs and all the adults are on roller skates."

Drugs were everywhere. Not just grass. Cocaine was abundant. You couldn't go to a record company meeting without some executive saying, "Let me take care of your nose." Hollywood made several movies at that time which can only be understood in the context of cocaine. In 1979, searching for a venue for Python to play in LA, I was shown several possibilities by a young, hip, tightly jeaned executive from a major live-event company. We went into the Pantages Theater on Hollywood Boulevard in the middle of a performance of *The King and I*. Yul Brynner was onstage. We walked through the auditorium and the young man talked normally to me, as if there were not two thousand patrons sitting in the dark spellbound. I marveled no one seemed to notice. Then we went to the Ford theater, an outdoor venue, where the Village People were onstage and the scent of amyl nitrate filled the air. Finally, we ended up for dinner at Carlos 'n Charlie's on Sunset across from the Chateau Marmont. A slight drizzle had begun, and as the executive pulled into the valet parking in his little silver Mercedes, he was rear-ended by the next arriving customer.

"All the kids are on drugs and the adults are on roller skates."

"Shit. I got to take care of this. Will you hold on to this for me?" he said, shoving a package into my hands.

"Sure," I said, and walked inside.

What was in the package he was so keen to get rid of before the police came? Did I know at that moment? The thought certainly occurred to me as I entered the restaurant. I decided it would be better to know, so I headed for the bathroom and opened the packet. I had never seen so much cocaine. I was looking at about fifteen years. Steeling myself, I calmly went and sat down at the table and ordered a strong martini. Soon he returned. I shoved the package onto his knees under the table.

"Thanks," he said.

We did not go with that company. We went with Denis O'Brien, who had figured out how to get a cheap Python movie out of us if we filmed our live performance at the Hollywood Bowl. We shot the show on a new 1,000-line Japanese video system, which we could easily convert into a movie, and our old BBCTV friend Terry Hughes, from *The Two Ronnies,* came in to direct.

The Hollywood Bowl was great fun, possibly the most fun we ever had together. We were spoiled rotten. George Harrison was there, Marty Feldman was there, Carrie Fisher was there, and Harry Nilsson was always there with Timothy Leary. Steve Martin, currently dating Bernadette Peters, threw us a party at his house, where Michael Palin was slightly embarrassed by a topless girl leaping into the Jacuzzi. I think he made some excuse about having to go off and read *The Daily Telegraph.* Terry Jones made no such excuse but plunged right in. To the water anyway. Though with Terry you never knew. He would always give a girl a decent chance.

Marty Scorsese threw us a party at our hotel, where he was working on *Raging Bull,* impressing me beyond belief by holding three separate conversations at once. Graham, who had rented a house in Brentwood, threw a party for his parents. It became star-studded and raucous and all of the Stones trooped in. There were slightly disapproving glances from elderly English people, and sharply at ten Graham's parents suggested to the Stones that it was getting late and time for them to leave. They all took the hint and cleared off.

"No problem, love," said Keith. It was probably still breakfast time for them.

After the show John Cleese and I stayed on to help Terry Hughes edit and adapt our two-hour, two-act live show into a ninety-minute film for Handmade Films. It was going to get a theatrical release.

Tania and I lived quietly in a bucolic canyon. One day Denis O'Brien came over. He had been eyeing me suspiciously, concerned about what I might have been saying to George about his many offshore companies and the mysterious, nameless people who ran them. I had indeed expressed some of these concerns to George. They were troubling. Now O'Brien told me I was fired from Monty Python. I laughed in his face.

"Denis, my dear, I think you will find you may cease to represent my financial interests, but you can't fire me from Monty Python. That's definitely not up to you. What will you do, sack a Beatle next?"

He was obviously very concerned that I was on to him and would reveal to George how shady he actually turned out to be. I think George must have asked him some questions and mentioned *my* name for O'Brien to have responded so abruptly. I had to go, and quickly. It would be many years before George finally learned the extent to which he had been bamboozled by his manager, and by then it cost him about thirty million dollars.

"Somebody should have warned me," he said. "Oh, that's right, you did."

By then, George hated Denis so much that he wrote and recorded a song called "Lyin' O'Brien." A few months after the Bowl, the rest of the Pythons decided that they too had had enough of him, and we all assembled for a conference at the Chewton Glen Hotel to decide how to tell him *he* was fired.

16

THE MEANING OF WIFE

There is only one edition of *Playboy* magazine from the Seventies that does not have a full nude on the cover. It features the beautiful derriere of a lovely lady in blue cutoff jeans on a bicycle seat. It is an unforgettable image, and it became iconic. The curve of her body. The elliptical perfection of those cheeks. The delicious delight of her golden globes. Reader, I married that lady.

Tania appeared on the cover of the September 1974 edition and, oddly, I too appeared in *Playboy,* in the November 1976 edition, only *I would be naked.* They reprinted an excerpt from my *Rutland Dirty Weekend Book:* "The Vatican Sex Manual," which shows you sixty-four positions in which it is impossible to have sex.

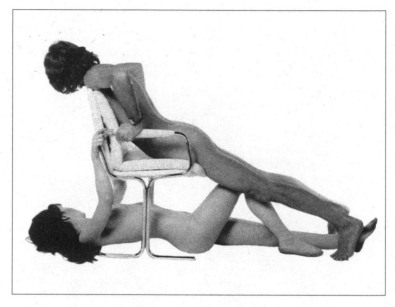

Position Number 14: The Chair.

I proposed to Tania after the Hollywood Bowl show in 1980, and high time too. I suddenly realized that I had been with her for four years and what the hell was I waiting for? Being a gentleman, I gave her till morning to consider my proposal. Luckily for me she said yes. Tania was the woman I had been waiting for my whole life, and I have been waiting for her ever since . . . I wrote on my graffiti wall at 41 Carlton Hill in the Seventies: *Time and tide wait for no man, but they do seem to make an exception for certain women.* This must of course be amended to *people* for our more correct times, because of course it is true of all sexes. I have been with Tania for forty-one years now. I gave that woman two of the best years of my life.

Tania was not only beautiful but very funny. She once asked me what I was reading and when I said, "The shorter Pepys," she asked me if there was a taller one. She could always crack me up. On her Twitter feed she describes herself as a "gagster's moll." She once entered England and wrote under Occupation: *Pillow*. In Sydney, she asked me what Australia Day was.

I said, "It's when Australians get together and drink."

"Oh," she said, "like nighttime."

Comedy was as vital to her as to me. Most of her friends were in comedy, particularly the Chicago improv theater Second City, and she became friends with John Belushi, Dan Aykroyd, Joe Flaherty, and Brian Doyle-Murray. She looked them up when she moved to New York, where *Saturday Night Live* was suddenly blossoming. This would bring us together.

I was fortunate that from the minute we met I inherited from Tania a large, loving family of American relatives. She grew up in the western suburbs of Chicago with her sister, Joyce, and two brothers: Mark, a cop who I saw box in the Golden Gloves, and Greg, a drummer who sold cars. There were three adorable nieces, Kris, Kim, and Sasha, and a whole slew of aunts and uncles. At Thanksgiving, there would be more than thirty sitting down for dinner.

Tania's mother, Algae, for whom I could do no wrong, was second-generation Italian from Napoli; and her father, Alex, was a Russian who had escaped from the Soviet Union in 1929, when the border changed overnight and it became Poland for a day. Alexander Kosevich drove a Chicago taxi most of his life, loved vodka and laughter and rescuing animals, and had a heart of gold. He played the accordion while his girls would dance the troika. He spent weeks bundling off packages of jeans to all the poor Russian relatives who lived near Kiev. Amazingly, he still thought Stalin was a good thing, which led to many heated arguments with me. Now I was surrounded by this whole argumentative, laughing, loving bunch of kin, who were perfectly prepared to accept that Tania had taken on this weird Brit. I was a very lucky bastard.

We were married in May 1981 in Susan and Lorne Michaels's

apartment in New York, with a party afterwards upstairs at Paul Simon's. All the relatives came.

Being married. Alex, my father-in-law, and Joyce, my sister-in-law.

We were married by a New York judge who brought her own vows. We both promised "to listen to each other's silences."

"Just married."

17

CINEMA: HALF SIN, HALF ENEMA

Before we fired him, Denis O'Brien had told John Cleese that after *Life of Brian,* if we made another movie he would never have to work again. This persuaded John to join us in writing what was then called *Monty Python's Fish Film.* The problem was we had no theme. For a while we worked on World War III, which was sponsored by advertisers, and then it became about a party of explorers in the Hindu Kush. While we attempted to bring some sense to a bunch of disparate sketches, Gilliam would sit doodling, pinning up images on a corkboard. One of his sketches was particularly memorable. It was a familiar sight, a typical London office draped with the canvas they use when washing buildings, except that it was billowing like a sail. It looked as if the building was just getting under way, and it was ripping out a huge anchor from the pavement. This image would form the basis of his *Crimson Permanent Assurance,* the short film that would open our next movie, if we ever got to make it, which was looking increasingly unlikely. We were getting nowhere.

We decided to go to the West Indies again for inspiration, this time choosing Jamaica. We spent a frustrating two weeks in a very pleasant house in St. Ann's Bay near Ocho Rios. But we were no closer to having a movie. It was still just a pile of sketches. No plot, no through-line, no consistent characters. We were on the point of abandoning the whole business and just having a holiday, when towards the end of our stay I came down to breakfast with an idea.

"I've been thinking that what this really could be all about is 'The Meaning of Life.'"

They loved that idea, even John, who said later it was particularly annoying, as he had been looking forward to the vacation. We set to work in the short time left to us, chopping, changing, and shaping our material to this theme.

We had taken some time off to explore the beauties of the island, and I spent a wonderful day with Terry Gilliam looking at Firefly, Noël Coward's delightful little house, with its fantastic view of the sea, and Ian Fleming's Goldeneye. I didn't know then that I would play Noël Coward in the movie and that "The Penis Song" would be called the "Not the Noël Coward Song." We moved on to Port Antonio, where we took an amazing river ride on a log raft down the Rio Grande, poled by a highly skilled young Jamaican, amongst some of the lushest and most perfect scenery I have ever seen. As we floated gently through this paradise, Terry would not stop moaning about Denis O'Brien, for whom he had also made *Time Bandits*. He went on and on until I finally said, "Terry, for God's sake, shut up and just *look* where you are. We can talk later."

When we got back to the house, we had a business meeting. Denis O'Brien owed us a million dollars from the Hollywood Bowl movie; what on earth were we going to do to pry it out of him?

"Why don't we seize his yacht?" I said. "We're in the Caribbean, it's moored not far away—we should just go and sail it off. He's not going to tell anyone that Monty Python has taken his yacht. He'll look like a total prat. We'll thank him for lending it to us and let him know that as soon as he pays us our money he can have his boat back."

To my surprise, everyone thought this was a great idea. They all voted in favor of it, except John.

"No," he said. "We can't."

"Why not?"

"It's piracy," he said.

That's the trouble with being trained as a lawyer. They know these minor little details about theft and piracy. I'm proud to say Monty Python voted five out of six to become pirates, but the Python veto rule held. Everyone had the right to veto a vote. A surprisingly effective and fair rule, which meant that no one could be forced into doing what they didn't want to do. But for that, Denis O'Brien would have sold off our TV series, for which we would still be paying him 20 percent. I dragged my heels. When we all came back a few months later, everyone had changed their minds. No wonder he hated me.

We returned to London with a theme and a title but no plot. I thought the screenplay still needed work, but John was reluctant to have any more writing meetings. I've always felt that was a pity, as it seems to me it could have used one more draft. It was really only a sketch film tenuously held together by a concept. It occurred to me later that we could easily have made it as *The Seven Ages of Man,* about the same central character growing from birth to death but darting backwards and forwards in time, so that his birth is in one era, his childhood in another and so on, but not in any historical order. I still think this might have been a good idea, but then hindsight is always perfect. I may have come up with this thought when I was working with John Du Prez to adapt it as a Broadway musical. The trouble was it already *was* a musical, but as an idea for the stage it was disastrous, as it had no common characters and no plot. It's a revue.

The Meaning of Life was shot in 1982 at Elstree Studios and in Scotland, where the Zulu warriors went on strike. Despite that, it was a fairly happy experience. Because we needed ten million dollars, we had sold the movie to Thom Mount at Universal. We refused to let him see the screenplay and simply gave him a budget and a short poem I wrote.

There's everything in this movie
Everything that fits
From the meaning of life in the Universe
To girls with great big tits.
We've got movie stars and foreign cars
Explosions and the lot
Filmed as only we know how

On the budget that we've got.
We've spent a fortune on locations
And quite a bit on drink
And there's even the odd philosophical joke
Just to make you buggers think.
Yet some parts are as serious
And as deep as you could wish
But largely it's all tits and arse
And quite a lot of fish.
Other bits are childish
And some parts frankly rude
But at least we've got a lot of nice girls
All banging around in the nude.
So take your seats, enjoy yourselves
And let's just hope it's funny
Because it's not only done to make you laugh
But to make us lots of money.
Yes, sit back and have a good time
With your boyfriend or your wife
Relax and just enjoy yourselves
For this is The Meaning of Life . . .

Amazingly, Universal said yes to this. Many years later, when I met Thom Mount again, I said what a brave punt I thought that was and he said not at all. Because he had green-lit our movie, many American comedians who were huge Python fans, amongst them Richard Pryor, beat a path to his door, and he made several very successful comedies. Ours was apparently not among them because, although it cost only ten million and took in twenty-five, the studio assured us for many years that it was still not yet in profit, even after the video release. Finally, in the Nineties when I had learned the Hollywood game a bit better, John Goldstone, our producer, came to me and said that Universal was requesting permission to release it as a DVD, and since these had not been invented when we made the movie, they didn't have those rights.

"Tell them no," I said, "we're still not yet in profit."

Miraculously, the next day the movie was in profit. Like God, the studios move in mysterious ways.

The film contains many great things, including "Every Sperm is Sacred," wonderfully choreographed by Arlene Phillips and magnificently shot by Terry Jones. I always regret I was in Australia when the final editing decisions were taken and they removed my blond French cooking lady, who I thought was funny. Still there were "The Galaxy Song," "The Penis Song," "Christmas in Heaven," and I'm fond of our title track, "The Meaning of Life," which I sang in a Charles Aznavour voice. John Du Prez and I were really getting into our stride composing songs, and "The Galaxy Song" is still one of my favorites.

"The Galaxy Song," from *The Meaning of Life*, 1983.

Terry Gilliam took his sketch of the office building under sail and turned it into a movie about rogue accountants, complete with our Accountancy Shanty.

It's fun to charter an accountant . . .

The Crimson Permanent Assurance was originally supposed to be a short six-minute insert toward the end of our movie, but no one has ever found it easy to stop TG filming and he took over a whole soundstage next door and kept on shooting till he ended up with an eighteen-minute film about old accountants, threatened by takeovers, who declare war on the City and set sail for adventure. It's wonderful but, of course, was far too long when we tried it in the main body of the film. Instead, we decided to put this Gilliam sequence before *The Meaning of Life*. At the Cannes Film Festival in 1983, it surprised and delighted the stuffy French cinephiles at our screening, and I'm convinced the brilliance of it persuaded the Cannes jury to award us the Jury Prize, although Orson Welles was on the panel and he must have loved Mr. Creosote.

For our press conference, as a send-up of Cannes, we had the bright idea of posing for the photographers on the beach exposing our nipples, a gag which was immediately ruined when a French starlet walked topless behind the rows of assembled cameramen and they all took off in pursuit of her. Terry Jones then shocked the festival by announcing that we were certainly going to win, because *we had bribed the jury*. They trumped his gag by awarding us their Jury Prize. At the closing awards ceremony, Terry went one better when he accepted the prize and announced that the jury would find their bribe money taped behind the plumbing in the gents' toilet. You've got to love Terry.

I have often found that bad movies are much more fun to be on than good ones. This was certainly true of *Yellowbeard*, written by Graham Chapman, Bernard McKenna, and Peter Cook. In those days executives seemed to feel that if you could lure one or two Pythons into a project, the audience would think it was a Python film. It never worked. What they failed to notice is that it's the *writing* in Python that makes the difference, and it takes all of us. Graham was very sweet to me now that he was sober, and said that if John and I agreed to be in his pirate film, he would get a green light. I agreed to do it if they would shoot my part in three weeks, so I wouldn't have to stay on location kicking my heels for months. John agreed to an even shorter time constraint, which meant he wouldn't even have to go to Mexico. The good news was that Marty Feldman was going to be in it, although when he came into our London kitchen, gaunt and chain-smoking, Tania and I were shocked by his appearance. He was emaciated, though very happy to be back in the U.K. working with all his pals again. It was like old times, returning to his homeland after a long and successful career in Hollywood. Well, it was certainly successful at the beginning when he worked with Mel Brooks on *Young Frankenstein* and *Silent Movie,* but when he began to write, star in, and direct his own films he had several flops. Hollywood thinks that failure is somehow contagious, and when he threw a party nobody showed up. Yes, it can be that cruel. Anyway, it was fun for him to come home and hang out with Peter and Graham and John and me. We had a delightful week filming in Rye before we flew to our location in Mexico, where Customs immediately impounded all our costumes until the right amount of money found its way into the right hands.

The movie had attracted a stellar cast of funny actors: Spike Milligan, Peter Boyle, Madeline Kahn, Kenneth Mars, Peter Bull, Cheech and Chong, James Mason, and Michael Hordern, whom Peter Cook dubbed "Hordern Monster" after he complained loudly and bitterly at the hotel's front desk for shrinking his laundry. The whole lobby watched in fascination. Peter said it was a better performance than his *King Lear.* Unfortunately, as we often say about Hollywood, the studio had chosen a newcomer to direct, a pleasant man whose previous experience was working as a sports director for American TV. Who knows what they were thinking, but Mel Damsky seemed certainly out of his comfort zone directing comedy. The comedians were flown in serially, so at no stage was there a general read-through for everyone to get on the same page about the style of comedy we were playing.

Yellowbeard was not a success but the "making of" documentary, *Group Madness,* is quite fun. Peter Cook was in great form and, as with all films, we had acres of time on our hands to spend hanging around in the pool at our luxury hotel. Peter would spend the day bobbing up and down in the water, improvising in that peculiar nasal E. L. Wisty voice:

"The funny thing about the Universe is, we know where the light comes from but where does the *darkness* come from?"

"The speed of light is 300,000 kilometers a second, but *what* is the speed of darkness?"

He had given up drinking, and one evening he suggested we needed to find some grass. I agreed to accompany him, but where to look?

"No problem," said Peter, "we shall find the nearest bordello."

My wife gave me an old-fashioned look, which Peter noticed, reassuring her with his incredible charm that I should come to no harm. Somewhat skeptically, she agreed to let me go, so off we drove to the local Mexican brothel. It wasn't far. A small door in a white-walled street led into a cantina, a square open to the sky with a band and a bar and lovely girls who were happy to dance, or there was a low cabana to the side with discreet rooms if you wished to dance horizontally. There were tables for drinking and strings of colored lights, and when we entered it had the air of a private party where the guests had yet to arrive.

Peter was an instant hit. He ran in shouting loudly in cod Spanish, shook the hand of the barman, seized a beautiful tall girl in a shiny red bathing suit, and stormed onto the deserted dance floor, where he began the most unimaginable shaking jitterbug. The girls went nuts. They danced around him and he boogied with them all, flinging his arms around, his hair wild, occasionally sinking to his knees or exaggeratedly twisting low. One minute it was a slow night in a naughty nightclub, and the next it was a one-man fiesta.

The whole place loved Peter; the band became animated, the barman grinned as he shook his cocktails, people flocked in to watch, and every girl was mad to dance with this wild, crazy Englishman who radiated goodwill and, yes dammit, innocence. It went on for hours with the band going nuts and the girls lining up to fandango with this wild spirit. We were filming the next day, and as midnight approached I made my excuses and slipped away. My beautiful young wife was waiting at the hotel; it would be hard enough to persuade her we only went to score some grass without staying all night. My last sight was Peter leading a line of ecstatic ladies in a conga line. He waved cheerily, tapped his nose, and yelled, "No problem, Eric, we're in . . ."

In the morning, we learned what had happened. Peter had taken the tall girl in the red bathing suit back to her room. Once inside, he asked casually if she had any grass. "Of course," she said, reached under the bed, and brought out a huge load wrapped in newspaper. Peter asked her how much for it. She cited a derisory amount and the deal was made.

"I have to go now," said Peter.

"*What?!*"

She broke into tears. How could he possibly leave? Didn't he think she was beautiful? She was utterly distraught.

"I only wanted some grass," Peter explained as gently as he could, but she was inconsolable. It wasn't a matter of money. It was honor. It was Mexico. It was her reputation. Poor Peter tried hard to convince her that, honestly, she was really beautiful, and normally he would have been torn up with desire for her, but he had only come for a dance and some grass. He had, he said, to spend a long time reassuring her.

"Been easier to shag her," said Marty, getting to the nub.

This would be Marty's last film, and he is very funny in it. He died on his final day in Mexico City, when he had a heart attack in the hotel and the traffic was so horrendous the ambulance couldn't make it in time. He would have lived had he been in LA. He was only forty-eight.

It would also be Graham's final film.

18

BRIGHT SIDE RETURNS

"Always look on the bright side of life" has probably been my subconscious motto throughout my life, but I never thought it would be a hit. And not just in the Top 10 charts. On January 20, 2009, it officially became the number one most requested song at British funerals, replacing Frank Sinatra's "My Way." It has remained there ever since. Beating out even Elvis. You've got to love the Brits. First of all, who would even *have* such a chart? And secondly, of course you don't get paid for funerals, but hey, you take it where you can. It probably replaced "Spam, Spam, Spam" at Viking funerals.

As far as I was concerned, "Bright Side" was just the end song of a movie, but now it began to take on a life of its own. It began at Graham's memorial. I was asked to sing it to close the event, as it was Graham's favorite song, and it was one of the hardest things I have ever had to do. I was still singing it to Graham, but now for the final time. He had died with exquisite timing on October 4, 1989, the eve of Monty Python's twentieth anniversary. We canceled a huge party we had planned, which wouldn't have been what he wanted, but it was how we felt. It was a shock. This was one of *us*. Mike and Terry J. were with him at the end. John wept inconsolably. I was at home writing a song for him, "Life Will Get You in the End." I finally finished it when George died.

A month before he died, Graham joined us filming *Parrot Sketch Not Included: Twenty Years of Monty Python,* a 72-minute celebration hosted by Steve Martin. I can still remember Steve's shocked look of horror as he watched an emaciated Graham being carried in. Nobody had warned him. Graham had lost a lot of weight after two operations on his cancer but he was his usual cheery self, cracking jokes about his condition, and we all did a sketch together with Steve interviewing us as schoolkids. We did another shot where Steve asked to-camera where all the Pythons were today and then opened a closet. We were inside. It would be the last time we were all together. One final gag, and after it we took one final photo.

Monty Python. The Final Photo, 1989.

I had bumped into Graham at the Beverly Center in LA that January, and he had a big wide grin and looked hale and hearty and said he had a slight thing in his throat, nothing to worry about, but he was going back to London for a procedure. When I visited him at Cromwell Hospital after his second operation he looked in a very bad way, but he surprised me when he told me he was thinking of opening a longevity center! Perhaps he was joking. Maybe he was trying to cheer me up. Who knows, but it would be the last time I saw him.

On December 3, 1989, we all gathered in the packed Great Hall at St. Bartholomew's Hospital for his memorial, where I had to sing "Always Look on the Bright Side of Life." It was particularly hard to get through and I almost lost it. It was even harder because, thanks to John Cleese, the memorial had become a roast. He brilliantly broke the somber mood and turned solemn grief into relieving laughter with an outrageous parody of their "Dead Parrot" sketch.

"Graham Chapman is no more. He has ceased to be. Bereft of life, he rests in peace. He has rung down the curtain and joined the choir invisible. And I say good riddance to him, the freeloading bastard. I hope he fries. And I say that because if I hadn't said something inappropriate he would never have forgiven me."

It was one of John's finest moments. It was inspired, it was fantastic, and he concluded by saying he would like to be the first to say "Fuck" at a British memorial. From that point on, the afternoon became uproarious. Michael spoke about how Graham was always late, and whenever he had to pick him up for rehearsal, various heads popped out of windows saying Graham would be down in about twenty minutes. Michael would sit fuming in his car for twenty minutes, until finally Graham would emerge for work. Michael ended his eulogy by saying, "I'm not very sentimental, but as I look around at all these great people, I like to think that Graham is here with us all today. Well, not *now* . . . but in about twenty minutes."

How ironic that Graham, who was always late, left so early.

That really should have been it for the song, except that it wasn't. Bizarrely, it was about to become a popular hit. I had become friendly with a neighbor, Gary Lineker, a brilliant footballer, the captain of England and Spurs and now the presenter of BBC's *Match of the Day*.

One day in 1991, Gary said to me, "You know they're singing your song on the terraces." Apparently, football fans had taken to singing it when their sides were losing helplessly.

With George Harrison on the set of *Munchausen*.

Silly Olympics. Flipper racing.

On location for *Life of Brian* with Terry Gilliam, Michael Palin, and Graham Chapman.

Lorne Michaels in Venice.

John Cleese with the Virgin Mary.

With my son Carey in France.

With David Bowie, his son Joe, and Adam Fisher at Mustique Airport.

With Pierce Brosnan in Yugoslavia.

With Paul Simon in France.

Stephen Fry, Peter Cook, William Goldman, and me. "Carry On Up the Nile."

"I want to be a pirate." With my daughter Lily on St. John's.

Steve Martin and Lily.

With Tania at the Great Pyramid of Giza.

With Billy Connolly at Candacraig, his home in the Scottish Highlands.

Lily with George and Ringo.

With Robin Williams and Steve at Candacraig.

Rotter with otter.

The fabulous Tania.

With John and cheetah, downunda.

With Her Majesty and Ann Howard at the *Royal Variety Performance.*

The amazing cast of *What About Dick?*: Sophie Winkleman, Russell Brand, Tim Curry, Tracey Ullman, Billy Connolly, Jane Leeves, Jim Piddock, me, and Eddie Izzard.

Carey and Lily at the London Olympics.

The Entire Universe in One Hour with Noel Fielding, Hannah Waddingham, Professor Brian Cox, me, Warwick Davis, and Robin Ince.

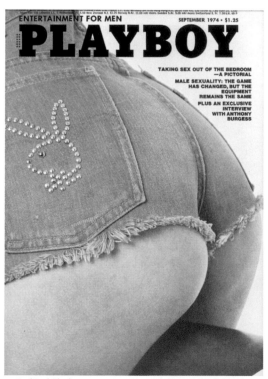

Tania's *Playboy* cover.

Always look on the bright side of life
Duh duh, duh duh duh duh duh duh . . .

Simon Mayo, a friend of Gary's and a BBC Radio 1 DJ, began playing the song every morning on his breakfast show, so it was getting a
lot of airplay. Because of this, Virgin Records rereleased it as a single
on September 23, 1991, and to my surprise it began to rise up the pop
charts. It was strangely exciting as each week it rose higher and higher.
It eventually got to number three, where it peaked after I had been persuaded to sing it on *Top of the Pops,* a deliberately chaotic performance
with John Du Prez leading the band. Simon Mayo said it was *because*
I had sung it on *Top of the Pops,* and he may well have been right, but
it did get to number one on the ITV charts, and, even more satisfying,
it became number one in Ireland, which was great because the movie
had been banned there, and the soundtrack album on Warner's was
withdrawn and pulled out of record stores after protests when it was
first released. A fitting revenge.

Because it was such a hit, ITV asked me to sing it for the Queen
on the *Royal Variety Performance,* an annual charity event, held that
year at the Victoria Palace Theatre. I had grown up watching this show,
which featured every top artist and the best comedians from Britain and America. Even the Beatles had been on it, and John Lennon
had said cheekily, "The people in the cheaper seats, clap your hands.
And the rest of you, if you'd just rattle your jewelry." Tommy Cooper, a wonderfully funny British comedian, had died on it, collapsing
backwards through the curtains at the end of his set to a huge laugh.
Everyone thought he was joking. Shockingly, he was dead. A great way
to go, though. So of course I said yes.

Traditionally on the show there was a classical moment from the
opera or ballet, where the audience would nod off for a bit. I decided
to use this to play a gag on them. David Frost introduced Ann Howard, my singer friend from the English National Opera, in an aria from
Madame Butterfly, and the curtain rose to reveal a beautiful set with a
little Japanese bridge on which stood Lieutenant Pinkerton in his naval

whites. Ann was dressed in a kimono with a black wig and knitting needles in her hair, and at her feet was a Japanese maid lying prostrate in a kowtow. She began the famous aria:

One fine day we'll notice . . .

I could feel the posh audience sinking down in their seats, beginning to take a nap. After a minute or two, Ann pulled out a Japanese sword to kill herself. At her feet, the little Japanese maid raised up.

"Stop," I said, for I was playing the maid. I began to sing:

Some things in life are bad
They can really make you mad . . .

The audience went nuts. They laughed themselves silly. Nobody had seen this coming. I could see the Queen in the Royal Box laughing out loud.

And . . .
Always look on the bright side of life . . .

Ann Howard watched in stunned amazement as six sumo wrestlers came on whistling. I pulled off my kimono to reveal an English football kit, and we began to fill the stage with some of the classic acts I remembered from when I was a kid: the Tiller Girls (the British Rockettes) high-kicking across the front of the stage, followed by the Dagenham Girl Pipers playing their bagpipes.

"*Why* the Dagenham Girl Pipers?" Prince Philip said to me afterwards, still giggling.

"Because no *Royal Variety Performance* would be complete without the Dagenham Girl Pipers," I replied.

We ended up with dancing men in top hats and tails, a full Welsh choir, and a British regimental band playing along loudly. Then I led the whole ensemble offstage and exited through the center of the stalls with the audience clapping and singing along. It was a lovely moment, and the gag worked even better than I had imagined. John Du Prez of course conducted and arranged the whole thing. Afterwards the Queen was still laughing when I was introduced to her, and what made it even better was that behind her was Lord Delfont, who had canceled *Life of Brian.*

"I told them, Bernie, I said, they'll never make their money back . . ."

19

THE QUEST FOR A MUSICAL

When I was young I was taken to see D'Oyly Carte Opera Company in productions of Gilbert and Sullivan. When he died, Pop left me full recordings on ancient 78s of my two favorites, *The Mikado* and *The Pirates of Penzance*. As a teenager, I had seen performances of both at the Royal Shakespeare Theatre in Stratford-upon-Avon, and now it occurred to me that *Pirates* would make a very good musical film. We ostensibly had a film company, so I stayed on in Tunisia after the end of shooting *Brian* to put the finishing touches to a Victorian screenplay, which opened at the Victoria and Albert Museum in modern-day London, where workmen stumble across a vault filled with cans of Victorian film. This turns out to be the first film ever made. I liked the idea of the first-ever movie being a Victorian musical, and it would all be shot like Pre-Raphaelite paintings on location in genuine Victorian settings.

After the modern-day documentary opening, we cut to the gala opening in front of Queen Victoria in a crowded Royal Opera House, the boxes packed with Victorian celebrities like W. S. Gilbert and Oscar Wilde. There is a big steam-operated film projector at the back of the auditorium with a grimy stoker shoveling coal into its furnace. Sir Arthur Sullivan himself is conducting the overture and when the curtain rises, it reveals not a stage but a movie screen with a sailing ship at sea, and pirates singing and dancing on deck.

My assistant Christine Miller and I scoured Cornwall and Devon for the perfect settings. We found our pirate ship in Torbay, and I got permission from Lord St. Leven, who owned St. Michael's Mount, opposite Penzance, to film there. My aim was to open the movie on the one hundredth anniversary of the operetta opening on Broadway, where it first ran, *before* London. This was to establish copyright in America, to avoid the piracy Gilbert and Sullivan had suffered from *H.M.S. Pinafore*. At one point, there were seven productions of *Pinafore* on Broadway, none of which paid a penny in royalties. They rehearsed *The Pirates of Penzance* in the U.K., gave one performance in Torquay to establish copyright, and then rushed the entire cast over by boat to open on Broadway, where it was a smash hit. I believe those are the roots of musical theater in New York.

I had become friendly with some cavalry officers of the Queen's Troop, a brigade of hussars garrisoned in St. John's Wood. After visiting their barracks, and discovering they were Python fans and loved Gilbert and Sullivan, I gained permission to film them bringing their horse-drawn Victorian field guns into action in Hyde Park, firing off a twenty-one-gun salute for the Queen's birthday. Better yet, they gave me permission to take a camera crew onto the Victoria Memorial, an ornate edifice on a traffic island directly in front of Buckingham Palace. Here I could get an unbelievable shot of the entire British Army marching down the Mall. Now, the British Army in full dress uniform is not all that different from a century before, so all I had to do was to avoid shooting anything that was not in period and I would have the most superb footage. I could shoot *any* part of this event, with the single exception of the Queen and the Duke of Edinburgh sitting on their horses taking the salute. Everything else would be perfect.

So, there I was on the Victoria Memorial with my shoulder-length hair, baseball cap, tank top, shorts, and a tiny crew. It was a blazing June day as we shot rank after rank of the British Army advancing directly down the Mall in wide-screen. In their red coats and their bearskins, the flanks of their horses gleaming, their brasses glinting, their sabers drawn, their bright breastplates flashing in the summer sunlight, it was a million-dollar shot. As the front ranks wheeled around us, we scrambled to the Buckingham Palace side of the monument to catch them marching directly in front of us. I directed my cameraman to close in on the horses' hooves, the glistening buckles, the glinting helmets, the gleaming swords, all tight shots I could use later.

I was running around enthusiastically pointing and jumping about with glee when I became aware I was being watched. Two pairs of gimlet eyes were staring at me: the Queen's and the Duke of Edinburgh's. They were both on horseback and they had become riveted by our activity. You have to understand that this was *their* show; the eyes of the entire world were on them; thousands of people had turned out to see them, lining the London streets for hours, TV cameras were broadcasting their image live round the world, while this loony ran around directly in front of them, not fifteen yards away, totally ignoring them. *What was he doing?* It must have seemed incomprehensible to them. Not once did I even turn my camera in their direction. They were the stars of the show and I was shooting the extras. They stared at me in mute incomprehension, this hippie ragamuffin, right on their patch, outside the gates of their palace, deliberately ignoring them! What was going on? What the hell was I doing? I could feel their eyes boring into me. I stopped and turned to look at them. I was watching the Queen watching me. Her hand raised to her hat in salute. The Duke next to her in utter disbelief. They stared at me while I froze. What to do? Impossible to explain in a look or a gesture that I meant no offense, that they simply couldn't *be in* my Victorian film. There was no way to convey anything at all. I smiled at them, shrugged, nodded in a vaguely reassuring way, and went back to shooting my inserts. They never stopped watching me. Two completely different worlds passed by, each utterly inexplicable to the other.

I had my finale of the entire British Army marching down the Mall, in their red coats and their bearskins for the Trooping the Colour ceremony; now all I needed was the finance. Handmade Films weren't remotely interested. Out of the blue, Joe Papp mounted a stage version of *The Pirates of Penzance* in the outdoor Public Theater in New York's Central Park. Kevin Kline was magnificent as a very athletic Pirate King, and Linda Ronstadt delightful as Mabel. (Three years ago, I got to play the Sergeant of Police on that very same stage with Martin Short as the Major-General and Kevin Kline repeating his amazing role in a gala performance to raise money for the theater.) It was a huge hit and would soon move from the park to Broadway, where it would play for years. Learning of my film script, a Hollywood producer flew me in on Concorde to see it. *Unfortunately,* a word I came to associate with the movie business, I got shafted by the producer, who bought the Papp show; but because I had written my screenplay specifically for locations in the U.K., he was forced to shoot his film inside a studio on a soundstage, thereby losing all the fun of a movie. A pity. No surprise it was a total flop.

I thought that was it for Gilbert and Sullivan, but one day, out of the blue, in July 1986, I got a call from Jonathan Miller. Would I be interested in playing Ko-Ko in his forthcoming production of *The Mikado* at the English National Opera? I hadn't foreseen becoming a diva. I asked him what on earth he was going to do with *The Mikado.*

"Well, I'm going to get rid of all that campy Japanese nonsense for a start."

"Chop it off, Ko-Ko."

This I had to see. That's like removing the Japanese from sushi.

"I'm not having any of those silly knitting-needles-in-the-hair rubbish," he said.

Did I say I adore Jonathan Miller? Of course, I said yes, and soon we were rehearsing in the freezing rain of a London summer. They made a documentary of this process called *A Source of Innocent Merriment,* and I got to make one of my comic heroes laugh. It's on-screen, too. Jonathan rolled about in hysterics when I began to grovel . . .

Instead of Japan, Jonathan had set the production in Freedonia, the location of the Marx Brothers movie *Duck Soup,* and the whole design, costumes and set, was in black and white. It was a massive hit and I was invited to repeat my role for a second season. I had never actually seen myself as appearing in opera before, but standing onstage at the London Coliseum with the chorus turned toward me expectantly, and the orchestra sitting up and paying attention, I really enjoyed myself. It went over so well that one night a member of the orchestra said to me, "Tell me, are you Jewish, or are you just very talented . . . ?"

There is a tradition that the words to the "Little List" song can be rewritten, so each night I delivered a new set of lyrics with lines pulled straight from the headlines. The huge laughs and the sheer fun of singing live was very exciting. I got to do *The Mikado* again a few years later at the Houston Grand Opera, where Jonathan revealed a surprising love for sentimental Mexican songs and baseball. We were watching the World Series live from San Francisco when the screen suddenly went blank. The earthquake had hit. Fergie, still then the Duchess of York, came to the opening, and we loved Houston and made good friends there. In fact, we had such a good time that when we left Texas, Tania was pregnant.

The experience of *The Mikado* excited me to search for a musical to write and perform for myself. I approached Mel Brooks in Hollywood with the suggestion we appear together onstage in a musical version of *The Producers,* he as Bialystok, me as Bloom, directed by Jonathan Miller, who was about to take over the Old Vic. Mel, though incredibly flattering about Python, was not persuaded: "I'm happy directing films," he said, not unreasonably. Many years later, at the Broadway opening of *The Producers,* I was very glad he'd waited, as he single-handedly revived musical comedy and I knew that night I would now be able to find people willing to put on *Spamalot.*

I was still searching around for a subject for a musical when I found myself in the West Indies with Mick Jagger watching England play cricket. I was shocked to witness the *News of the World* setting not one but two honey traps for Ian Botham, the team's biggest star. Mick warned him of the first lady, but sadly he was entrapped by the second, a former Miss Barbados whom I knew, called Lindy Field, who was dropped right in it by the vultures, and the next day poor Ian Botham was faced with screaming headlines and forced to cancel his lawsuit against them. I was shocked by this blatant entrapment, and I didn't know what to do with this information, so, naturally, I wrote a musical. I created *Behind the Crease* with John Du Prez. It was about a shoddy journalist, played by me, pursuing an English touring team in search of scandal. My former Katisha, the late, great Ann Howard, played Princess Joan, a slightly tipsy Royal lady who had a home on the Isle of St. Jonas, where it was set. We recorded it before a live audience. It is a lot cheaper doing a musical on the radio because you don't need sets and costumes and dancing, and it was duly broadcast on BBC Radio 4.

Working with John Du Prez inspired me. He was the perfect partner. In 1982, I had written a lyric for *The Meaning of Life* placing ourselves in the Universe, a pulling-back of perspective which shows how truly inconsequential we are:

> *Just remember that you're traveling*
> *On a planet that's evolving and revolving at nine hundred*
> *   miles an hour.*

I had written a fairly simple tune for it, but when I played it to John he said, "That's not how this song goes, *this* is how this song goes," and laid down a wonderful melody.

The hit from *Spamalot,* "The Song That Goes Like This," began with

John playing around with some chords while I was on my way to the bathroom.

"Wait, that's it," I said, running back in and clicking on the tape machine. I began ad-libbing an overacting Broadway singer.

"Once in every show, there comes a song like this, that starts off soft and low and ends up with a kiss. Oh *where* is the song that goes like this? *Where is it? Where, where?*"

We improvised the whole song.

So, we had done a radio musical, and for a time London Weekend Television played with the idea of doing it on TV, but now we needed another subject. We found it in Edward Lear's poem "The Owl and the Pussycat." We adapted this as an animated movie, since we realized they were the only musicals being made by Hollywood. I pitched it to Steven Spielberg. He looked puzzled, and when he kept talking about Barbra Streisand, I realized that Americans had no knowledge at all of the Edward Lear poem. So I adapted it as a children's book for my five-year-old daughter, Lily, and we recorded the tale with ten songs for Dove Audio as *The Quite Remarkable Adventures of the Owl and the Pussycat.* I even got a Grammy nomination for it. But we were no nearer our Quest to make a musical.

Meanwhile, I continued working as an actor. I told you bad films were more fun, and I should know, I was in quite a few. I will spare you the full list, though sadly, IMDb never forgets. *Burn Hollywood Burn* won five awards, including Worst Picture, at the 1998 Golden Raspberry Awards, though I got nothing, not even a nomination. It was originally titled *An Alan Smithee Film,* and I played the eponymous Alan Smithee, the name the Directors Guild puts on a movie when the director takes his off. Irony of ironies, then, when Arthur Hiller removed his name from the final cut and the Alan Smithee film ended up being directed by Alan Smithee. However, it was quite fun filming with Sylvester Stallone, Ryan O'Neal, and Jackie Chan, to name-drop but three.

Dudley Do-Right was filmed in a monsoon in Vancouver, and it rained so much that I turned a screenplay into a novel (*The Road to Mars*) in the hotel in which I was holed up for several weeks. *Too Much Sun* was a low-budget caper directed by Robert Downey Sr., starring his son, Robert Downey Jr. Junior was quite young and very funny. One day Senior asked him, "Robert, when do you learn your lines?" Robert replied, "Oh, usually by the third take . . ."

Robin visiting me on the set of *Too Much Sun*.

I did, however, have a hit movie, and oddly it was funded by Denis O'Brien. He had approached me at Cannes to make something for Handmade Films. "How appropriate," I said. "I made the first Hand-made Film, now I can make the last." He looked pained, but it was! Johnny Lynn, my old friend from Cambridge and the director of my play *Pass the Butler* in the West End, had written a funny script about two West End gangsters hiding out in a nunnery. He wanted me to play it with Michael Palin, and when Mike turned it down I suggested Rob-bie Coltrane. It was a wonderful partnership. Robbie was hilarious as Sister Euphemia, while I played Sister Inviolata, and it was even fun to film. Once, Robbie sat dressed as a nun, smoking a cigarette with his habit up to his knees, when a lady came up and asked him for spiritual advice. Oops.

There were never such devoted Sisters. With Robbie Coltrane.

Nuns on the Run was a big hit in the U.K. and made a lot of money, but here is the magic of cinema: the movie took three and a half million pounds at the box office in England, and not a single penny found its way into my pocket. Two of the distributors, whose names I have kindly removed so that their wives and children may live without shame, had been screwed by Denis O'Brien on another deal, so they refused to turn over any money to him. We made not a cent. Maybe we made God laugh. We certainly didn't make Siskel and Ebert laugh, who pronounced our film utterly unfunny and went out of their way to abuse us in print and on television. Well, at least we had a good time. And I always thought Ebert looked like an old nun.

One of the best times of the Eighties was filming Passepartout alongside Pierce Brosnan's Phileas Fogg in *Around the World in Eighty*

"But sir, zis *is* a silly French accent." With Pierce Brosnan.

Days, which NBC made as a miniseries in England, Hong Kong, Macao, Thailand, and Yugoslavia. Pierce is a hilarious man and we had a lot of fun. Often, Tania and I would join him for dinner at his request, as he was literally hounded by females. They would look very disappointed as we turned up yet again.

There are only two rules in show business for actors: never appear in a Stanley Kubrick movie, and never appear in a Terry Gilliam movie. I broke this rule when Terry invited me to appear in *The Adventures of Baron Munchausen,* which he was shooting at Cinecittà Studios in

With Sarah Polley on *Munchausen.* Worse than boarding school . . .

Rome. Summer in Italy, at Fellini's studio, with further locations in Spain, what could possibly go wrong? Well, actually, everything. I shall draw a veil over nine months of torture, but it would have taken a crate of Boukha to numb the senses. Of course, there were many fine times, but how no one died I have no idea. I would often find myself having to stand in front of Sarah Polley, the sweetest little eight-year-old girl, when things got rough.

Once I was with Sarah and Jack Purvis at the back of a small boat, and directly in front of us was a stunt double on a huge white horse. Suddenly explosions went off, the horse panicked, reared up, and began backing into us on its hind legs. I thought we were done for but the rider, brilliantly, tugged the reins and took the horse overboard. I recently had some correspondence with Sarah, now a very fine film director, and she said she still had anxieties from those times. When she read a tweet of mine about the dangers we underwent, she wrote to me:

> It was one of the only times I've had someone validate my feelings and memories of the experience of being on that set. I can't tell you how much it meant to me to read it.
>
> I'd love to hear your take on the whole experience.
>
> You were always so so kind to me. I remember you creating so many moments for me to feel like a child, playing music, buying me a synthesizer, taking me on walks, making sure I stayed warm. I've always been incredibly grateful and think back often to your care for me when I really needed it and my children know every word to "just remember that you're standing on a planet."

20

THIN WHITE DUKES

I have met many people in my life and, sadly, many of them were not famous. I agree it's not their fault, though they might have tried harder. Anyway, I'm not writing about them because you don't know who the hell they are, and I'm tired of little notes from my English or American editor saying, *Who's this?* Surely, they've heard of the Queen . . . ?

I believe it is wrong to be prejudiced against people just because they are not well-known. Fame can bring a sad misunderstanding about the nature of life. As George Harrison never failed to point out, "Even the famous have to die," although I think in America they do suspect it gives you a pass on the death thing. Anyway, I have always tried not to hold fame against those who suffer from it. It's really not their fault that just because they possess some talent in a popular performing art, people look up to them, worship them, stalk them, hunt them down, and kill them. "Fan," after all, is short for "fanatic." So I try very hard not to discriminate against the illustrious and eminent.

In any case, it is only after you have achieved fame that you realize that it is a piece of shit. As Bob Dylan observed, "It's only really useful for getting tables in restaurants." It can be very confusing when you see people smiling at you across a room and you panic, thinking, *Have I met that person—or are they remembering me for something I did in a frock a long time ago?* So you end up hopelessly nodding at strangers in airports, and saying "Nice to see you again" to the wife. "Nice to *meet* you" is always a minefield and to be avoided, unless you can remember with some certainty that you never actually have met a pope before.

America used to be about the pursuit of happiness, but they seem to have exchanged that for the pursuit of money, fame, and Twitter followers. Once you become a celebrity, in today's culture, not only do people feel they have the right to bother you or shoot you, or demand you pose for "selfies," and scribble your name on grubby bits of paper, but they get your identity wrong, confuse you with other people, tell you shows you weren't in, and then ask you what your name is. I always tell them I'm Michael Palin and to go fuck themselves, so I can help ruin his reputation for niceness.

Whenever I checked in to a hotel in the Eighties, I would check in as Mick Jagger. It's better to be mistaken for a better class of person, don't you think? Nowadays I don't do that. I need my sleep. And I bet so does Mick. For a while I was his Bunbury, when he would tell Jerry he was out all night with me. *Yeah, right.* Some of his friends believed it, and David Bailey wouldn't have dinner with me because he and his model wife, Marie Helvin, thought I was leading Mick into trouble! As if. Eventually Tania cleared my good name, which was only right since I was home every night with her.

Perhaps the best way to ensure that people leave you alone is registering at hotels under the name of a novelist. Although I don't recommend Salman Rushdie for security reasons. I recommend his *books,* and I was rather startled to find myself entering his latest, *The Golden House.* Yes *me,* personally. It's a bit scary to be quietly reading a novel in bed and find yourself coming into the scene. I even sing "Always Look on the Bright Side of Life" at the dinner party in the book. I have known Salman for some years, since we met at a Billy Connolly concert in Hammersmith, where his dates were four hefty guys from Special Branch, and we sat singing Beatles songs with Gerry Rafferty. You don't have to believe me, but *who could make this shit up?*

Anyway, you can register away in hotels as Martin Amis and Ian McEwan, confident in the knowledge that people will leave you alone. I once tried registering as Meryl Streep, but then I felt guilty because she is so damn nice and smart. Notice how cleverly I introduced the fact that I know her. That's name-dropping at its finest, as I said to Prince Charles only the other day. He wasn't there, but I like to talk to myself and if I pretend he's in the room it feels classier. I used to talk to myself in French so that people would think I was quoting Rimbaud. No. *Not* Sylvester Stallone. Nowadays I talk to myself in a Birmingham accent, like Jeff Lynne's, because I like talking like that and if people overhear me they will assume I am rehearsing for some kind of Midlands sitcom with Lenny Henry, or an episode of *Peaky Blinders*. I've been pals with Jeff for a long time now, and we've played guitars and drank a lot of red wine. One night, quite late, we'd had a few and were playing away when Jeff said:

"Let's form a group."

"Okay," I said.

"What should we call ourselves?"

"The Fuck You Two!"

So began a legendary duo that was dedicated to never writing, recording, or releasing anything at all, and was constantly on the brink of splitting up. The FU2 is still my favorite group. Even though I did once write "Toad the Wet Sprocket" in a sketch and nearly drove off the road when I heard them announced on the radio in California. They sent me a platinum record. I think "Blind Lemon Pie" was also borrowed, from *The Rutles*.

What has this to do with the price of cheese? I hear you ask. Well, it's all by way of being a preamble to my meeting with David Bowie, and how we became friends in the Eighties. I wasn't particularly a Bowie fan when we met, and early on he asked me to collaborate with him in making a Ziggy musical, handing me a tape of *Diamond Dogs* to listen to. I didn't know how to respond so I said, "It's very loud." Luckily, he laughed. That was the great thing about David. He would simply explode into laughter. He was surprisingly normal and he loved comedians. He pursued comedians like he pursued musicians, like he pursued everything really, with a high seriousness. I met him for tea in Hollywood through our mutual friend Bobcat Goldthwait, the rowdy comedian and now brilliant director, in the Pink House we stayed in above Sunset.

We had almost met when we were on the road in the U.K. in 1973.

His tour went up the east coast while Python's went up the west, and both tours collided in Edinburgh, where we all stayed at the same hotel. There were carrot-haired weirdos at breakfast, but only Terry Gilliam was smart and hip enough to go to his show. I ran into David again in the Eighties when we were both guests of Lorne and Susan Michaels on St. Barts in the Caribbean. David and Coco Schwab, and his young son "Joe," now Duncan Jones, the amazingly good movie director of *Moon, Warcraft,* and *Mute,* were staying with Lorne and a house party of friends. We immediately launched into North Country gay dresser chat, and spent two days improvising camp dialogue.

"Well," I said, "you're not going to wear *that* onstage, are you?"

"If looks could kill I'd have been a slab of herring."

"Oo, get back in the knife box, you're too sharp to live."

David was very funny, and for days we bantered interminably in these panto voices until the rest of the group became thoroughly sick of it and begged us to stop.

Back home, David invited Tania and me to visit him and Coco at their Swiss villa in Vevey. One night they took us to dinner with Oona Chaplin. Here we learned the story of how after Charlie Chaplin died, and was buried locally, two Polish men had the idea of digging up and kidnapping his corpse. They called Oona and demanded two million dollars for the return of the body.

"Keep it!" said Oona brilliantly.

Two days later the body was returned. Not a brilliantly thought-out crime.

Because of our friendship, I wrote a short scene for David in *Yellowbeard* and he came down to join the party in Mexico. I even jumped into his jock strap once when he casually canceled his appearance as the Pied Piper in Shelley Duvall's *Faerie Tale Theatre,* and she called me in tears to fill in for him. You have not seen disappointment till you have tried on a jock strap for a dresser who has designed it specially for

David and Mick and the cake. Far right, Tania's mom, Algea, and niece Kris.

David Bowie. So it was me who had two hundred rats crawling over him in Toronto, and not him. Not just any old rats either, but *Hollywood* rats, trained in LA and flown to Canada on a one-way ticket, a journey which for them ended up as snake fodder in the Toronto Zoo. A perfect metaphor for showbiz. One minute you're in a movie, the next you're being fed to the pythons . . .

Tania and I spent many good times with David. He and Mick both came to our wedding reception. They sweetly brought out the cake for a very nervous Tania to cut. There was a huge bouquet of flowers from Mike Nichols, and on his card to Tania he gave her excellent advice for her wedding night: "Act surprised."

Tania and I went to Welwyn Garden City in 1983 to see David on his Serious Moonlight Tour, and to Cannes for the opening of *Merry Christmas, Mr. Lawrence,* where the French medical students were on strike and had put plaster of Paris and bloodied bandages on every statue in town. We even went on two cruises with him, the first to the Windward Isles, where we were marooned on Mustique with Iggy Pop, as the rented yacht hadn't made it across the Atlantic, and they stuck us for a week in Princess Margaret's rather pretty Oliver Messel villa. Before dinner I made the mistake of asking for a rum punch and Mrs. Lane, Princess Margaret's steely-eyed cook, said severely, "We. Don't. Meddle. Wid. Rum."

Oops. Bet she didn't say that to PM, as everybody on the island called the Queen's sister. She would put religious tracts under our pillows with red warnings about the devil. I kept a sharp eye out but I never saw him. At least under the pillow. One day there was a terrific shrieking from a terrified cook. A bird had gotten into Mrs. Lane's kitchen and she was freaking out. I went in and calmly opened a window and it flew out. She never bullied me again. I think she thought I had saved her from the devil.

Finally, the boat arrived and we left the island on a wonderful yacht. One night we hoaxed the crew by telling them it was going to be Drag Night. With Bowie and Idle on board they decided they had better make a real effort, and so at cocktail time a fully glammed-up staff emerged on deck, dressed to the nines, with the captain leading the way in a blond wig, twinset, and pearls. When we emerged, dressed normally, they realized they had been had. Being British, they were still game to go ashore with us for dinner in their frocks and wigs.

Drag night. With David, Iggy Pop, and a conned crew member.

Another time, we cruised the Italian coast with the beautiful Iman, and David took us to Campo di Thermi, where he had done his first gig. He spoke movingly about his dad and how proud he had been of him. David was himself a proud parent, bringing up Joe, of whom I am a strangely useless godfather, and I was always happy that he had a daughter with Iman.

I could never get him to be friends with George Harrison, though. I would say to George, "He's wonderful and brilliant and funny," but then George would become very much a Beatle, "Oh *Bowie*," he would say contemptuously, to rhyme with "Bowwow." I even got David as far as Henley once, but George would not admit him. Stubborn buggers, Beatles.

In 1987, Tania and I were on holiday in the South of France with Robin Williams and family, and David invited us to come for lunch to see his new yacht. Steve Martin and Michael Caine were nearby filming *Dirty Rotten Scoundrels* and we all turned up at the quayside to find a simply enormous boat, with David waving from the top deck. We all stared at this huge vessel in stunned amazement.

"Fuck me, Eric," said Michael Caine. "We're in the wrong business."

David was always extremely generous, and in early 1991 he lent me his wonderful house on Mustique to write a movie. Tania and I spent an idyllic six weeks in this lovely Balinese home of many waters that he had built high on a hillside, overlooking a beautiful bay, with our tiny new daughter, Lily, floating around in the pool. I'd had the idea for the film when a friend told me he had been found as a baby in a telephone booth in Sloane Square. This seemed so very Oscar Wilde (*a handbag??*) and it reminded me of some friends of ours who had too good a time at a party and left, forgetting their baby was asleep in a bedroom with the coats. Of course, when they got home they remembered and panicked and raced back, but what if the baby had been gone? I liked the idea of a wealthy, hippie, Sixties upper-class couple forgetting their heir in a restaurant. Searching desperately, they were given the wrong baby (Rick Moranis), who grew up to become the Duke of Bournemouth, while the rightful heir (me) grew up with an Indian family in Southgate. Universal liked my script and I came back to England with eight million to spend, but it was January and it was three weeks before I could find anybody to work.

That Easter, John Cleese invited us to join his expedition to Egypt. It was tough, I can tell you, on a luxury boat with a Jacuzzi on the top deck, floating gently up the Nile, with no one for company but John, Peter Cook, William Goldman, Stephen Fry, and forty other assorted friends. John and Alyce Faye very generously paid for the entire trip and even arranged for the British Museum to give us a private tour before we left London, and for the Cairo Museum to open early so we could gaze undisturbed at the sarcophagus of Tutankhamun. (He didn't look a bit like Steve Martin.) The boat itself had air-conditioned bedrooms, each with a private bathroom and a little balcony, where I could sit and play guitar. Tania won the Easter Parade with a hat composed of the many medicaments she had taken with her to avoid almost every known form of tropical disease. People were very grateful for that hat. Peter Cook was in great form and would usually skip the day tours of the temples and pyramids so he could be hilarious in the evenings. He was, but the temples and burial sites were unbelievable, some of them so recently excavated they looked as if the painters had just left. I crossed the Nile at dawn on a tiny boat to fly in a hot-air balloon, as the sun rose over the Valley of Kings. Each day, at teatime, Stephen Fry would read us a chapter of *Billy Bunter on the Nile,* a popular Fifties kids' book, as we glided past villagers in colorful robes winnowing, straight out of illustrated scenes from a children's Bible. Oh, it was rough let me tell you, but I had to get serious and return to London to begin work on *Heirs and Graces,* whose title Universal had changed to *Splitting Heirs.*

We shot the movie in the glorious summer of 1992 at Longleat, the

John Cleese gave a very fine nuanced performance.

magnificent palatial home of the Marquess of Bath. Barbara Hershey played the Sixties hippie, and John Cleese a shady lawyer, seen on the previous page, giving one of the most emotionally charged performances of his career.

Catherine Zeta-Jones, in her first movie, played the love interest. Catherine was adorable, and Rick made special canvas backs for our chairs: ERIC ZETA IDLE, RICK ZETA MORANIS, BARBARA ZETA HERSHEY. The film went very well and I got to do a nude scene with Catherine, though sadly it was I who was nude.

Halfway through the shooting, Tania and I flew to Florence for the marriage of David Bowie and Iman. David had asked me to make a speech at his wedding, and Tania kept asking him for me just how low I should be. Tell him to make it as low as he wants, David would reply. I, of course, went too far as usual, and I blush to think of it now, but it went down very well with the guests, who included Ono, Eno, and Bono.

The studio was very happy with *Splitting Heirs*, and it was chosen by

"Mawwige, is what bwings us together today."

the French to be the British representative at the Cannes Film Festival. "Chosen by the French" I emphasize, because some of the British press got their knickers in a twist. What was this *comedy* doing representing Britain? Well, getting laughs for one, since it played very well at the screening, but at the press conference I was publicly attacked by Baz Bamigboye and Alexander Walker. The rest of the world's press looked on amazed as the British tried to eat their own. How dare I? Who did I think I was? I have no idea what Baz was up to, but I reckon Alexander Walker was still seething because we had pilloried him in Monty Python as a pretentious fart with silly hair, even building a special wig which grew taller as Graham spoke. I was very happy when later Ken Russell took a stick to Walker on *Film Night*.

Back home, the tabloids were hounding Catherine Zeta-Jones over a boyfriend issue, and at the last minute she pulled out of attending the festival. I don't blame her, but it meant I had to take the long walk up the famous Palais staircase all on my own. I think it was the loneliest I have ever felt. I decided there and then, *Right, that's it, fuck it, I'm leaving.* If that's how you behave when someone brings eight million back to spend in the country, I shall take my flops to America, where they don't even mind if you are successful. The unexpected press response to my movie in the U.K. caused Universal to have cold feet about the American release, and they pulled back on the spending. I think a lot of the attacks on me were because they discovered I was fifty, and therefore by their reckoning too old for the lead. I had outed myself by writing a cheeky letter to the Prime Minister.

The Rt.Hon. John Major M.P.
10 Downing Street
London SW1A.1AA

12th January 1993

Dear Mr. Major,
On the 29th March you and I will both be fifty.
Has it ever occurred to you that, but for a twist of fate, I

should be Prime Minister and you could have been the Man
in the Nudge Nudge sketch from Monty Python?

I do hope you don't feel too disappointed.

Happy birthday anyway.

Eric Idle

He wrote me an amusing reply about how his cricketing friends always said the first fifty was the hardest, and invited me to 10 Downing Street, but sadly the newspapers found out and had a go at me for being too old. It was enough for me. Tania and I decided to bring up our daughter, Lily, in California. I felt I couldn't survive another fifteen winters in St. John's Wood, and the idea of driving her to school in California seemed far more appealing. It was.

21

RUN AWAY!

As a young teenager riding on top of the 148, a double-decker Midland Red bus from Studley to Birmingham, I would pass through a suburb improbably called Hollywood. How could I possibly imagine fifty years later I would end up living in Hollywood, California, in a rambling old 1920s Spanish house? We moved to LA in 1994. Tania and I had been discussing it for some time. She had spent seventeen years in England; only fair if we spent the next seventeen years in the States. We had frequently wintered there, staying in a huge old pink house above Sunset with Garth and Euva, lovely friends who rented out three or four suites to itinerant actors like Albert Finney and Greta Scacchi. The house and the pool were filled with beautiful models, like Janice Dickinson and Lauren Hutton. There was music, ping-pong, dancing, art, food, and excellent conversation. We had stayed there with the infant Lily, but now we would need to find somewhere to live. We would escape the Schadenfreudian nightmare of the U.K. and do a runner. It was almost as if I regretted not running away from boarding school all those years ago. Thaweesee (Wee), our adorable Thai nanny, who made the most exquisite food, would come with us. It wasn't exactly Ellis Island, but I still had to wait downtown with immigration lawyers for green cards and driver's licenses. The only difference? Celebrity. You get spoiled rotten. Finally, a good use for fame. Since I have a pathological fear of filling out forms, waiting in lines, and all officialdom, it was a great relief to be discreetly marched round the back and asked for autographs.

It wasn't until I moved to America that I truly discovered I was funny. Suddenly I was making Steve Martin and Robin Williams laugh. Chevy Chase told people he wished he were really funny like me. Garry Shandling said he adored the Rutles. It's appreciation by your peers that counts, and being in a group can make you feel insecure. My own TV show after Python, *Rutland Weekend Television,* had no live audience and so I never knew if it was funny or not. Several people went out of their way to assure me it wasn't. My play *Pass the Butler* was hammered by some of the West End critics, though it ran for six months to gales of laughter. My solo film, *Splitting Heirs,* now also suffered critical abuse. In England, my future was behind me. It was time to leave.

I went to California initially to make a speech for John Cleese at the Beverly Wilshire Hotel, where he was presented with the Screen Actors Guild's second annual Jack Oakie Award. The first was to Walther Matthau. There wasn't a third.

Good evening, ladies and gentlemen.

Actually, I am here rather in error. The transatlantic phone line was very bad, it was Christmas, my mother was visiting so I was shit-faced, and I could vaguely hear someone inviting me to a Jackie Oakie evening, and what I heard was "a karaoke evening": so naturally I was very excited.

Imagine my disappointment when I find it is instead some kind of salute to John Cleese, a man who has consistently ruined my life by being funnier, better known, and better paid than me.

A man who hurt me deeply by giving the role I would have been perfect for in *A Fish Called Wanda* to Jamie Lee Curtis.

A man alongside whom I have spent several days being crucified, perhaps the worst job you can get in show business, with the exception of working for Jeffrey Katzenberg.

Well, I have known John now for thirty-one years, which is perhaps the longest of anyone here. So, while it is an excellent opportunity to make some cheap cracks about him and reveal some tasteless and extraordinary bits of gossip about him that I have picked up over the years, I think I can embarrass him far more successfully by being sincere.

John is quite simply, and it pains me to say this, the best.

Perhaps even more irritatingly, he has turned himself into not just a nice person but a morally fine, caring, thinking, teaching, incredibly generous, wise, and loving human being.

And now he's dead.

Oh, I'm sorry, that's something I was writing for later.

John responded with a very funny speech complaining how nobody ever mentioned his fucking humility, a line Mike Nichols found so hilarious he told John he was going to steal it.

Shortly after this tribute, Tania, Lily, and I were in Encino when the Northridge earthquake hit, on January 17 at four thirty in the morning. We were just four and a half miles from its epicenter in Reseda, in the San Fernando Valley. It had a 6.7 magnitude and lasted for an interminable twenty seconds.

I was awoken by Nikolai, the dog, just after four in the morning, and took him outside, but he just stood there looking confused, so I went back in with him. No sooner had I climbed into bed than the earthquake struck. It was like the sound of an express train coming through the bedroom. I held on to Tania while the bed bounced, until the whole house finished shaking and we could run and check on Lily. It seemed like an eternity and we found her underneath a clown picture, which had fallen off the wall but fortunately missed her. Downstairs the house was a mess, but Wee and I turned off the gas, swept up the broken glass, and we all went back to bed. The house continued rocking and swaying with aftershocks all night long. Even the dog jumped into our bed after a particularly big tremor. We were on Balboa Avenue, which at one point that night was both flooded and on fire. The wail of car alarms echoed round the valley. It was eerie.

The house belonged to our friend Dave Stewart (of Eurythmics) and, fortunately for us, he was seriously paranoid about earthquakes, and had built it to three times code, so while it bounced a lot, it withstood the initial earthquake and the three weeks of aftershocks. The power was back on by noon the next day and we sat in the Jacuzzi and discussed what to do. Nobody was very keen on returning to an English January. The general consensus was that since that was "the big one," we might as well stay. Eventually I took some geological maps and discovered where granite and limestone intersected and bought a house there. I would start again.

22

GOOD AT DINNER

It was a strange thing to emigrate at fifty, but America truly is the land of opportunity. It took me a while to learn you don't need to take *all* of the opportunities. At first I was confused about what I should do, and a friend told me I was depressed and recommended therapy. That was a smart suggestion and I have benefited from it ever since. There is nothing finer than paying someone to listen to you moan every week, and it helped me enormously. It still does to this day. I know the Brits think therapy is some kind of moral weakness, but we don't come with a manual and it's good to find out what makes you tick.

This time I wanted to stay home for Lily and not be an absentee father, which I was a lot of the time for Carey. By this age I was less obsessed with career and self, and I had more time to be a father, a role I had to learn anyway since I had no model and didn't do a great job first time round. Carey has forgiven me now, I'm happy to say, and I tried very hard to get it right on my second stint at fatherhood. Life in America was different. The school system was different. The kids were told to respect each other's feelings. *Feelings?* Not a word you'd hear in British schools in the Fifties. I'd come a long way from Wolverhampton.

The nicest thing about living in Hollywood was that it was no big deal being in showbiz. At my daughter's school, seventy percent of the parents were in some way connected to the entertainment industry. It's like living in an auto town: that's just what people do. I am what they call in LA a hyphenate. I write, act, sing, perform, direct, produce, and generally show off in all sorts of desperate ways. I have always been a little puzzled as to my true métier, and I once asked my wife what I did best.

"Well," she said, after a moment's thought, "you're very good at dinner."

Soon after moving, I got a great role in *Casper*, a big-budget studio movie, which was encouraging, but I'm not really cut out for acting, as I get bored easily, so I began to work as a screenwriter. I made quite a good living writing scripts, and for many years Hollywood paid me handsomely, providing me with an enormous income developing things that never got made. In the end frustration got the better of me, and I quit. I was tired of being lied to at lunch. I will say, however, that while I am not a very good writer, I am a good *rewriter*, and I learned that particular skill in Hollywood.

After the earthquake, first thing I did was buy myself a very expensive guitar. It was a handmade Musser and had fallen off the wall at NORMS. No point in dying with a cheap guitar. It's still a beauty. Now we had dinners where people came over and played music.

I knew I finally lived in America when I got a dog. I didn't mean to. Lily and I went out to buy a balloon and we came back holding an exquisite beagle puppy. The minute I put him on my shoulder there was no way I could put him back in that cage. We drove home with Lily holding this tiny soft thing in her hands. Tania was reasonably pissed off because she wasn't consulted, and stormed off for an hour, because she'd always wanted another German shepherd, but she soon came back and of course she fell in love with Bagel the beagle. Tania eventually got her shepherd. Shadow was wonderful. Powerful, protective, and very thoughtful. One day Mike Nichols was leaving our house and looked closely at him.

"You know, your dog Shadow really reminds me of Julia Roberts," he said.

We both looked at him. *What??*

"You can see exactly what he is thinking."

I taught little Bagel to sing. Being a beagle, he howled like a hound,

Bagel's birthday.

and one day I picked up my guitar and encouraged him to howl along with me. A few treats later and I had a singing dog. From then on, he sang at every party. Toward the end of the evening, after dinner, he would make his way next to me, looking at me expectantly. He was ready. I would pick up my guitar and begin to play his song:

> *Bagel, Bagel, Bagel, Bagel, Bagel,*
> *Bagel, oo, Bagel, oo*

He would put his head back and howl. It never failed to kill. He sang to Beatles, he sang to Stones, to Eagles, and of course, to many comedians. That dog sang to the uncrowned heads of Europe. He even sang for Lily at a school concert, the only dog ever allowed in.

The great thing about California is you are close to the sea, to the mountains, to the desert, and of course to Las Vegas. Carrie Fisher took us to Vegas for the first time, to attend her mother's latest venture. Debbie Reynolds was opening a small hotel just off the Strip. We were startled when we got there at eleven in the morning to find her all dolled up and singing "Tammy" to a small party of Japanese tourists. She had her pianist Rip Taylor with her and was performing her whole cabaret in the tiny lobby. It was very odd. The hotel opening was a disaster. The fire department came to check on safety equipment and the sprinklers went off in every room. Oops. Still, we got to visit the Liberace Museum and gaze at his rhinestone Rolls-Royce, and we went to see Siegfried & Roy and their amazing white lions and tigers. A few years later I met them on *Regis*, a breakfast TV show in New York, and I was relieved to find that Siegfried was absolutely terrified of their cats and wouldn't go near them. Shortly after, Roy was almost killed by one of his animals. Mercifully, he recovered, and came to the *Spamalot* opening in Vegas.

Still, there is no escape from show business. There is no exit. You can only get out feet-first. Vegas reassured me that as long as I could stand up, I would have somewhere to perform. And what was it but a glorified Blackpool? I thought I would prefer to end my days in the fake glamour of the desert rather than the fake splendor of pantomime in Eastbourne—it's a better class of glitter. Panto was in any case spoiled for me in Wolverhampton when they took us to the Grand Theatre and the female chorus spent the entire matinee in tears. It was puzzling and very odd. On the way back to school, we learned the reason. One of the chorus girls had been murdered . . .

I got to play Las Vegas a few times, once with Kevin Nealon joining Clint Black at a Country convention, once with Steve Martin and Tom Hanks as the "Too Warm Trio" singing "The Galaxy Song" for a global warming convention, and once for *Penn & Teller's Sin City Spectacular* singing "Bright Side," chained upside down in a straitjacket suspended over a vat of boiling oil. I always loved visiting Penn & Teller. Apart from the genius of their magic show, I knew that afterwards you would always have a great discussion for hours in their dressing room about the Universe.

Another time in Vegas, Steve Martin had an exhibition of his own private art collection at the Bellagio Hotel. His paintings ranged from Picasso to Hopper. Steve is a polymath, which is *not* a parrot good at algebra. His intellectual range is astonishing. He writes plays and novels and screenplays and funny pieces for *The New Yorker,* and hosts the Oscars and knows everything about art. *Of course, he is a banjo player,* but then no one is perfect. Actually, he is even perfect at that and has won at least three Grammys for his banjo playing. We began to play together, at his house in Montecito, and, both being a little shy, we encouraged each other. He always wanted me to sing "The Galaxy Song," and we did it first at Marty Short's Christmas party, and then publicly. Actually, after Marty Short's Christmas party, everything is easy. I saw even Marty nervously smoking a cigarette outside his own party, before he went on. But he is always funny. That's because *he tries very hard.* We shared a dressing room at the Public Theater for a charity performance of *The Pirates of Penzance,* and we both agreed that the best moment in showbiz is when it is over. It's somewhat like sex in that regard . . .

Once, Steve was being honored by the Kennedy Center in Washington, and there was a gala dinner at the Smithsonian, in a huge art gallery hung entirely with American masters. Carl Reiner, who introduced Steve, said he was so knowledgeable about American masters that he could probably go around the hall and name every single artist on the wall.

"Well," said Steve, modestly, "I'm not sure I can . . . well . . . Let's see . . . Homer?"

"Yes," said the curator.

"Wyeth."

"Yes."

"Copley."

"Yes."

"Durand?"

"Yes."

"Stuart."

"Yes."

He went around the walls of the entire room correctly naming every single artist. Unbelievable. But then, he is a magician. We spent some very good times together. He had an amazing house in Montecito where we would go for long weekends. Often Ricky Jay would come for these holiday weekends and we would be perplexed as he produced constant aces, or, using cards as weapons, propelled them across the room into watermelons. Steve was once prevailed upon to do a magic trick at a party at our house, which he did with great aplomb. A few days later one of Lily's young friends said, "Hey, I saw your magician on TV."

I'd hardly been in LA a year when we went scurrying back to London to make a movie. Terry Jones was filming *Wind in the Willows* and asked me to play Ratty, a big step up from Second Field Mouse, where I started my career. I even got to sing "Messing About on the River," an English hit from the Sixties. Terry had written the script and was directing and, best of all, he was playing Toad, a role he was born to play. The hilarious, multitalented Steve Coogan played a very sweet Mole, and between takes he taught me to do Michael Caine impersonations:

Steve Coogan as Mole, Terry Jones as Toad, and me as Ratty.
Wind in the Willows, 1996.

"I don't fucking well believe it. No no Eric, I *don't* fucking well believe it . . ." What bystanders thought of Ratty and Mole doing loud Michael Caine impersonations as we passed by, I have no idea.

Tania and I were fortunate to be on Carrie Fisher's guest list, which meant we were invited by Paul Allen, the Microsoft billionaire, on several amazing trips. The first was a pirate-themed party on Cap d'Antibes, where the Louisianan luthier Danny Ferrington pulled out handmade guitars and we all jammed Beatles songs for hours. Paul is a very shy man, but stick a guitar in his hands and he is happy. We played together on several occasions. Once he took us all on a cruise down the Middle Passage of Alaska, where at lifeboat drill Tania and I were lined up next to Bill Gates. I thought, *Wow, this increases our chances of survival.* Until, arriving late, along came James Cameron, the director of *Titanic.*

"Oh no," I said, "not on our boat."

He went and found another. You can't be too careful at sea.

On another occasion, Paul took us to an unforgettable masked ball in Venice. We floated down the Grand Canal in gondolas at sunset, in glittering eighteenth-century costumes. It was like being in a different century, except for the desperate cries from the paparazzi, who of course couldn't recognize anyone because of their masks. "Robin?" they would yell hopefully. He and I took to calling out fake names to confuse them. "Stephen?" "Tom?" "Betty?" "Your Holiness."

Perhaps the most extraordinary Paul Allen trip was a visit to St. Petersburg. We set off overnight from Helsinki on a large cruise ship, and steamed into the city the next morning. I had no idea it would be so beautiful. Peppermint and pistachio palaces, bridges, art galleries, and canals. It was even more fabulous than Venice. This dream city was created by Peter the Great, who wanted a port for his new fleet and moved all the nobles out of Moscow to this swamp and made them build palaces and houses. After a two-year siege by the Nazis in World War II the city was a ruin, and only Communists could have spent what they did to restore it. Even the tapestries had been pains-takingly re-created in France at their original eighteenth-century ateliers. Not a ruble had been spared. It was an extraordinary restoration job and we lucky few enjoyed it. St. Petersburg was indeed mind-blowing. One day we were getting on a ferry to ride to another palace and this very sweet little old lady boarded the boat. I was already seated, and she very politely came up and asked me if she could sit next to me.

"Well, alright," I said, "*but you keep your hands to yourself.*"

Michael Kamen nearly fell overboard laughing.

The opening event was a cocktail party in a gilt-and-glass salon built by the Empress Catherine the Great. Tania and I were admiring this mirrored salon, as guests quietly assembled, when I became aware of Deepak Chopra, the prominent New Age guru, bearing down on me. I recognized him from Dave Stewart's wedding a few months before, when he had married Dave and Anoushka Fisz on the beach at Juan-les-Pins. We had also attended the opening of Dave's unlikely sex shop, Coco de Mer, on Melrose Avenue in LA. Dave had a whole new line of expensive vibrators and strange toys, and he had invited Deepak along to say a little prayer and bless the sex shop. As you do.

"O Lord, please bless these thy unguents and vaginal jellies, that together we may see Heaven."

Well, of course Deepak didn't say that, but he did make Tania and me giggle that day, as he was wearing rhinestone sunglasses and looked uncomfortably like Peter Sellers in *The Party*. So, I was well aware of who he was. George had even warned me: "Watch out for Deepak. He only really loves money." Not the greatest character reference. Now he was bearing down on me, smiling. He had mistaken me for Dr. Watson. Not Sherlock Holmes's Dr. Watson, but Francis Crick's. He thought I was James Watson, one of the pair of molecular biologists who had discovered the structure of DNA in 1953 at the Cavendish Laboratory in Cambridge.

"Oh, Dr. Watson," he gushed directly to me. "This is such an honor. I am so thrilled to meet you. You are the reason I became a doctor, I have always been inspired by your work. That's why I started medicine in the first place. This is truly a great moment for me in my life."

There was an uncomfortable silence. Tania was looking at me. I could see the mischief in her eyes as she enjoyed this moment. How was I going to respond?

"Well, Deepak," I said. "For a start, I'm not him. Secondly, he is at least fifteen years older than I am, and thirdly, he is standing right there."

Deepak did a double take, turned on his heels, and raced over to continue his gush. So much for cosmic consciousness.

Professor Brian Cox and I have always enjoyed teasing Deepak. We call his chatter "The Quantum of Bollocks," for he manages to mix cosmology and bullshit.

"There are no extra pieces in the Universe. Everyone is here because he or she has a place to fill, and every piece must fit itself into the big jigsaw puzzle."

So much for physics. Brian is kinder than me, but Deepak's form of quasi-scientific religiosity gets to him too.

Tania and I loved Jim Watson when we met him, a charming and funny man, and we shared a couple of meals with him on that trip. It was nice to remember how I would pass the Cavendish Laboratory every morning in Cambridge on my way to lunch at the Footlights, or go for a drink at the Eagle, the famous old pub where Watson and Crick first burst in, excitedly saying they had found the meaning of life.

"We should never forget that DNA backwards is AND."

Sorry, Deepak, I'm just not good at this bollocks.

I got a great job on a 4-D interactive movie called *Honey, I Shrunk the Audience!*, working with Rick Moranis again. Marcia Strassman, the eponymous Honey, got me the job at the last minute when Raul Julia fell ill. They were making a twenty-minute "ride" of the movie for Disneyland. It was shot on a huge 70mm camera in long takes, as most of the gags were special effects added later. Huge snakes slithered off the screen in 3-D. Lifelike rats ran out of the picture, down through the audience and into the seats. Little weedwhackers flicked their ankles, so the screams started at the front and proceeded through the auditorium. These gags were very effective, and we went with Lily to Disney World for the opening. They even took us to Paris when it opened there, and of course for a kid, the whole VIP tour thing is magic. There is no waiting in line, and you can go on a ride again and again. Paradise.

A year later, Anheuser-Busch approached me with an offer to write one of these 4-D things. They wanted a pirate film for their Busch Gardens theme park in Williamsburg, Virginia. I was intrigued by the technology so I wrote one. In mine, when seagulls flew overhead, water would drop like bird poop on the audience. I wrote the lead for Leslie Nielsen and he said he would do it only if I would be in it too. You mean filming in the West Indies on a pirate ship with Leslie Nielsen? Well, alright then. So off we went to Puerto Rico, eventually ending up filming on a boat in Caneel Bay off St. John, where I had stayed so happily with George and Liv. At the end of each day's filming I would dive overboard and swim back to my hotel.

I loved every second with Leslie. He was extremely funny. He would play with his own fame and had found a clever way of coming to terms with it. He had a fart machine. He kept it hidden in his hand. He used it to perfection on a crowded elevator in our tourist hotel.

People would enter the elevator and suddenly notice that there was Leslie Nielsen, deep in thought, staring into the middle distance. You would see them recognize him and nudge each other. He would gaze placidly ahead, completely unconcerned, not noticing. They would be trying to make up their minds to say something, but his benign concentration held them back. The doors would close. A moment of silence and then suddenly there would be a loud fart. Louder than socially polite. Impossible to ignore. But who was it? Leslie would continue to stare straight ahead. His face would not move a muscle. There would be another loud fart. The passengers would begin to look uncomfortable. Was that . . . Leslie Nielsen . . . *farting*??

Now it was awkward. They could hardly burst into "Aren't you Leslie Nielsen, we loved *Airplane,* can I have an autograph?" while he clearly had this epic bowel problem. Another couple of floors of silent descent and there would be another extremely loud fart. This time there was no mistaking the source. Leslie would give away nothing. Not a glimmer. Not a twinkle. The tourists' eyes would meet. They would clearly just have to pretend it wasn't happening. They would give this poor farting star the anonymity his unfortunate entrails deserved. Mercilessly, as the ground floor approached, Leslie increased the tempo. He would play a whole range of farts, little ones, big ones, short ones, long ones, melodic ones, Handelian ones, starbursts, frog farts, his repertoire was lengthy and relentless, his face a study of intense concentration as this terrible barrage unfurled. Deeply embarrassed for him, the other passengers in the elevator looked studiously at the floor, avoiding each other's eyes and this terrible secret. Finally, the doors opened and the passengers burst out, leaving Leslie saying nothing, revealing nothing. It was the most brilliant controlled display of deadpan acting I ever saw.

Another time, Jack Black asked me to sing at Festival Supreme on Santa Monica Pier, a whole-day concert he was organizing for comedians who played instruments. My pal Jeff Davis did the set with me with the assistance of my hilarious assistant Alana Gospodnetich. I had a gag I wanted to try. To introduce us, Jack Black came on and gave me the biggest showbiz intro ever. "You know him from this, you know him from that, one of the original Montys, will you all please welcome Eric Idle!"

Thunderous applause, and on came Billy Idol.

The crowd did a double take. What? And then laughed themselves silly. Billy played up the moment perfectly, strutting around the stage, pouting, pumping his fists, singing "I'm a lumberjack . . ."

After a few minutes I came on, looking daggers at Billy.

"What the hell are you doing?"

"I'm doing the show."

"It says *Eric* Idle."

"No, it doesn't. It says Billy Idol."

"Not on the poster."

"Yeah, on the poster."

We argued. We pushed. We shoved. We fought until Jeff brought out the poster and showed him.

"Oh. Alright then."

Reluctantly, he left the stage to an enormous ovation. We continued our set without him, but he came on at the end and sang "Bright Side" with us. It was one of my favorite gags ever. A visual pun. Billy was such a pro, he came to my house three times to rehearse the bit.

Idol and Idle.

I eventually repurposed almost everything I ever wrote for Hollywood: *The Road to Mars* became a novel, *The Rutland Isles* became a CD, and *The Remains of the Piano* turned into a concert film of a radio play called *What About Dick?*, which we filmed with the incredible cast of Eddie Izzard, Billy Connolly, Tim Curry, Tracey Ullman, Russell Brand, Jane Leeves, Jim Piddock, Sophie Winkleman, and me, live before a howling audience for three nights at a sold-out Orpheum Theatre in LA. As Dick Vosburgh, my early mentor, would always say as he filed away rejected gags, "Nothing's wasted."

But no matter how comfortable and at home I felt, always there would be the inevitable question:

"When are you Python guys getting back together again?"

23

PYTHON REUNION?

In the States, I found that Monty Python was really popular. Everyone knew *The Holy Grail*. It seemed to be a college rite of passage. Now, I helped 7th Level turn it into a CD-ROM game. They had been very successful adapting our TV series into *Monty Python's Complete Waste of Time,* an interactive CD, and now I got to rethink *Grail*. I loved this new high-tech world. I had sniffed contemptuously at Timothy Leary in the Eighties, when he said one day everyone would have a laptop computer.

"Why would I want that?" I said in my snobbish ignorance. "I have a pencil."

Now, not only did I have a computer, but I visited Microsoft in Redmond, and ESPN, and several other companies, looking for a home for a Python website. In the end, 7th Level generously offered to bankroll it, and in July 1996 I founded *PythOnline* on the newly burgeoning Internet, where even spam was named after one of our skits. Running *PythOnline* was a quotidian task that eventually became promethean. My ambition had been to create an amusing site to which the Pythons could contribute and where I could vent my occasional spleen and unfold my propensity for satire, but as the Python contributions soon dried up and I was left to deal with it solo, the task became increasingly frustrating. Each day there would be an ever-growing mountain of Python questions, and when I attempted to answer them, the fans would argue with me.

"You're not Eric Idle," they would say.

"Yes, I am," I would reply.

"No, you're not," they would insist.

"Then fuck off," I would add.

"Oh. You *are* him."

It was an early form of Twitter. How to drive yourself crackers. I found I had given myself a highly unpaid job, a monster that daily demanded new food. But the popularity of *PythOnline* made me think that Python was not dead yet, and I came up with an idea for a final Python movie called *The Last Crusade*, where a bunch of grumpy old knights, loosely based on ourselves, are rounded up reluctantly to go off on a crusade, taking King Arthur's ashes to Jerusalem. They didn't want to do it.

"I can't, I'm too old."

"The thing is my mother is coming."

"This is my year off to read a book."

Promised beautiful women and cash, they are lured to Venice, where they are screwed by the Italians.

Everyone seemed to like the idea of playing older versions of their younger characters, and I went for lunch and a walk on the beach in Santa Barbara with John Cleese, who sounded quite positive about the notion, and so we arranged for a Python Conference at Cliveden, a neo-classical manor hotel on the River Thames in England. Once the Astors' old family home, in 1963 it had been the setting for the Profumo scandal. Involving sex, call girls, government ministers, and Russian spies, this helped bring about the collapse of the Tory government.

The meeting began rather disastrously when John announced at the outset that he was not interested in making another Python movie. Terry Gilliam, who had just flown overnight from California, where he was prepping a film with Johnny Depp, asked rather acidly if he couldn't have said that *before* he flew all the way from LA. John then said he was very tired and went off for a nap, so the rest of us began working on the idea anyway. It was just like the old days of *Do Not Adjust Your Set,* and we were going quite well when John returned and said he wanted to have a business meeting instead. We had a hilarious dinner, and afterwards the four of us (minus John) had an uproarious game of snooker on the very same billiard table where Christine Keeler had contributed to the Tories' downfall. She hadn't been playing snooker, but the balls were definitely Conservative.

Next morning, we discussed doing a live show and, as we had all been getting along very well, we decided to accept an invitation to attend the Aspen Comedy Festival. A few months later, in April 1998, we assembled in the thin Colorado air and filmed a Q&A session in front of an invited audience at the Wheeler Auditorium for an HBO Special. On John's recommendation, I went to see Eddie Izzard perform and loved him so much that I went back the next night. He was truly funny and unique, and I asked him as a gag to come onstage with us at the beginning of our show. When Robert Klein introduced the Pythons to a cheering audience, Eddie came on as well and took one of the chairs.

"How did you all get together?" was Robert Klein's first question.

"Well," piped up Eddie, "we were all in the RAF and we first met in a railway carriage in 1943 and . . ."

But we interrupted him.

Michael and Eddie in Aspen. Executive transvestites.

"Fuck off, Izzard," we said, and threw him off the stage. He went off reluctantly through the middle of the audience shouting bits of old Python sketches.

We had one other gag set up. We brought Graham's ashes out on-stage with us, in an urn, and placed them reverently on a low table, with a picture of Graham. We answered a few mild questions, and John was in the middle of a long reply, when Terry Gilliam crossed his legs and "accidentally" knocked the urn off the table, scattering ashes all over the stage. The audience laughed in total shock. We got up and did our best to clean up the mess, shoveling the ashes under the carpet, sweeping them into a tiny dustpan, and even bringing on a vacuum cleaner. The laugh went on for four minutes and grew even bigger as they realized they had been duped. It was certainly the longest laugh we ever got. And of course, we finished the show singing "Always Look on the Bright Side of Life."

The joyous response of the audience seeing us together inspired some of the group to suggest we do a reunion show, and at a business meeting the next morning this proposal became more concrete. Mike and Terry were for it, John seemed keen, and even Terry Gilliam didn't seem to mind, though he was mainly there to hang out with Hunter S. Thompson, whose *Fear and Loathing in Las Vegas* he had just filmed. It seemed the Pythons were really keen on doing some kind of a stage show, and I was designated to explore the options. Believing them to be serious, I set off to find the finance. I came back with a solid offer of ten million dollars from Alan Tivoli, who had been our promoter for *Monty Python Live at City Centre*. Python was to play six nights in Las Vegas, culminating in a live TV performance on New Year's Eve. Not a bad idea and a very decent offer. We were talking dates, venues, and deals. There was a long Python conference call while I was on holiday in Venice. Everyone was in. Then, a month or two later when I returned to LA, Michael suddenly reneged. He *had* said yes, of course, but what he had meant, apparently, was no. He had *always* had anxieties about doing a live show, though he had not shared these anxieties, and he had apparently been very reluctant all along. Of course, it would have been nicer if he had said so earlier. I had spent a lot of time taking meetings and dealing with businesspeople, and now that the offer was concrete he pulled out. But life is too short to fight with friends, and I find at my age I can barely remember to hold a grudge, so although I confess I was a little pissed with Mike for wasting my time, of course I forgave him. It's impossible to dislike him for long. He *is* after all a National Treasure, although, in his case, perhaps a bit of a *Hidden* Treasure.

The fallout from Aspen liberated me. Finally, with Python definitely not going on the road, I was now free to play my own songs. I had been working constantly on music with John Du Prez, and we performed a concert at LA's J. Paul Getty Center in 1999 with backup singers and a band, which became a record, *Eric Idle Sings Monty Python*. The following year this turned into a full-blown two-month, twenty-city tour of the U.S. called *Eric Idle Exploits Monty Python*.

On the road with John Du Prez and twenty-one other people—what was I thinking? Certainly not money. William Morris made more than I did, but in hindsight this was a smart move. I enjoyed playing to live audiences across America. It was a nice change from developing movies that never got made. I loved making people laugh, and I really

With my longtime pal and partner, John Du Prez.

liked singing my songs. Wherever we went, the audiences sang along to "Bright Side." At Carnegie Hall I stood onstage in full drag as Dolly Taylor, singing "Sit on My Face."

"Follow that, Brahms," I said as I looked at his portrait in my dressing room.

In the 1997 James Brooks movie *As Good as It Gets,* Jack Nicholson sang "Always Look on the Bright Side of Life" to a dog.

"Thanks for ruining our film, Eric," he said to me.

"Thanks for ruining my song, Jack," I said back.

We had met Jack through our friend Anjelica Huston, and hung out quite a bit with him while Stanley Kubrick was busy driving him and Shelley Duvall mad filming *The Shining* in London (*see Rule One for actors*).

Hans Zimmer, who scored Jim Brooks's movie, asked Art Garfunkel to sing "Bright Side" over the closing credits, and Artie was kind enough to come onstage and sing it for me both nights at Carnegie Hall. A year later Monty Python was inducted into the Hollywood Bowl Hall of Fame, and John Du Prez and I went along with our touring company to accept the trophy. There were wonderful nostalgic clips of us at the Bowl twenty years earlier, and then Robin Williams came on like a blast from a blowgun and torched the audience with a high-octane tribute.

Originally Terry Gilliam was going to join me onstage to accept the award and then we were going to sing "Sit on My Face," but the Bowl nixed that naughty song, saying it was inappropriate for a gala, and so, sadly, Terry Gilliam pulled out. He has very high moral standards when it comes to low moral songs, so that moment of particular public tastelessness would have to wait.

Meanwhile I took the trophy from Robin and said:

It's wonderful to be back at the Bollywood Hole after all these years.

I am proud to be here on behalf of Monty Python to accept this honor.

I bring messages and thanks from the others. Terry Gilliam sadly can't be with us tonight as they won't let him show his ass, which has been very favorably compared with Spielberg's ass.

Graham Chapman can't be with us tonight, as sadly he is still dead. And John Cleese is finishing a movie.

He has to get it back to Blockbuster by tomorrow.

So that just leaves me here tonight.

And so, I'd like to thank *me,* without whom I too wouldn't be here this evening.

I'd like to thank everyone at the Bowl for honoring us in this way.

I'd like to thank Robin for friendship above and beyond the call of comedy.

But above all I'd like to thank America and you Americans for accepting Monty Python's essentially British silliness so warmly, so wholeheartedly, and so surprisingly.

Because, you see, I never wanted to do this for a living.

I always wanted to be a . . . lumberjack . . .

—and on marched a chorus of Mounties to sing the inevitable with John Mauceri and the Hollywood Bowl Orchestra. Of course, as we exited we naughtily sang "Sit on My Face" . . .

After Monty Python they honored Stevie Wonder, introduced with a spot-on impersonation by Smokey Robinson. At the end, there was an incredible curtain call, where I appeared holding hands with Stevie Wonder and Smokey Robinson. *I can die now,* I thought as the crowd went wild and two of my heroes held my hands and we bowed onstage at the Hollywood Bowl.

Little did I know I would return within a year for a less happy occasion.

24

GEORGE

The new millennium began terribly, with a horrible attack on George. Tania and I were in Montecito, staying with Steve Martin, when we heard the news that a crazed intruder, off his meds, had broken into Friar Park and fought with George and Olivia until she smashed him across the head with a Tiffany lamp. Some people said, "Oh it was just a burglary that went wrong." Some burglary. Some wrong. The reality was horrendous. George and Olivia had fought desperately for their lives for fifteen minutes, against a man armed with a kitchen knife. George had been stabbed multiple times. When the police arrived, he was at death's door. Now, mercifully, he was out of the emergency room. I called him.

"Would you like me to come over?" I asked.

"Where *are* you?" he said.

Tania and I caught the next plane.

We were relieved to find them alive. We kept thinking we could so easily have been flying for their funeral, but mercifully they were home, though bruised, wounded, and shocked. George had seven stab wounds, which he displayed rolling up his shirt. Some wounds were exit wounds where the blade had simply gone right through him. One stab had punctured and collapsed his lung, leaving him dangerously short of breath, lying on the floor chanting while his lung filled up with blood.

"I thought I was dead, Eric," he said.

Carried out to the ambulance on a stretcher covered in blood, and quite possibly dying, he said to his two new housekeepers, who had just started working for him and whom he had not yet met, "So, what do you think of the job so far?"

The first I knew he was going to survive those dreadful early hours was the unmistakably George quote displayed on the BBC website. When the police asked him about the intent of the intruder, he had said, "Well, he wasn't auditioning for the Traveling Wilburys."

"Why doesn't this kind of thing happen to the Rolling Stones?" he had asked me wryly on the phone.

It was the ultimate nightmare, an armed intruder in your home at three thirty in the morning, breaking windows and screaming loudly at you to come down.

"I wrestled hand-to-hand with the face of evil for fifteen minutes," said George.

Fifteen minutes is an awfully long time to struggle for your life against a man with a seven-inch kitchen knife while receiving multiple stab wounds.

"He came racing up the stairs, screaming dementedly," George told me.

Having called the police, Olivia ran out with a poker to find her husband on the ground and a man attempting to kill him. She bashed the intruder on the head fifteen times with the poker, but amazingly he was able to get up and turn on her. He knocked her over, and she lost the poker and retreated to their bedroom, where he followed her. Although stabbed by then, George was able to get up and go to her aid. At which point Olivia picked up a huge Tiffany lamp and began to bash the man about the head.

"It was like a movie," she said. "He wouldn't stop. There was blood everywhere. I kept yelling at him to stop, but he'd just get up again."

He grabbed the cord of the lamp and came at her with it. "I thought he was going to strangle me," she said. She knew there was another, heavier poker by the fireplace and ran downstairs.

He meanwhile picked up the lamp and began to beat George with it.

"I'd had it by then," said George. "I just tried to put my feet up to stop him." But he took several blows to the head. Then Olivia heard the man coming after her. She felt she could outrun him, but to her relief she heard him suddenly collapse. All his head wounds had finally caught up with him. Later, to his great joy, George learned she had managed to stab him in the butt. He was to have twenty-two stitches in his head, a measure of the success of Olivia; but right now there were three totally exhausted combatants. The battle was over. George was lying upstairs desperately wounded, his lungs filling with blood, chanting Hare Krishna. The intruder was collapsed on their balcony, and Olivia was sprawled at the foot of the stairs as the police entered. It was a scene from a horror movie. Blood was everywhere. Dhani, their twenty-one-year-old son, was faced with this dreadful scene. He kept his father conscious during the long wait until the ambulance came. He can always be proud of this, but no son should have to face what he did.

By the time Tania and I arrived at Friar Park, George and Liv were patched up, but angry, like all victims of violent crime, and in need of good friendship. Nobody had more good friends all round the world, and flowers and faxes poured in. We played guitars and sang. George was very shaken. I had never seen him like this. He needed constant hugs.

We were present for a puja, where a Vedic priest performed a short ceremony to thank Shiva for their survival and to clear the lurking presence of evil from their home. We went upstairs and walked around the various sites where the violence occurred, which is where I lost it. Many of us were weeping. It was impossible to be with them at these places and hear them say, "This was where it got really bad," without weeping. But after the ceremony even an old agnostic like myself felt cleansed. It is the power of ritual within us that is so important, and how wonderful to see George, Olivia, and Dhani receiving blessings. We felt very uplifted by their bravery, their honesty, and their grace in dealing with such an experience.

George died of cancer in November 2001. Impossible to believe he wasn't weakened by the attack. The first I realized he wasn't going to live was when I spoke to him on the phone in Switzerland. He had finished an album.

"What are you doing now?" I asked.

"I'm working on the liner notes," he said, "but if I don't finish them, then you will."

What did he just say? "If I don't finish them"?

I went to visit him a few times as he was dying, in a house in LA owned by Paul McCartney, to whom he had already said a tearful farewell. Jim Keltner told me that when I walked into the room it was the first time he saw George perk up and smile. We talked, though interrupted by his terrible hacking coughs.

Tania and Lily had flown to Chicago for Thanksgiving, but I wanted to stay close to George. When they returned we made a little package of food to take over to the house. We were twenty minutes too late. We were met at the door by our security friend Gavin de Becker.

"He's just gone," said Gavin simply.

The sight of him peacefully laid out in saffron robes with a bindi on his forehead was too much. I stepped forward to kiss him goodbye and totally broke down. I held him, my shoulders shaking with grief.

We were all weeping.

"C'mon," said Dhani, "Dad wouldn't have wanted this."

His funeral was a simple affair at the Hindu Temple on Sunset with the familiar incense from Friar Park, a large photo of George, and his recordings of the chants of Ravi Shankar. Afterwards, friends gathered at the nearby home of Mo Ostin, where I tastelessly said, "I'd like to thank Marlboro, without whom we wouldn't all be here today." Later the next year I was proud to eulogize George at the Hollywood Bowl.

When they told me they were going to induct my friend George Harrison into the Hollywood Bowl Hall of Fame *posthumously* my first thought was, *I bet he won't show up.* Because, unlike some others, he really wasn't into honors. He was one of those odd people who believe that life is somehow more important than show business, which I know is a heresy here in Hollywood, and I'm sorry to bring it up here in the very Bowel of Hollywood, but I can hear his voice saying, "Oh very nice, very useful, a posthumous award, where am I supposed to put it? What's next for me then? A posthumous Grammy? An ex-knighthood? An after-lifetime achievement award?"

I think he would prefer to be inducted posthumorously because he loved comedians, poor sick, sad, deranged lovable puppies that we are, because they, like him, had the ability to say the wrong thing at the right time, which is what we call humor.

He put Monty Python on here at the Hollywood Bowl, and he paid for the movie *The Life of Brian*, because he wanted to see it.

His life was filled with laughter and even his death was filled with laughter.

In the hospital, he asked the nurses to put fish and chips in his IV.

The doctor, thinking he was delusional, said to his son, "Don't worry, we have a medical name for this condition."

"Yes," said Dhani, "humor."

And I'm particularly sorry Dhani isn't here tonight because I wanted to introduce him by saying, "Here comes the son," but sadly that opportunity for a truly bad joke has gone.

What made George special, apart from his being the best guitarist in The Beatles, was what he did with his life after they achieved everything. He realized that this fame business was, and I'll use the technical philosophical term here, complete bullshit, and he turned to find beauty and truth and meaning in life, and more extraordinarily, found it. This is from his book *I, Me, Mine*:

"The thing that most people are struggling for is fame or fortune or wealth or position, and really none of that is important because in the end death will take it all away. So, you spend your life struggling for something, which is in effect a waste of time . . . I mean, I don't want to be lying there as I'm dying thinking, *Oh shit, I forgot to put the cat out.*"

And he wasn't. He passed away, here in LA, with beauty and dignity, surrounded by people he loved.

Because he had an extraordinary capacity for friendship. People loved him all over the planet.

George was in fact a moral philosopher; his life was all about a search for truth, and preparing himself for death.

Which is a bit weird for someone in rock and roll. They're not supposed to be that smart. They're supposed to be out there looking for Sharon. Not the meaning of life.

He was a gardener, he grew beauty in everything he did, in his life, in his music, in his marriage, and as a father.

I was on an island somewhere when a man came up to him and said, "George Harrison, oh my god, what are *you* doing here?" And he said, "Well, everyone's got to be somewhere."

Well, alas he isn't here. But we are. And that's the point. This isn't for him. This is for us, because we want to honor him. We want to remember him. We want to say, "Thanks, George, for being. And we really miss you."

And this is the big drag about posthumous awards: there's no one to give 'em to.

So, I'm gonna give it to the love of his life, his dark sweet lady, dear wonderful Olivia Harrison, who is with us here tonight.

Liv, you truly know what it is to be without him.

Thank you, Hollywood Bowl, you do good to honor him.

A year later, on the anniversary of his death, Olivia and Dhani mounted a wonderful memorial concert for George at the Royal Albert Hall in London. Never have I seen so many grown men in tears. George had the capacity to reach in and take your heart. Eric Clapton had organized the music with Dhani and they had rehearsed for three weeks with some of the greats, like Tom Petty and Jeff Lynne and, of course, Paul and Ringo. They all played George songs, a very nice touch. Olivia had asked me to ask the Pythons to sing "Piggies," but I said, "Liv, we can't, we're not musicians, that's not really what we do." I persuaded her, and bless her forever for this, to let us come on instead as waiters and sing "Sit on My Face." It was such wonderful bad taste, and a laugh is exactly what you need for sadness. At the end, we all slowly turned around and bowed to the huge photo of George behind us, revealing to the entire audience our ancient bare posteriors. I'm so proud of that moment. You often hear the statement "It's what he would have wanted," but never, I think, was it more appropriate. He would have loved the sheer tasteless joy of what we did. Although we were without John, we hadn't been onstage together in London for almost forty years, and in the dark before the lights came up, the crowd somehow sensed we were there and went crazy. I felt the hairs on my neck stand up. When we did "The Lumberjack Song," Tom Hanks came on quietly as a Mounty in George's role.

There were many tears backstage during that concert. I had to resort to the bathroom on several occasions, but Paul in particular was wonderfully comforting, like a big brother:

"Come here, you need a hug."

At the end, when we all stood quietly onstage while Joe Brown sang simply and unforgettably to his ukulele, "I'll See You in My Dreams," and rose petals began to fall from the ceiling of the Royal Albert Hall, I think everyone fell apart. I can still hardly remember that moment without tears. We all knew what we'd lost.

25

BRIGHT SIDE ON BROADWAY

John Du Prez and I did a second North American concert tour in 2003. The point of a Greedy Bastard Tour is that, having taken twenty-two people around America, the next time, in order to make money, you take only yourself. The next time I took only *two* other performers and a band, but William Morris still made more than me. Eddie Izzard and Billy Connolly were encouraging me to do more stand-up, more improv, more talking about myself, so I did. We went all the way across North America on a rock-and-roll tour bus, traveling fifteen thousand miles in three months, playing at beautiful old theaters. *The Greedy Bastard Diary* is my daily account of this journey. In Vancouver as the holidays approached, I tried out a new song John and I had written called "Fuck Christmas." It was like throwing a hand grenade into the crowd—the audience response almost blew us offstage. Each line killed. Especially the end:

> *Go tell the Elves*
> *To fuck themselves*
> *It's Christmas time again.*

Apparently, we could still write funny songs. Just as well, because John and I were working on an exciting new project. In the Nineties, I had worked on a Python CD-ROM game of *The Holy Grail*. If it could become a game, I wondered, why couldn't it become a musical? *Grail* was perfect for a musical. Every sketch seemed to demand a song. It appeared to have all the elements of a great comic stage show, a mock-heroic pastiche of Wagnerian grandeur, with bickering knights riding around on imaginary horses—but would the Pythons ever give us permission? Only one way to find out. I wrote a play, adapting the ninety-eight characters in the movie to a more manageable eight, and then John and I recorded half a dozen songs and sent them off to the guys. Amazingly, they were all intrigued by the idea, they loved "The Song That Goes Like This," and wonderfully they said yes.

Spamalot was born.

I'd had some previous experience of Broadway in the late Nineties when Garth Drabinsky, the Canadian producer of *Ragtime,* asked me to write the book for *Seussical,* a musical based on the Dr. Seuss books. I was shamefully ignorant of Seuss, so I read everything, including some interesting biographies, and set to work writing a treatment for Lynn Ahrens and Stephen Flaherty, brilliant songwriters who had a huge hit with *Ragtime.* I decided Horton should be the central story because I loved the tiny Who world, desperately seeking help. Inside that plot I crammed as many references to the other stories as I could, eventually delivering a heavily illustrated treatment in the summer of 1998. Lynn and Stephen loved it and set to work writing the score, which they did remarkably quickly, and it was soon filled with brilliant songs.

But then the fat lady sang.

Garth Drabinsky sold his company to Mike Ovitz, the former CAA agent, who soon found a *second* set of books with the *real* figures, and now faced an uphill task of trying to turn around a debt-ridden theatrical company. Garth himself fled from the feds to Canada, where he would eventually do some time, but the experience set me on the path to Broadway, and my own Holy Grail. I was supposed to write the book for *Seussical* but, once Garth departed, new management came in with a different idea. I did play the role of the Cat in the Hat for the Broadway investors' tryout, and Lynn and Stephen wrote me a special song, "How Lucky You Are," which took place in total chaos as the set fell apart, but at no stage was I tempted to swap my wife, child, and home in LA for eight shows a week on Broadway, and I turned down repeated offers to play the Cat. *Seussical* taught me a lot about musical theater and what it takes to make things work, from having good producers to getting the book right, and how to advance the plot through the music and dance, a lesson choreographer Casey Nicholaw would repeatedly drum into me on *Spamalot*.

Now, I had more experience of Broadway, and I also had a script, a title, and the rights for *The Holy Grail*. What next? My lawyer and good friend Tom Hoberman suggested I approach Bill Haber, another founding father of CAA who was venturing onto Broadway. It took me twenty minutes to sell the idea to Bill in my LA home, where I had laid out the *Holy Grail* dolls and some of the tons of merchandise from that movie. I played him a couple of the songs that John Du Prez and I had demoed and handed him the script. He was in before he was out the door.

"What about a workshop?" I said.

"We won't need a workshop," he said. "This stuff has been playing successfully for thirty years. We'll go straight into rehearsal."

Wow.

"Who would you like to direct?" he asked.

"I'd like Mike Nichols," I said.

"Who wouldn't?" he agreed. "But it takes Mike ages to respond."

"I know him, and he loves the music of John and me."

"Alright, I'll send it to him."

Mike called me three days later.

"Yes, yes, yes," he said.

From the beginning, Mike was determined to have "Always Look on the Bright Side of Life" in *Spamalot*. He had come to the Greedy Bastard Tour in New York and seen how the audience responded to the song, joining in and singing along happily. He wanted *Spamalot* to end that way too. For him it would simply be the finale, but Casey and I put the whole song into the play while Mike was away in California opening *Closer*. I couldn't get Act Two to work and I felt we needed something familiar near the beginning, something the audience could relax to, a little moment for Patsy, where he tries to cheer up the despairing King Arthur. So, "Always Look on the Bright Side of Life," which started off in *Brian,* eventually ended up in *Grail,* and on Broadway.

Spamalot changed my life. I thought the play would be funny, but I had no idea it would be so successful and so well received. Mike Nichols was, of course, the key. Not only did he reassure the other Pythons that here was someone responsible enough to be left in charge of their baby, but as he was both a comedian and a fantastic director, the play would be in the very best of hands.

I had met Mike back in 1975 at a party at Paul Simon's, where I talked to a stranger for two hours and found him the funniest and most interesting man I'd ever met, and we yakked away until he finally left.

"Who was that?" I said when he'd gone.

People looked at me like I was nuts.

"That was Mike Nichols!"

Oh, duh.

Ironically, as Mike would always say, when I was at college I was a big fan of his records with Elaine May, but I had never seen either of them live or on television, so I simply hadn't recognized him. One of the great delights of life from that moment on was lunch or dinner or theater or anything at all with Mike. Once, in San Paul de Vence, we passed an art gallery selling a sculpture by Salvador Dali. Mike stopped and went in.

"How much is that Dali in the window?"

He loved being funny. And outrageous. He was late one day for rehearsal and was apologizing profusely to me:

"The traffic was horrendous. The whole of the Upper East Side was *yidlock.*"

He would look so happy, with that lovely smile, when I cracked up. He was always fantastically generous to his writer. I have never been so encouraged by anyone. He wouldn't let anything pass; he'd badger you until you'd finally send him an email with a new proposal he liked, and he would simply respond, "Perfect."

Mike's most brilliant decision was picking Casey Nicholaw for choreographer. It was Casey's first Broadway show, helming the Terpsichore, as *Variety* might say, and it was an utterly inspired choice. His choreography, a perfect balance between sweet and silly, and his own amazing calmness and leadership inspired the whole company. As for the actors, many of them came to Mike. David Hyde Pierce called and *insisted* on being in it. Hank Azaria said he had known his lines since he was twelve. I had always wanted Tim Curry for King Arthur, and when Mike heard him read the part at my house, so did he. The Lady of the Lake was the hardest part to cast. I had created the character as an African American diva and later she often was, but Mike said one day, "There's someone I want you to look at." So we all assembled in the Shubert Theatre and Sara Ramirez came onstage and sang a Sondheim piece. She blew us away. She was so powerful, so passionate, and so goddamn sexy. Every man in the room was smitten.

Oh yes, Mike!

Next year she won the Tony.

Mike brought a high seriousness to *Spamalot*. He insisted the actors *always* take it seriously.

"If *you* don't take it seriously, why should the audience?"

Sitting behind him, watching him give notes, was a master class in directing. I had almost five years of it. He told them to *listen* to what the others were saying. Often, he would have them lie on the ground and just say the lines, no acting, no emphasis. If they found a new laugh or a new piece of shtick and kept it for another performance, he would make them take it out.

"You must kill your babies" was his refrain.

He insisted they believe in their characters. Often, he was quite severe. Some actors he insulted. A very small number he made cry. He would not let anything through. His rule in productions was "No Assholes." We had one, who thought it funny to slap another actor. Mike fired him at lunch.

One day he was being very severe about a scene:

"You must make them real!"

"But Mike," I said. "You are talking about the Knights Who Say Ni!"

He laughed. But he was right. I think he had noticed something about Python. We always *believed* in everything we did. After all, the Minister of Silly Walks is only funny if he believes he really is a minister with hard choices to make on a declining budget. If for one second he doesn't, then the sketch falls flat.

Something rather special was happening in the large mirrored rehearsal room on Forty-Second Street. The great news had come in before we even started rehearsals that we had sold out the entire run of previews in Chicago. I kept writing to the other Pythons, *Don't miss this.* But they did, except for John, who came to visit. He walked in just as they were rehearsing his song "Knights of the Round Table," and he was totally delighted. We hugged and it was really sweet to see him. The cast saw him too and perked up and performed the life out of the number. There were tears in our eyes as we sat side by side and watched them, thinking how amazing it was to sit here thirty years later and watch people doing this. John was affable, charming, and complimentary. It was a joy to see him back in the studio as he recorded the lines with Tim Curry. He was hilarious. His God has a wonderful testiness about him.

"Of course it's a good idea. I'm fucking God, you idiot!"

Mike suggested the billing should read: "and John Cleese as God."

Subj: Rehearsals
Date: 10/31/2004 6:35:35 AM Pacific Standard Time
From: Eric Idle
To: The Pythons

I just thought you should all know that Spamalot is not only progressing well it is a positive blast. I sit in a warm rehearsal room on 42nd street watching pretty young women in leotards bending, bouncing, and stretching. And the show is pretty good too.

In fact, I sit next to Mike with a big silly grin on my face and tears in my eyes. I can't explain exactly the appeal: it is something to do with compounding the silliness.

John C came in the other day just as they were rehearsing "The Knights of the Round Table" song he wrote with Graham all those years ago, and he just beamed and glowed. He came to play God. And won. His voice is now in the show.

So the reason I am writing, is to encourage you to drop by the process if you can, I think you'll find it marvelous and uplifting, and even moderately arousing.

The script, particularly Act Two, was changing daily, but has now locked down into a better shape, and everything seems to flow, though often into unexpected quarters. You'll see what I mean. I'll keep you updated in any case. We have another four weeks in NY and then move to the theater in Chicago, where we just announced an extra week of performances. Tim Curry, Hank Azaria, and David Hyde Pierce and all couldn't be funnier. Or nicer.

Mike says he hasn't been so happy since The Graduate.

Hugs to all

E

Subj: Re: Two weeks of rehearsal
Date: 11/1/2004 8:08:46 AM Pacific Standard Time
From: Terry Jones
To: Eric Idle
Sent from the Internet

Dear El

Ah the magic of the theatre . . . sounds wonderful . . . warm and inviting and arousing . . . it's the girls in leotards bending and stretching that really convinces me that the whole thing is going to be a thundering success.

I wish I could get over . . . but on the other hand, if Bush gets in tomorrow I think I'll give the US a miss for another four years.

I hear the extra week has sold out already—can this be true?

Fingers crossed all over my tense yet still young body.
Lots of love
Terry
xxoxo

I responded . . .

Say it ain't so, Tel. You can't let the bastards win, and you really must see *Spamalot*—it's your creation too.

Would a Hitler victory have stopped you going to Berlin for the Ludo finals? Of course not. Where's the man I once saw conducting a German band while stripping in front of Nazis at a beer festival in Munich?

I agree anger would be a correct response, but I remain foolishly optimistic.
Miss you
E

There were three blizzards in Chicago during the previews and the cast bonded—we all loved each other and there were many parties and much dancing. Mike had only one major concern. I had written a lyric that contained the hook "You won't succeed on Broadway if you don't have any Jews." He was worried about how this would be received by an audience.

"Well, we'll just have to try it," I said. "Only way to find out."

So, at the opening preview in Chicago the show took off like a rocket. The audience was so into it. "He Is Not Dead Yet" made them yell with happiness. "The Song That Goes Like This" killed. "Find Your Grail" was electrifying. We were all smiles at the intermission. Act Two opens with "Bright Side," and they actually whistled along.

"Now for it," said Mike next to me, as what he insisted on calling "The Jew Song" approached. David Hyde Pierce sang, clearly enunciating:

> You won't succeed on Broadway . . .
> If you don't have any . . . Jews.

There was a moment of stunned silence. The audience rocked back in their seats mouths open, and then instantly rocked forward again screaming with laughter. At the end of the number they applauded and applauded and applauded. Some people even stood. It was a mammoth hit.

"Well, I guess that's okay then," said Mike, beaming that wonderful beam.

Mike and me.

By the time we moved to Broadway, thanks to reviews and word of mouth from Chicago, we had a huge box-office advance. We opened on St. Patrick's Day. All the Pythons attended. There was a glittering audience. Mike had pulled in quite a crowd. Mountains of opening-night gifts flooded into my hotel room overlooking Forty-Fourth Street. My wife, daughter, and sister-in-law Joyce were all getting dolled up. Resplendent in a new charcoal cashmere coat from my exceptionally generous producer, Bill Haber, I walked to the theater from the back entrance of my hotel down Forty-Fifth Street and across Times Square, thinking to myself, *I must remember this and how it feels*. I was elegantly dressed in a brand-new Issey Miyake tux with an outrageous Day-Glo shirt with a fake tie in luminescent green. Smart but silly. I was aware that the picture we were about to take with the Pythons would be the one used of us for the next six years, or forever if we never met again. It had been seven years since the last photograph of us together at the Aspen Comedy Festival. We only seemed to get bigger.

Shubert Alley was closed off, with security people who recognized me and let me through. Backstage there were happy laughing people from *Fiddler on the Roof*, and Harvey Fierstein was there for the Gypsy Robe presentation, a Broadway opening-night tradition that Harvey in his wonderfully precise voice explained to me. They handed the traditional robe to the youngest of our chorus ladies. Then they hugged us and wished us good luck and left, and Casey said, "Alright everybody, just one chorus of 'Knights of the Round Table,'" and right there they all snapped into the closing song-and-dance routine. This was so sensible and so centering and such a smart thing to do that I admired Casey and his brilliance all over again. We were bonded and centered and ready. Nothing much for an author to do except hang around and wait for the PR folks to deliver me up to the media.

I was taken out and grilled in front of the theater for the world press, then back along the alley into the Booth Theatre, where the Pythons were being held downstairs. They seemed to be at ease and looking forward to seeing the show, sipping drinks in the mirrored bar, and I hugged them all. John was looking particularly distinguished. We were all anxious to get on with it, and soon the relatives were shepherded away and we were left waiting on the stairs. It all felt strangely familiar. John pushed Mike around like a schoolboy.

"You still can't keep your hands off him, can you?" I said, and we were once again that odd group of strange men backstage waiting to go on.

We were led out to the front of the Shubert to face the electrical storm of the cameras amidst cheering and screaming from the crowd across the street. The Pythons were all gracious and affectionate and then we disgorged into the celebrity-packed theater. Whoopi Goldberg said hello. Lorne Michaels smiled. I spied Barbara Walters and Mike Wallace from *60 Minutes,* and there was a general air of anticipation. Soon the lights dimmed, the overture played to laughter, and we were under way with "Finland."

I thought the show went really well, especially for an opening night. Mike hated the audience, and the cast thought they were down, but the people there experienced the most joyous and wondrous opening night in a long time. At the end, the cheers were deafening and Tim Curry very kindly called the author up onstage; I got a huge ovation and then Mike and then Casey and then John Du Prez came up too. We all took a bow and then I said, "I must ask up a group from Britain without whom we wouldn't all be here today: John . . . Paul, George, and Ringo," and then we pulled the Pythons up onstage. I was looking at my daughter's face in the front row and winking at her and just feeling this warmth and enormous love for all the Pythons together again. Finally, we cued the music and we all sang "Always Look on the Bright Side of Life" until the curtain came down and there was a great deal of hugging. Mike Palin was in tears; John too had a tear in his eye and kissed me and said well done. I told everybody that the Pythons coming made the evening for me, and it was true. It was all fantastic really.

The Ratfuck (Mike's ubiquitous term for any black-tie event with rubber chicken) was held at Roseland and was loud and big and meaty with roast beef and Yorkshire pudding and a huge castle built out of Spam cans with a cartoon Holy Grail in the center of it. I was interviewed and photographed and then was caught near the door by a series of well-wishers. Nice people crowded around me. Irene and Buck Henry were glowing with enthusiasm. Tom Hoberman was in tears. A lawyer crying! Elliot Brown said, "Do you know how rare this is?" In twenty years of going to the theater, only three times could he remember an opening like this. I was happy to see Roger Waters there and glad he loved it, as he was one of the original investors in the movie. Coco Schwab came to get me and drag me over to a grinning David

Bowie standing with Lou Reed and the adorable Iman. Both musicians thought Sara Ramirez a gold mine and had the idea to make money from her. I told them they were too late. Also there was Eddie Izzard, Python fan extraordinaire, who had flown in to New York from Scandinavia for one night only to attend our opening on Broadway, and then immediately returned to his tour in Sweden.

The next day, I walked into Sardi's and the producers were all having lunch and they stood and applauded me. By then the box office was going nuts. The reviews were apparently sensational, though I stuck to my guns and didn't read them. We had done over $900,000 in the morning. By 2:00 p.m. we'd passed the million-dollar mark in a single day, and by the evening show we were already over two million and making Broadway history. So not just a great show, not just great reviews; great box office too. We had pulled it off. The grand slam.

Did I learn anything? Certainly. First, Mike's Law: *Only work with the best.* Second, Mike's Second Law: *Never give up.* Third: *Always work with Mike.*

26

THE TONY FAIRY

One morning in the Eighties when I lived in St. John's Wood, I received a large package with an invitation which said in big gold letters:

> Congratulations, Eric Idle, Tony Award Nominee. You, Eric Idle, have been nominated for a Tony Award. We would like to invite you to New York for the Tony Awards Ceremony and we are very happy to inform you that you have been nominated for Best Female Performer on Broadway.

I have to admit that this was a shock. I certainly hadn't expected it, but I am a polite man and I wrote back.

> I am so thrilled to receive this nomination. It is one of the greatest honors of my career. It is particularly thrilling for me because not only have I never appeared on Broadway, I am not even a female. I would be delighted to attend your awards ceremony. Would you like me to wear a frock?

There was a series of embarrassed phone calls, and sadly it turned out it wasn't for me at all. It was for Chita Rivera. Well, it's a mistake anyone could make, Eric Idle, Chita Rivera . . . I very much enjoyed the confusion and for a long time I counted that nomination as one of the most unlikely near-achievements of my career. So, it was some-

thing of a surprise when I actually did receive two real Tony nomina-
tions, for Best Book and Best Lyrics in a Musical Play on Broadway for
Spamalot.

I had never actually seen a Tony show before I attended Radio City
Music Hall for the 2005 Tony Awards. Most of the audience of all sexes
were drooling over Hugh Jackman, the host. *Spamalot* had been nomi-
nated for thirteen Tonys and had already lost six when I spotted Mike
Nichols heading urgently up the aisle toward me.

"They're going to stiff us," he said. "You have to think of something
to say."

In a previous life, I wrote ad-libs for David Frost, so I didn't panic.
David would say, "I need a line to get me over to the junkies," and I'd
scribble away and, live on air, David would say the line I'd given him
exactly as if he had just thought it up.

"I'll have a go," I said, wondering if the junkie line could be of any
use.

Mike returned glumly to his seat, and I was so busy racking my
brains for something amusing to say that wouldn't sound bitter and
twisted, but incredibly mature and suitably grateful for being ignored
and passed over completely, that I barely noticed when I personally lost
the next award for Best Book of a Musical. My lovely wife, looking adorable in Harry Winston diamond earrings, on loan for the night, gave
my hand an encouraging squeeze. Advised by the virtually irresistible
Hugh Jackman that this would be a good time, Tania then exited to the
bathroom during what was promised as a long commercial break, only
to be replaced in her seat by a mature-looking lady in a large and very
bizarre hat, which resembled a ginger tomcat squatting on her head.
It is axiomatic that there must be no empty seats visible at TV awards
shows, and highly dressed extras are employed to deftly slide into the
gaps when people pop out for a smoke or a pee. Of course, this was the
very moment the cameras singled out me and "my wife" for our close-
up as I bravely lost for Best Lyrics in a Musical. I was so busy trying not
to laugh at this strange woman smiling proudly by my side, giggling
in the knowledge that people all over America were going, "Whatever

happened to Tania?" and "Has he gone mad taking up with a weird Cat Woman?" that I didn't even have time to feel disappointed. We had after all already been winners at several major Broadway awards ceremonies, and Mike had picked up a variety of oddly shaped statuettes and made a series of increasingly funny speeches. My favorite, when once again his name was announced as the winner, was watching him walk up slowly, look genuinely puzzled at the audience, and say sadly, "I miss failure."

On Tony night, the Pigeons of Irony were coming home to roost as we continued to miss out on Best Choreography, Best Score, Best Actors, Best Sets, Best Lighting, Best Costumes, Best New Shoes, etc., etc. Finally, the Tony Fairy relented and the utterly deserving Sara Ramirez headed up the aisle to accept her award for Best Performance by a Featured Actress in a Musical, thanking us, her parents, and Claritin. And then, of course, Mike's nightmare was over as he won yet another Tony for Best Director. I crumpled up my pathetic half-written one-liners in relief.

But fate had one more surprise in store for us. After a very long and occasionally interesting evening, the inestimable Hugh Jackman read out the name of Best Musical of 2005 and, incredibly, it was *Monty Python's Spamalot*. Wow! Who would have thunk it? Our cast of knights and wenches spilled out onto Hugh Jackman, whooping and hollering, and the auditorium was filled with smiling producers hurriedly heading for the stage. I beat them to it by a good yard. Mike gave me a proud hug and I barely restrained myself from kissing Hugh Jackman. There would be time for that later.

We danced and partied in the brilliant way our company had perfected. It was a wonderful evening. I, who had been sober for five years, had "just the one" glass of champagne to celebrate, and that one glass went on for twelve years, as they do. I'm back on the wagon now, much to the disgust of some of my friends, especially in France. I'm far less fun but I get more done, and at my age the less you fall over the better. Gravity, once your friend, becomes your enemy. Sorry, people, you can say "break a leg" but it'll have to remain metaphorical. I broke a leg last year, and I hadn't even had a drink. It cost so much that I seriously considered marrying my surgeon. He was cute, too. I guess it might have been the painkillers. Once after ankle surgery they gave me a morphine button, which I could just press to top up. I knew I was doing too much when I became aware that I thought Regis was the funniest, smartest, and wittiest man on TV. Wait! Could it be the morphine?

At the end of the night Tania, like Cinderella, had to return the loaner jewels to Harry Winston. A long line of limos outside their Fifty-Eighth Street side entrance meant they'd had a busy night. At the Tonys, discreet security guards had hovered everywhere. Discreet if you consider seven-foot linebackers clearly packing heat a form of discretion, but for heaven's sake, they were lending *actors* jewelry. So, as we pulled up, Tania reluctantly kissed good night to the glittering diamond earrings and the gorgeous diamond-and-amethyst ring, and I took them inside and dropped them in front of a man in shirtsleeves. He had a snub-nosed .38 sitting on the desk in front of him in case anyone changed their minds. I changed my mind the next day and snuck back to Harry Winston and bought the diamond-and-amethyst ring for Tania. I mean, how often do you win a Tony?

27

DIVA LAS VEGAS

It's eight o'clock in the morning and already stinking hot in Las Vegas. Not just hot, it's blindingly bright. There is simply too much sunshine bouncing off the golden walls of the Wynn, blown by the strong wind shuffling across the desert, which lifts the awnings on the striped pavilions and ruffles the tassels and snaps the umbrellas. This is the only time you can be alone in Vegas. One or two early risers sit in the white ranks of loungers by the pool. The waiters chatter over the endless heartbeat thump of the disco, the gardeners spray water on the Provençal shrubbery, even the crickets are chirruping, though I am suspicious and see they have been piped in. There are tiny little speakers everywhere. Yes, the devil is in the details. There is half a forest of huge pines impressively green on the hillside, hauled in and tastefully replanted amongst the artificial grass, fake rocks, and carefully constructed waterfalls. I think I prefer the fake to the real. Hardly surprising: I am in show business, which is all about faking the real. The beauty of ancient places is accidental; the ugliness of Vegas is planned. Yet to stand in front of the phony Doge's Palace at eleven and hear the chimes of Big Ben from London, the pealing of the bells from Paris, and the explosion of a volcanic waterfall is to experience something unintended. A random Universe created by a thousand monkeys. It makes you ask, "Why am I here?" The answer is *Spamalot*.

Spamalot was the first time in my life I experienced big money, and I liked it. That wonderful summer of having a hit on Broadway, Bill Haber, our producer, invited me and Tania to stay at his chateau in the

Loire Valley. He showed me to our suite. There on the mantelpiece was a check for five hundred thousand dollars. To an English guy brought up poor, that was incredible. Next year he invited us again. I took our bags up and came back downstairs.

"Bill," I said, "there's no check . . ."

Thanks to Steve Wynn booking the show into Las Vegas, we had made our money back in record time. Only 18 percent of Broadway shows ever do that. What F. Scott Fitzgerald said of American lives is definitely true of Vegas: there are no second acts. Partly this is because they want you back in the casino, but mainly it's because they want you back in the casino. In fact, with our low ticket prices ($49, $69, $89), I figured out that you will actually *save* money if you go and spend ninety minutes in *Spamalot*. Even on the cheapest slots. And if you sleep during the show, you can save on a room.

I'm a little concerned about how our show will play out here in the desert, so as part of my research I visited all the major attractions. Nothing quite matched the intensity of *Jubilee!*, which gripped me with its thrilling story of 150 bare-breasted ladies seducing Samson and causing the *Titanic* to sink. Sometimes the plot was hard to follow. As the huge ship went down on stage firing off rockets of distress, I knew just how it felt. To me the most interesting part of the evening was watching a show where the girls start nude and gradually put on more clothing. An oddly effective technique. One thing for sure, you cannot out-Vegas Vegas. There is simply no parodying this. There is no over-the-top. Only over-the-topless.

At the world-famous Crazy Horse, all the girls have short blond wigs, perfect derrieres, and genuine French names like Fifi and Suki. They remind me of what the Seventies was all about: light shows and shagging. But this show too is a little thin on plot. And clothing. The rest of the entertainment is all French Canadian, from Céline to the many Cirques. Monty Python was a Flying Circus but does that qualify us as a Cirque? We have no acrobats, no contortionists, and only a few French people farting in our general direction. How will the nipple-hungry Nevadans take our show?

At the press launch I say, "I'm missing my wife so much here in

Vegas that last night I paid for a woman to come up to my room and ignore me."

Steve Wynn says he has been trying to finish Broadway in Las Vegas and what better way than to put on *Spamalot*? He had recently put his elbow through his own Picasso in front of a small crowd of stunned guests. As a gag, I tried to persuade him now to put his elbow through a fake painting.

"It'll kill," I said.

"No way," said Steve. "Bad enough I'm known as the Inspector Clouseau of the art world."

Instead John O'Hurley, from *Seinfeld*, who is here to play golf and King Arthur, in that order, comes onstage. Together we do a tango. Why? Because neither of us could do the paso doble. And of course, we brought on our beautiful showgirls, wearing only white lingerie. *Why? Do you need to ask?* I announce that, as an added attraction, some of our shows will be topless, but only in John O'Hurley's part.

Next day we are in a rehearsal room in the less salubrious side of Las Vegas, amongst the bail bonds and the pawnshops—the last place you see before the desert. Our modern studios are pleasant, and the cast is confident as they read my edited version for Mike Nichols and Casey Nicholaw. It's not bad, but we caucus thoughtfully in a conference room. On Broadway the play was fifty minutes, then a nice intermission, and then sixty minutes of Act Two. Now it is ninety minutes straight through, and that's a completely different dramatic shape. There is work to be done. It's not that we are long, but with a ninety-minute shape you have to feel the driving force of the plot. It must never feel like a sketch show. We roll up our sleeves and set to work. I have a wonderful feeling of nostalgia. It's like two years ago when we were on Forty-Second Street. Ah, happy days.

Mike gives a master class. He talks to the actors for about fifty minutes, but in that talk he says everything they will ever need to know about drama. He is spectacular. Not just about truth telling in acting, or storytelling, or about the shape and types of scene, but how to ask: *What is this like? Who am I being like? What does this remind me of?*

He ends by reminding them not to be funny. Just say the words. Don't act. Meanwhile, I am cutting and pruning and trimming and there are glum faces as I remove favorite bits.

Then I bring in my secret weapon: Terry Gilliam. I confess to the cast that what I had told them about all the other Pythons being dead is not true. They are thrilled to meet the legendary Gilliam, who has brought down more financial institutions than Enron. Even he is bowled over by the Grail Theater and the new Python Hall that leads up to it. Large cutout iconic figures of Silly Walks and Colonels and Naughty Vicars decorate the entrance, and there is a plethora of Gilliam art. Terry says he is going home to persuade Michael Palin to come for the opening. Ironically, Michael has announced he is staying home because he's writing a travel book. John Cleese is scheduled to attend but then he plays God, and we know they both move in mysterious ways. Sadly, Terry Jones can't make it. He is apparently wrestling with chemo. I rather hoped he would be here wrestling with keno.

Will *Spamalot* succeed? Who knows? Dare I say, it's a crapshoot. We have, by Vegas standards, a huge advance, but the word of mouth will be everything. If we make 'em laugh, we'll have a shot. If not, well, we have the North American tour, we have Broadway, we have London and soon Australia, and I shall just have to get used to *not* having dinner with billionaires again.

The first preview went great. In fact, it took ages to clear the theater afterwards as they were lining up to buy merchandise—Killer Rabbits, Coconuts, and Flying Cows. Even the Wynn-folk were impressed.

On the third night of previews we had a major glitch. Our elevator failed and, instead of the Lady of the Lake and her Laker Girls emerging from a pond in their skimpy fronds, nothing happened. King Arthur stood gesturing to an empty stage.

"She's a bit late," said John O'Hurley, exiting. "I'd better see where she is."

Galahad and Patsy and Mrs. Bedevere looked alarmed.

"Me too," they said and they all went off, leaving an empty stage. Great. Nice improv, people.

From below we could hear the Lady of the Lake singing away with all the chorus girls, but no one emerged. Backstage, they had forgotten to build stairs from the basement to the stage level, and now the onstage lift was jammed. The stage was empty, the audience was growing restless, and nobody came on to explain anything. Oh dear. We were going to have to stop. Some deep show-off instinct kicked in and I found myself rushing down through the audience and up onto the stage. The place went wild. The easiest standing ovation I ever had.

"This is what technically in theatrical terms we call a fuckup," I said. "A huge helicopter was supposed to land . . . Oh, no, that was another show."

I ad-libbed for about ten minutes, thinking how Eddie Izzard would be proud of me doing improvisational stand-up in front of 1,600 people. Luckily the glitch ended before I did and I escaped back into the audience and the show continued. Opening on my sixty-fourth birthday, March 29, 2007, *Spamalot* would run in Las Vegas at the Wynn for sixteen months, and when we closed, I said we were some of the few people ever to leave the city with money in our pockets.

28

BRIGHT SIDE GETS BRIGHTER

In 2005, John Du Prez and I won a Grammy for Best Musical Show Album for *Spamalot*. On Thanksgiving Day that year, our New York cast sang "Always Look on the Bright Side of Life" on a float all the way down Broadway in the Macy's parade. Soon after, we opened a highly successful North American tour in Boston. *Spamalot* would eventually open in London, Germany, Spain, France, Sweden, Holland, Norway, South Korea, Australia, and even Japan, where I sang "Bright Side" in Japanese on Japanese TV:

> *Gin Se Lacuni E Qui YoYo . . .*

Well, that's how they wrote it out for me phonetically. I attended many opening nights in cities I had never yet visited—Barcelona, Madrid, Oslo, Stockholm, Malmö, Copenhagen, and Budapest, as well as a delightfully sexy production in Paris and a brilliant mad version in Mexico City—and always ended up onstage singing with the cast.

John Du Prez and I put "Bright Side" into our next show as well, a comic oratorio called *Not the Messiah (He's a Very Naughty Boy),* based on *The Life of Brian,* which we premiered in Toronto at the Luminato Festival, conducted by my cousin Peter Oundjian, the principal conductor of the Toronto Symphony Orchestra. Peter had encouraged me to find something two improbable cousins could do together. When I suggested *Not the Messiah,* he loved it. Christopher Sieber, our wonderful first Galahad, came up from our Broadway company to play Brian. He would later play Galahad again for us in London. We did a further two performances outdoors at Caramoor with the St. Luke's Orchestra and Chorus at the bottom of Martha Stewart's garden. The oratorio went down so well that later in the year we added a second act, and John Du Prez conducted his own brilliant score on a tour of New Zealand and Australia, including two performances at the Sydney Opera House. A year later we went on a U.S. tour to Houston and Wolf Trap—an outdoor venue near Washington with a 7,000-seat theater—culminating in two glorious nights at the Hollywood Bowl before 24,000 people, where John wrote some special encore music for fireworks, based on our "Galaxy Song." We finally filmed *Not the Messiah* for DVD at The Royal Albert Hall in 2009 with Michael Palin, Terry Jones, Terry Gilliam, Neil Innes, and Carol Cleveland, to celebrate the fortieth anniversary of Monty Python.

I was asked to sing "Bright Side" again for Prince Charles's sixtieth birthday concert in November 2008. This was a charity show for the Prince's Trust at the New Wimbledon Theatre, with many funny people, including Joan Rivers and Robin Williams. I decided to play a gag similar to the one I had pulled on his mother. I was closing the show, and John Cleese introduced the English National Ballet, warning the audience it might be rather tedious. A beautiful Brazilian ballerina danced the Dying Swan surrounded by a bevy of young girls in tutus from the English National Ballet School. As the Swan expired I popped up from the middle of the corps de ballet in a tutu and said, "Cheer up, ducks, you know what they say . . .

Some things in life are bad . . .

Once again, we totally surprised the audience and they all laughed and happily sang along as we filled the stage. Unfortunately, as this was the closing number and there were to be drinks afterwards, I hadn't realized I would be trapped onstage to meet Prince Charles while still dressed in a tutu. If you want to be really laughed at by people, try wearing a tutu to a Royal cocktail party.

The photo that went 'round the world.

I had met Prince Charles at Billy Connolly's Highlands home, where we would gather with comedians like Robin Williams, Steve Martin, and Eddie Izzard. The Royal Heir loves comedians. One night he came to dinner and everybody was being a bit polite as we sat down, and nobody said anything. There was an awkward pause as we sat around the huge dining table.

"Billy," I said eventually, "is there anything to eat?"

Well, that kicked off Robin and the evening became uproarious. Later on, wiping tears from his eyes, Prince Charles said to me, "Eric, why don't you become my jester?"

Everyone looked at me. No pressure.

"Why would I want a fucking awful job like that?" I said.

He laughed his head off. In another century, he could have laughed *my* head off, but I guess that's the job of the jester anyway, to put you back in the moment. Secretly, of course, I was very flattered, which I guess is why I wore a tutu and a bloody swan on my head for him.

Perhaps my favorite time singing "Bright Side" was in June 2010 at the American Film Institute tribute to Mike Nichols. It was a glittering Hollywood occasion and again I was to close the show. I decided to come on dressed as Emma Thompson from Mike's superb production of *Angels in America,* in a wig, a white frock, and huge angel wings. At the sound check I tried out my costume and decided to surprise Paul Simon and Art Garfunkel, who were onstage rehearsing "Mrs. Robinson."

"Hello, chaps," I said behind them.

They turned around, saw me in full drag, and couldn't continue.

What are you laughing at?

On the show, an announcer said, "And now to close the show, here is Oprah," and I came out dressed as Emma and began to sing. I left the stage descending on a host of stars, including Steven Spielberg, David Geffen, and Oprah herself. I remember thinking, *I like my life,* as I searched for Emma Thompson. As I approached her, she fell off her seat. Mike had tears in his eyes as I ended up singing the final chorus to him. At least I didn't have to stay dressed up like that at the after party.

Ah, dear Mike. I was proud to be invited to speak in his honor at a seventy-fifth birthday dinner thrown for him at David Geffen's remarkable art-filled house in Bel Air and attended by Diane Sawyer, Mike's wife, gracious and beautiful as ever, as well as the Hankses, Larry Ellison, David Mamet, the list went on. When it was my turn to speak, I stood and pulled a piece of paper out of my pocket, and began seriously.

"Is there any greater pleasure in life than having your face licked while ejaculating into the body of a younger woman? [*Pause*] Oh. I'm sorry. That was for something else."

I threw the paper away and produced another from my pocket. I began again.

"Is there any greater pleasure in life than having dinner with Mike Nichols? Well, yes. Obviously, there is one. But apart from that . . .

"When I asked my wife what it was about Mike Nichols that was so special, she said, 'Oh, just hurry up and come.'"

I added a few more low comments before concluding: "Here's a little poem I wrote for you, Mike:

> *"Love makes the world go round*
> *Love conquers all*
> *True love will never forget*
> *The world loves a lover*
> *Love's all you need . . .*
> *And I am Marie Antoinette."*

I was asked to sing my song once again, to my surprise, at the closing ceremony of the London 2012 Olympic Games. My friend Patrick Woodroffe, who lights up the stars, from Dylan to the Stones, said,

"You have to do it, Eric, it's a classic." And so, one August night in 2012, I found myself standing by one of the six wide entrances that dotted the arena. The turf was damp beneath my feet. I could see Russell Brand on top of a garishly painted double-decker bus, accompanied by brightly colored Beatles figures. The Spice Girls passed me, standing on top of London taxis.

"Fucking hell that was scary," said Posh.

"Time to go," said an assistant, and I made my way in darkness past hundreds of extras held back by tape. The enormous crowd was painted in colored light. Patrick would be given an OBE for his incredible work. I made my way towards the wooden scaffolding holding up the impromptu stage that had arisen in the last sixteen hours in the center of the 90,000-seat arena, filled with the sweat and memories of thousands of athletes from around the world.

I had been hiding in a small holding area somewhere under the massive new concrete stadium, in a caged-off space with a fridge, a tiny truckle bed, and a kettle. I was reading Camus's *L'Étranger* in French all day to prevent any anxious English thoughts intruding. Pretentious? *Moi?* Actually, it was very calming. I had been there since ten in the morning waiting for the chance to rehearse my number. It never came. Tonight, live on worldwide television, would be the first time I climbed out onto that stage. No point in panicking. Back to the Algerian beach with brother Albert. I popped my head out briefly as the show started. Timothy Spall came by as Churchill.

"That was terrifying," he said.

I retired to my French. Still forty minutes to go.

Suddenly it's time. I'm dressed in what is supposed to be a cannoneer's outfit. A body double of me is to be fired out of a cannon in a deliberate misfire that will land him in a hole center-stage. It will be me who emerges.

I'm led out amongst hordes of changing dancers. They glance only briefly at me. I smile and nod. I do this every day, right? Somewhere high above, in a box, are my wife, son, daughter, and cousin Nigel. Don't think of them. It's just another show.

I cross the damp grass of the stadium, reaching the mineshaft entrance, where I'm greeted by friendly Cockney voices.

"'Ello, Eric."

Huddled under the stage opposite was an unbelievable sight: seven of the most beautiful girls in the world, stunning in white, feathered angel costumes. The crew could hardly take their eyes off them.

"Is this heaven?" I asked a stagehand who was staring at them openmouthed.

"Oh yes," he said.

"Funny, they don't look like virgins to me."

Odd how a gag can calm you before you face the storm. I'm in a hole under a stage in the center of the Olympic Stadium. Suddenly the wooden ceiling slides open. We're getting close now. I can hear my old pal Jeff Lynne singing on the PA. "Mister Blue Sky." My cue to move.

I'm led forward and crouch at the foot of some low stairs.

Now I can see above me a huge circus cannon. A man dressed identically to me climbs in. The cannon fires. He tumbles out of the mouth of the cannon and falls into the hole in the ground. Unseen mattresses break his fall.

Time to go over the top. A voice in my ear says, "Here it comes." Then, "Cue Eric."

I'm on.

I wait a beat.

Make sure the cameras have had time to focus. I pull myself up groggily into the brilliant lights.

"Some things in life are bad, they can really make you mad . . ."

The crowd roars in surprise as they see me.

"And . . . Always look on the bright side of life."

Too fast. The audience has taken off ahead of me. I concentrate on bringing them back to the tempo of the track. In one ear, I can hear the orchestral backing; in the other, annoyingly, the director, talking me through every move.

Shut the fuck up, I'm thinking, *so I can hear the damn track.*

I have never done this in-ear singing before. I want him to be quiet so I can hear the band, but there's nothing I can do. I have to keep going. The audience is singing along joyfully now. I've managed to slow them down. Now we're all in sync.

If life seems jolly rotten, there's something you've forgotten.

I turn to the lovely models, who have risen up behind me. They are supposed to react to me but they are frozen, staring glassy-eyed at the spectacle of a packed arena, filled with lights. *Move on.* I skip round 150 Welshmen from a male voice choir, dressed in traditional Welsh female costume (a reference to "The Money Song," the first number I ever sang on *Python*). I skip and dance around a chorus of 550 singers and dancers. I skirt the skating nuns (another Python reference).

"Turn right, Eric," says the annoying voice in my ear.

I know that. For fuck's sake, shut up.

There's a whole new lyric coming up about the Olympics. Mustn't forget the words. I've only been rehearsing them in my head for months.

> *When you're stuck on the world stage*
> *With lots of weirdos half your age*
> *And everything is starting to go wrong*
> *It's too late to run away*
> *So you might as well just stay*
> *Especially if they play your silly song!*

Nailed it. Over the dangerous bits now. Ahead now, my favorite moment. Forty Bangla dancers come racing in. Great idea of our director's, this. Thank you, Kim Gavin! They lift me up and sprinkle me with Holi, throwing dry colored paint at me.

"Remember to throw it hard," I'd said to them before the show. *"It's only funny when it hurts."*

They do. It does.

Now this dry paint is in my mouth, in my eyes. I'm blinded, I'm choking, I'm lifted off the ground and manhandled. But it feels funny. I recover my voice as they set me down and there ahead of me is my Britannia, soprano Susan Bullock, who was with me in Jonathan Miller's *Mikado* at the ENO. She heads towards me and I grab her hand gratefully. Nearly there.

"And always look on the bright side of life!"

I am led away blinded by the paint and deafened by the earbuds. I stumble towards the exit and pull out my plugs. Sue is beaming.

"How did it go?" I say.

She looks at me wonderingly. *"Really?"*

The stadium is still applauding. *I guess it went okay then.* I head for the showers, enjoying that blessed moment in show business: when it's over.

Only afterwards, as all of the performers gathered together upstairs, did it feel better. I said to the Who: "You know who we are? We are the sort of people who will work for nothing." True, too. Every single major rock star was supposed to attend, but found the financial rewards unattractive. Of course, it wasn't really *nothing.* It was a pound. I kid you not. They wouldn't even pay for airfare. Even that quid wasn't easy to come by. It took three months of negotiations with an expensive LA lawyer, and they produced a 300-page contract I had to sign giving them, well, everything. One of the clauses required me to insure the audience against any act of terror or physical harm during my performance! When Tom Hoberman, my lawyer, asked how I could possibly afford that, they said blandly that most acts carried such insurance. When John Cleese and I toured, the most we could guarantee was they would be offended.

And there were no cars after the show. For all those glamorous performers, they had arranged a bus! I think that was the clincher for Elton. A bus ride home. For *Elton?* He dropped out. Actually, the bus turned out to be surprisingly good fun because Tania brilliantly arranged with the caterers to stuff it with champagne and it became quite a party and we did get very rowdy. Lily tells me the young people I partied with all the way home were amazingly famous, One Direction, and Elbow, and such. They partied on when we reached our hotel, but for me, blissful sleep.

Of course, the Olympic Committee never even paid the pound. Some months later, I decided to call them on this and got my California lawyer to send them a letter demanding immediate payment of the fee of one pound. They did see the humor of this and sent a letter of apology with a one-pound coin Sellotaped to it. I told Tom my lawyer that, instead of his usual percentage, he could keep the *entire* fee. So yes, he has the whole pound proudly framed in his office. I'm generous like that.

29

THE LAST LAUGH
The Python Reunion, O2 Arena, London, July 2014

Of course, we said we'd never do it. It could never happen. It wouldn't be possible. We were too old. Graham was still dead, and until he came back we would wait. What we hadn't foreseen is we would all be in our seventies and a million quid in debt. So, the Python reunion was really thanks to the man who pursued us for seven years in a free partnership with a lawyer, looking for ways to get more money out of Python's income from *Spamalot*. A success of any sort always brings people crawling out of the woodwork, and *Spamalot* was no exception, but I must say I was surprised when one of the producers of *The Holy Grail* sued us, despite the huge amounts of money we had already given him.

In the end, it cost us over a million pounds in legal fees simply to defend ourselves, and even though he'd lost or abandoned most of his claims by the time the trial began, surprisingly the judge accepted his one extraordinary claim that we had promised to treat him as "the seventh Python." As if? Despite the fact his contract said otherwise, and that Mike, Terry J., and I testified in court that it was nonsense, and John Cleese gave a scathing deposition that "he had more chance of being considered the fourth Kennedy brother than the seventh Python," the judge shocked us when he upheld this claim. As I said at the time, "it has restored my faith in British injustice." But we were still a million pounds in debt.

I tracked down my old friend Jim Beach, now cunningly spinning *Queen* around the world with Adam Lambert, and asked him if he'd come to London for an emergency Python meeting and give us his advice. He flew in from Switzerland, listened to our story, and delivered his professional opinion.

"You're totally fucked," he said.

"However," he added, "if you played one night live at O2, you could pay this debt off immediately."

There was a very swift response.

"Yes," we all said.

So, the final Python reunion began.

Our promoter Phil McIntyre immediately persuaded us to do five shows. Might as well, we thought, although John was very doubtful we could sell that many seats. Since everyone else was busy, I volunteered to put the script together and direct the show, and pissed off to the country to work on it. I asked everyone to let me know which sketches they wanted to do for the last time, and had some interesting responses. (John chose "Gumby Brain Specialist," which we rehearsed but cut before opening.) I set to work to create a show with corkboards, cards, and colored Sharpies.

My problem was the O2. It's a huge arena. Even if we were on big screens, we would still be dwarfed by the sheer size of the stadium. I didn't want our final appearance to look like a rip-off of our last live outing at the Hollywood Bowl thirty years earlier, or simply be bad. This was the Python farewell; it simply *had* to be good. And different. But how?

Fortunately, my Broadway experience came to the rescue. Of course, it had to be a *musical* show, with a big band and lots of singers and dancers to surround us ancient septuagenarians with energy and dancing. That way we could do popular Python songs, some publicly for the first time, and, more important, I could add the amazing Arlene Phillips as choreographer so she could re-create "Every Sperm Is Sacred," which she had done so brilliantly in the *Meaning of Life* movie. Having Arlene and her tireless energy made all the difference. Now we had a real show, with a live orchestra and singers and dancers. We could do a big final version of "Lumberjack" sung by Michael and end up with "Always Look on the Bright Side of Life" as a grand finale. I linked things together as in the old Python days: Yorkshire miner, into the Blackitts, into the pope, into "Every Sperm Is Sacred" . . . etc.

When I returned to London for the read-through it was a love fest. The Pythons were all very pally, greeting familiar faces in the packed room. I'd realized we must have Carol Cleveland—of course, she really *was* a seventh Python, and had been with us all those times on the road. In a tiny, packed hotel room off St. James's, we read the script aloud to our new department heads, stage designers, set designers, costume designers (including the wonderful Hazel Pethig, our original wardrobe lady), choreographer, wigmakers, lighting designer, sound, video, musical director (John Du Prez, natch), and producers. The read-through went very well and the Pythons requested only one change: John wanted to cut the Yorkshire miner sketch, which, though one of my favorites, was fine by me. I was happy they liked the script.

We did a day of press announcements and interviews, and then appeared on *The Graham Norton Show* with a slightly tipsy John, who was very naughty after sneaking a sly vodka in the greenroom. Inevitably, another two TV documentaries were commissioned—one by Alan Yentob for the BBC, and another that would follow the making of the show with backstage access.

The first inkling we had that something very exciting was happening came while I was working in my hotel room with Arlene and John Du Prez on the musical numbers. Holly Gilliam, Terry's younger daughter and one of the Python managers, rang to say that the tickets had gone on sale and they had sold out in thirty-four seconds!

What?

They were immediately releasing the tickets for the next four shows. She called back. *Those* had all sold out in thirty minutes.

What the hell?

Now they were asking would we consider doing five more shows. *Holy shit.* We were thrilled and a little humbled and went back to our meeting.

"We'd better be good," I said.

The first stage design was a disaster. It was a high-tech, rock-and-roll set with multiple levels and stages rising and descending from below. The thought of any of the Pythons falling into one of the holes during a blackout was insupportable. The show would be over instantly. So I suggested low roll-out platforms with sets built behind, all on one level, with a high bridge for dancers, no holes to fall into, and a Gilliamesque Victorian cutout theater look. Ric Lipson and STUFISH, the amazing design company, did a fantastic job. Their new set looked great, like a child's toy theater, incorporating an enormous central screen for film and animation, plus two side screens for live close-ups. It wasn't cheap but then again, we were inundated with offers to tour the world.

Directing the show took up most of my time from September to July. Unfortunately, because they were all busy, I would only get the Pythons two weeks before the first performance. We would get just three days of us alone in a rehearsal room to work on the sketches, and then we would be on to our big stage, rigged up in Acton in a large rehearsal space, with all the video and lighting and sound crews present. Knowing this time limitation, I had doubles for all the Pythons so we could rehearse their entrances, exits, and blocking with the dancers. It meant too that lighting could have something to focus on and the video projectors could learn their cues. When they appeared on set for the first time, they had someone to hold their hand and walk them around for their individual cues. This was good, as the set was huge, and the costume changes quick and complicated. I also wanted an invited audience for three nights up in Acton, so we could at least get used to playing together again, and the whole company could get the feel of a live show. Fortunately, I had great help from my assistant director, the indefatigable and tireless C. J. Ranger, and of course, the delightful and always supportive Arlene Phillips.

Before the Pythons came in, I spent an incredible June day filming on the banks of the Cam by King's College, with Stephen Hawking and Professor Brian Cox under a perfect cerulean Cambridge sky. Brian and I had been friends since he came to a recording of *What About Dick?* in LA. He was a Northerner like me, from Oldham, where my parents had married. When my mum came to visit me on the set of *Baron Munchausen* in Rome, I said, "Mum, Rome is built on seven hills."

"Oh," she replied, "just like Oldham."

Brian and I shared a love of cosmology, champagne, and Chinese food, which we found went well together. We could talk for hours because he knows everything and I know nothing, which, of course, doesn't stop me arguing. Once you get to the Universe and whether life in it is common or unique, you leave the realms of science for philosophy and I can bullshit philosophy with the best of them.

> *Immanuel Kant was a real pissant, who was very rarely*
> *stable.*
> *Heidegger, Heidegger was a boozy beggar who could think*
> *you under the table . . .*

I have always loved the fact that the wonderful Christopher Hitchens knew every word of the "Bruces' Philosophers Song," and would often sing it publicly at the end of his talks. You can see him do it on YouTube.

Professor Brian, so called to distinguish himself from the *actor* Brian Cox, whose twinkling buttocks we once saw bouncing naked in a kilt running full pelt toward a castle in Scotland, would always complain that my lyrics to "The Galaxy Song" were wrong. I kept telling him that they were scientifically correct thirty-five years ago and it was science that had changed. More precise measurements have been made since then, but these figures were accurate for 1982 when we wrote the song. But even though I updated them, he still wouldn't have it.

"The sun is *not* the source of all our power, there is uranium in the core of the earth . . ."

"Yes, but there wouldn't be uranium there but for the sun."

"That's not true."

"Well, there wouldn't be a solar system for it to be in but for the sun . . ."

He wasn't having any of it, so I decided to tease him and wrote a film piece for him, where, immediately after I sing "The Galaxy Song," he appears on-screen complaining about my lyrics on the riverbank at King's College. In the middle of his complaint he is run over by Stephen Hawking in his wheelchair. Brian is such a good sport, he was totally up for this. He emailed Stephen to ask if he would consider doing it, and Stephen immediately responded yes, so there we were shooting this gag on the banks of the Cam. We used a stunt double for Stephen for the actual running over of Brian, although he himself fell gamely and perfectly eight times like a pro. We then went to Stephen's incredible modern Cambridge science department to film him against green screen with wind ruffling his hair. While we were talking to him, Stephen was busy writing something. He then played it back.

"Way too pedantic," he had ad-libbed.

Luckily, we were filming him and, we used that line on the audio after he runs over Brian.

In the car on the way home Brian said, "We just spent a whole day filming with one of the most extraordinary minds on the planet, and all we did was a silly gag."

"Brilliant," I said.

Professor Hawking came to the final night at O2. There was a huge laugh as he ran over Brian on-screen, then a laugh at his own line, and applause as he set off into space in his wheelchair singing "The Galaxy Song." In 2015, with his permission, we released a special single version of him singing the song. When he died in 2018, that image of him singing in space was all over the Internet. Now, at O2, we stuck a spotlight on him and the whole place exploded. They cheered him to the rafters. It was so moving it made me cry, and when his nurse raised his arm to wave and acknowledge the applause, I felt the hairs stand up on the back of my neck.

After the show, he came backstage to the party and seemed really happy to be there. I said to him, "I think you, me, and Professor Cox have a great future in comedy."

Before we opened, thanks to our lighting guru Patrick Woodroffe, Mick and the Stones released a wonderful video ad-lib rant about the sheer nerve of wrinkled, British oldies coming out of retirement, charging exorbitant prices to gouge the public. A video so funny and accurate that many newspapers altogether missed it was a gag.

On July 1, 2014, eighteen thousand people were packed into the impossibly vast space of the O2 Arena for opening night, the first of ten sold-out shows. We were there by the skin of our teeth: now, were we ready?

We were ushered into our slightly renamed TARDIS as the overture began to play. We sang along quietly, each in our own thoughts. Terry G. giggling nervously.

"Oh, shut up, Gilliam," said John to his old friend and bête noire.

They opened the door and sprayed smoke on us. Might as well have been gas. I felt incredibly close to these four men dressed as Mexican mariachi players, accompanied of course by a kangaroo, the rather brilliant Samuel Holmes, whom we had co-opted from *Spamalot*. God knows what he must have been thinking.

We heard the overture ending and the audience yelling in anticipation. The TARDIS was shoved forward onto the enormous stage.

Here we go.

The doors open. Jonesy bursts out in front of me. The crowd goes wild. We step forward into the bright lights, basking in the shower of love. Anticipating we wouldn't be able to start speaking for quite some time amidst the loud response from the audience, I had put in a pacing moment right here. *Photo Opportunity,* it said behind us, triggering thousands of cell phones blistering into flash as we posed. A vast wave of sound. A huge bark of approval.

We're back!

Though it had cost a lot, I was confident we could amortize this expense on the road, because we had strongly tempting offers for tours of the U.S., Australia, and South Africa. Michael Palin, however, was not keen and nixed all proposals. That was certainly his right. Although some taller members were a little cross. Especially when he immediately set off on a solo tour of Australia . . . but I understood what Mike felt. Backstage one night, with both of us dressed in glam drag for "Camp Judges," he had said, "This has been fun, but we don't want to keep on doing this do we, El?" I knew what he meant. It *was* fun, but come show eighty-seven and *where are we again tonight?* I didn't fancy it that much either. So when it became clear that we would not be doing any more, I suggested to Jim Beach that we make the last night a big worldwide event, screening live on TV and in cinemas all around the globe. I liked the idea of doing a final show. We still liked each other, we had had a lot of fun, and we had made thousands of people very happy. Terry J.'s memory was fading fast and I think that was the smartest way to end. It seemed classier than petering out in Peterborough or Cleveland, and so the metaphorical curtain came down on Monty Python on July 20, 2014. Eighteen thousand people for ten nights at London's O2 Arena had come to see us live onstage, performing together again for the first time since the Hollywood Bowl in 1980. The final night was live on TV and in selected theaters around the world. You couldn't have written a better exit than us all singing "Always Look on the Bright Side of Life" for the very last time together. It was a fine farewell to Monty Python.

The final curtain.

30

THE SPEED OF LIFE

Shortly after our final show we learned the terrible news that our friend, the wonderful, funny, extraordinary Robin Williams, was dead. And unbelievably, by his own hand. I will never be reconciled to his death, but I will remain forever grateful for his life. He brought me so much joy, so much laughter. For thirty-four years he was my pal. Nobody was ever quite like Robin. He was sui generis, which is Latin for *fuck off and don't be pretentious.*

I first saw him in May 1980, in a seedy ex–strip club in Soho, where he was inviting a British audience to pray for the death of a heckler. The previous comedian, Alexei Sayle, had fought desperately against a loud, drunk, aggressive crowd and had virtually given up.

"But," he said, with a twinkle, "I have a secret weapon."

Did he ever. He brought on Robin, who from the moment he bounced onstage turned this dangerous, hostile crowd into a docile chorus of grateful adorers who hung on his every line and laughed at his every riff. I have never seen a funnier man. It's as if Einstein suddenly decided, "Fuck it, I'll do stand-up." It was high intelligence, perverted for purely mischievous ends. I've seen a few funny people in my time, and I can tell you there was never a one like this. After the show, while I was still gasping for air, we met and went across the street for a meal that started a lifelong friendship.

Life would never be the same again. In conversation, he was so fast you could barely get a thought out before he would seize it, gloss it, show you the opposite, turn it upside down, show you the left and right of it, run multiple variations on it, and then, properly examined, hand it back to you. It was like Mozart improvising on a theme.

In the fall of 1980, around the time we played the Hollywood Bowl, Tania and I visited him and his first wife, Valerie, in rustic Topanga Canyon amongst their goats. Soon afterwards, Robin took me on a wild comedy ride that went from large clubs to small clubs, to extremely tiny clubs in both LA and San Francisco. He never stopped. Every night, he had to work out. Along the way, there would be refueling stops at rich mansions where powerful people bent over powdered mirrors. For it was the time of cocaine. Mountains of it. He would burst on the scene, reduce them to laughter, hit them up for some lines, and we would be off. Finally, in front of as few as six startled customers in some seedy comedy club, he would bounce onstage at three in the morning to excite and ignite, to hit and run and leave them wondering what just happened. Pity the poor young comic he had just preempted and left in his wake to follow him. He was not always popular amongst comedians, because sometimes, while ad-libbing, he would remember someone else's line, but no one could doubt his status. Finally, toward dawn he would run out of clubs, the coke had by then conclusively clogged his mind, he would cease to be funny, and we could slink off to roost.

We spent a lot of time together before he finally trusted me enough that he didn't have to be funny every second. I could write a novel about him. In fact, I did: *The Road to Mars.* When it was published, Steve Martin wrote the best-ever blurb:

"I laughed. I cried. And then I read the book."

When Robin and Valerie came to stay with us in France, *Mork & Mindy* was the most popular show on American TV and Robin could go nowhere without being mobbed. In France, he was completely anonymous. He couldn't believe it. He stood in open disbelief in the middle of a Provençal fete, amazed and thrilled that not a single soul recognized him. Finally, he jumped up and down in the middle of the dance floor yelling, "I'm Mork! I'm Mork!" Nobody turned a hair. The French danced by with hardly a Gallic shrug at this crazy foreigner.

The freedom of anonymity is what you lose most with fame. I told him it's very important to get away from it all, so your life isn't just showbiz. There's got to be a place where you can be you. It's vital not to lose that sense of yourself, and to get away from time to time so you know who you are. Seeing our French hideaway encouraged him to buy a country place for himself up in Napa. He even managed to escape the shackles of alcohol and cocaine shortly after John Belushi overdosed in a bungalow at the Chateau Marmont. What a terrible waste of a great talent. So many more gifted young comedians would follow. Robin had been one of the last people to visit John and see him alive that night. Now a grand jury was investigating. Time to clean up. No drugs, no alcohol. Robin only became funnier.

Shelley Duvall asked me to write and direct the premiere episode of *Faerie Tale Theatre* for cable TV, and Robin played a frog for me, which won me a CableACE Award. I wrote "The Tale of the Frog Prince" for Robin as the eponymous amphibian and Teri Garr as a petulant princess. One morning on set, I saw Robin in his frog mask with huge tears in his eyes, reading in *Daily Variety* that *Mork & Mindy* was being canceled after five years. Nice executive touch, that. *Shall we tell him? Nah, let's just put it in the papers.* He was very upset, and he gathered the crew around him and just let go on ABC. He was hilarious and brilliant, deeply hurt and dressed as a frog, and he just let it all out, trashing the network, lambasting the executives, naming the names and taking no prisoners. Ten minutes in which he killed us with his wit, scraped out every last scrap of resentment for our laughter, turned all the hurt inside-out with the truth exposed, so that at the end he was whole again and ready to work. What better example of the healing power of comedy?

I had the pleasure of introducing him to Peter Cook at our London house at a dinner party on April 7, 1992. Here's the cast list:

Eric and Tania Idle
Robin Williams
Barbara Hershey

Gary and Michelle Lineker
Charles and Kay Saatchi
Lin and Peter Cook

I almost wrote *casualty list,* for many of us nearly died. None of us could eat. We could hardly breathe. It was the big bang of comedy. The funniest and most original Brit meets the funniest and most original American. They were so hilarious, they sucked all the air out of the room. Comedy kills, they say. That night we were lucky to survive. Billy Connolly, who himself comes close to the title, said Peter Cook was the funniest man in the world. Robin certainly challenged them both.

Often, I would go shopping with him in Beverly Hills, because he was a clothes freak, and he would swish around the stores being outrageously gay.

"Oh Eric, this is *so* you, it goes with your eyes. *Red . . .*"

He reduced shopkeepers to helpless giggles.

He did it again with me shopping for shoes in Florence, speaking fluently in cod Italian, and then spending ten minutes on Michelangelo in a little old Russian voice.

Two Gentlemen of Versace.

"So, *this* is David? What, he can't *afford* underpants?"

He came to visit us in Rome when we were filming Terry Gilliam's epic misadventures of Baron Munchausen at Cinecittà. The production was a legendary disaster. We were all suffering. The arrival of Robin cheered us all up, and amazingly Terry persuaded him to come back and play the part Sean Connery had just abandoned. His managers didn't want him to do it, so he appeared under a pseudonym, Ray D. Tutto. This was great news for our little gang of actors. We had been suffering from Valentina Cortese, an Italian actress of the old school. No matter what the scene, or what we had rehearsed, on hearing the word "Action" she always headed directly for the camera and the center of the shot, shoving everyone out of her way. Poor adorable, seventeen-year-old Uma Thurman in her first film was constantly being pushed aside by a very determined Valentina. Robin, who is by no means easily upstaged, instantly arrested this tendency by plonking his foot firmly on the hem of her costume so she couldn't move, and then shoving a peach in her mouth so she couldn't speak. Oh, how we applauded.

One weekend we escaped on what we called "The Big Jobbie Tour," named after a Billy Connolly routine about a floating turd, and I drove Robin, his wife Marsha, and Tania in my fab Citroën CX Turbo from Rome to Sorrento with improv all the way. We got lost and ended up accidentally in a funeral cortege in some little village, crawling along behind the mourners.

"Don't laugh," said Robin. "It's Don Corleone."

He gave us a misguided tour of the deserted ruins of Pompeii in his flamboyant phony Italian, leaving our real guide doubled over, gasping for air.

"You see they is no roofs on any of these houses because it was so very hot that they never finished building anything. They never finished building the whole city, because all they do is have sex all the time . . ."

We took a horse-drawn-carriage tour of Sorrento, where the horse was so skinny that Robin suggested we put it in the carriage while we pulled. Next day we took the chair lift to the top of Capri and gazed across the Bay of Naples at Mount Vesuvius. Of course, we took a boat into the Blue Grotto, where even the boatman became hysterical as Robin improvised Tiberius encouraging his naked nymphs to nibble on his testicles, in mad Italian.

On Capri.

It was a wonderful weekend but then it was back to the chaos of Cinecittà, where each week our drivers became better dressed and drove newer cars. Someone was making money. At first it was fun driving past the Colosseum on the way to work, but soon it turned into a nightmare that lasted six months. I had my head shaved every morning and then three hours of makeup. Gilliam swore to me he would shave his head if I did, but the minute I did he reneged, the bastard. Often the cast would get made up and then be told, oh no, they wanted the *younger* version. Back for another three hours of makeup.

Munchausen was a long and difficult shoot. I said I'd rather go back to boarding school, but Terry has the most amazing stamina and willpower, and how he kept it together I have no idea. Seeing him recently

I realized he is only happy in chaos, and he made me laugh so much talking about directing while incontinent with a catheter on his latest film, *Don Quixote,* which he had amazingly just finished. He laughed at his own folly, but he is still the funny, crazy Terry Gilliam I've known all these years. Although he does seem to attract trouble . . .

Robin taught me the meaning of private-jet lag. We were always off on holidays or cruises, to the West Indies, to the Bahamas, to Venice, and to Greece. Occasionally we would have some nice private times together, when he could just be sweet and serious. I can remember swimming ashore with him from a boat in the Aegean. It was a lot farther than we thought, and we both struggled. We hugged as we finally reached the beach. Always a bit too far out.

Suffering from private-jet lag in the Aegean.

Once, for his birthday, he picked me up in his jet from Montreal and flew me to Paris. Just the two of us. We shopped, we dined, and we went to the Crazy Horse. He was scared Marsha would find out, and I said, "Don't worry, she will, because I'll tell her. We're looking, not shopping."

Next day was the final day of the Tour de France, where for the last two laps we had the unbelievable treat of being in the little red Renault that is the lead car, a seat usually reserved for presidents but on this day filled with three very excited men: me, Robin, and Michael J. Fox. It was the most exciting thing I have done with my pants on. The lead riders were eight yards behind us sprinting up the Champs Élysées. We couldn't believe we were that close. We screamed and yelled like ten-year-olds. It was the best seat for any sport ever. As we passed the Louvre and headed down into the tunnel, a hundred riders were pedaling hard behind us for the final bell. As we climbed out of the little red Renault totally exhilarated, Michael J. Fox said, "We will always have Paris."

Robin took me to the Tour de France three times and we always had fun. He excelled at cycling and would go riding with Lance Armstrong's team on their day off. It was sad about Lance. The French always said he was cheating. Seven Tours in a row?

Robin and I were computer geeks, and both of us used the same Toshiba dealer in Beverly Hills. One day I was in the shop and I heard the guy answer the phone, "Oh *hello,* Robin." I could tell by the tone it was *The* Robin. I said to the guy, "Let me talk to him," and he handed me the phone. So I started talking in a very cod, over-the-top comic Indian accent.

"Hello, who is this, please? Oh, Mr. Villiams. Oh yes, sir, this is Ramshid, sir. I understand you have a problem. Oh yes, I can help you, no problem. Vat is the issue?"

Robin is speaking in this serious little-boy voice because he really wants help; his hard drive has crashed and he's lost all sense of humor. He explains what has gone wrong while I say, "Oh yes, yes, yes, oh dear, dear, dear. Vell, I am thinking you are having problems with your Ram Dass Dat Bat file. Yes, sir, your Ram Dass Dat Bat file. It's under the Dis Dat Rom Bat file. Well, can you see the Dos Dat Dot Rom Com file? You can't find it. Okay, let's look for it in the P file. The P file. You don't have a P file? Oh dear, well we can make one, but first of all I want to try a little test, sir. I have a quick fix that may just work. Put one hand on your computer. Yes, right. Now take your other hand and touch the wall. Yes, stretch out and touch it. This gives better grounding, sir, for the electro static. Which may be part of the problem. So, now you're touching the wall? Good. Now I want you to take your hand off the wall and just very quickly touch your bottom. Yes, sir, near the buttocks. Yes, sir, this will discharge some of the electro static buildup. It's what we call the Bombay Fix. Yes, sir, the Bombay Fix. By the way, do you know who you are talking to? No, sir, this is not Ramshid, sir, this is your friend Mr. Idle, and I just got you."

A howl of anguish on the other end and Robin laughed for five minutes.

We spent wonderful family holidays at the Connollys' lovely Scottish home, Candacraig, just a fart away from Balmoral. Billy and his wife, Pamela, organized ceilidhs (Scottish dances) where young and old danced together after dinner, and we wore kilts and went to the Lonach, the local Highland games, where Robin joined the fastest and toughest for the grueling three-mile hill climb, and always finished in the top ten. On the morning of the Lonach an entire company of armed Scotsmen with pikes and kilts marched up the drive behind a bagpipe band. It was a tremendous sight. While we all watched, Billy would take the salute from the wonderful Sir Hamish, who had escaped from Colditz Castle in World War II. Then they would all be given a dram of whiskey, salute, and march back down the drive to another twelve large houses. Behind them there followed an attendant with a small donkey cart, to collect those who could not take the whiskey. They would enter the arena later proudly proclaiming, "There is nae one in the cart!"

With some of the funniest people in the world staying just up the road, Prince Charles would sometimes call up and say, "Billy, I hear you have some interesting people staying. Can I come to dinner?" One night at Billy's dinner table with Judi Dench and Prince Charles, there was a heated conversation about the movie *Mrs. Brown* and whether or not Queen Victoria had actually slept with Mr. Brown. Two said yes—Billy, who played Mr. Brown, thought yes, while Judi Dench was adamant: "I'm sure they did." Only one insisted the answer was no. But then, for the naysayer, she was his great-great-great-grandmother! I think I'd trust the actors on this, and since the main job of Royals *is* shagging (to produce an heir and a spare), I imagine they have become quite good at it. Queen Victoria apparently was very fond of it: she had nine children.

So, in Scotland at the castle of the Connollys, young and old had fabulous and hilarious times. I dubbed their court Pamelot, because it was all organized by the amazing (now appropriately *Lady*) Pamela Connolly. I emailed Billy recently, congratulating him on his knighthood. He wrote back:

> Dear Eric,
>   As you rightly observed, I was knighted this morning, and, in my new position as Knight of the Realm, I have decided that I will no longer squander my good time by hanging out with scruff like you.
>   So you can fuck off.
> Famous comedian, and friend of the great,
> Sir Billy Connolly, CBE
> Unbearable Shit (Don't you forget it)

I accepted his kind invitation to fuck off. He always gave us the best of times. Once they flew us all to Fiji to celebrate Billy's sixtieth birthday! The first year we went to Scotland I wrote and recorded a song called "Candacraig" with Peter Asher, in order to thank them. Steve Martin played banjo, and Robin ended up ranting in a Scottish voice about the colon-unclogging effects of haggis.

"Haggis, nature's way of saying slow down."

I was asleep when Eddie Izzard called me from the Edinburgh Festival to tell me Robin was gone. I had been trying to get him to come over to London to do the final night of the Python Show at O2 and be our Guest Celebrity in "Blackmail," but he wrote back anxiously begging off. I should have guessed something was up; Robin *not wanting to perform*?

Listen, I wrote him, *you don't have to come onstage, just come here for our last show.*

But he didn't. And now he was gone. Forever. It was hardly three years since we had danced at his wedding to the lovely Susan. He seemed so happy. "Eric," he said to me, "I have finally found my Tania." And now this.

I went through all the emotions. Shock. Denial. Disbelief. Anger. Guilt. Could I have done something? Could anyone have done something? I knew he was depressed. But then who knew how badly? The manner of his death was so awful. His suicide seemed inexplicable until finally an autopsy revealed that he had been suffering from an unusually severe case of Lewy body dementia. In the months before his death, Robin was besieged by paranoia and so confused he couldn't remember his lines while filming a movie. He was wrongly diagnosed with Parkinson's disease, and the telltale signs of Lewy body dementia in his brain were not discovered until the autopsy. Now all we have left are memories. It was too sudden, too soon, and too awful. At his memorial that September in San Francisco, my daughter Lily and I sang a little song for him.

Goodnight, Robin
Thanks for all the laughs . . .

It still doesn't seem real. I can't bear it. It's too fucking sad. Shortly afterwards Mike Nichols died, and then Garry Shandling, and then Carrie Fisher. It was all too much.

Rage, rage against the dying of the light.

31

TOGETHER AGAIN AT LAST . . . FOR THE VERY FIRST TIME

$\mathfrak{S}$hortly after the Python farewell, John Cleese asked me if I would interview him for Writers Bloc Presents at the Alex Theatre, Glendale, about his new autobiography, *So, Anyway . . .* Of course I would, though I read his book with some trepidation. We are all pretty good at giving out stick. One of the tabloids has insisted for many years we all hate each other, despite all evidence to the contrary, so when it came to his final chapter about the O2 Farewell, I was a little concerned. What might John say about me? I needn't have worried. He gushed. I blushed to read what he had written. It was the kindest and most personal review I have ever read, from someone who means the most.

John's book event at Glendale was sold out. Fourteen-hundred eager fans were waiting, and the black-market price was over a couple of hundred dollars each. I know, because I sold 'em.

John and I met up at the stage door of the Alex, our tall daughters immediately bonding backstage.

"What on earth are we going to do?" I asked him.

"Oh, just go on, we'll be funny."

We walked straight on, bowed, and then walked straight off again. It was Footlights time. We sat in two red, comfy chairs, and began to chat. Two hours flew by. Memories, anecdotes, jokes; John even threw some sketches at me to cold-read with him. The audience loved it. I loved it. Our daughters loved it. I had known this man since 1963 and here we were back onstage, simply chatting.

In February 2013, on the anniversary of our meeting, I had written a blog about our fifty years together. I think it was the first time he read what I really felt about him. I'm not sure he knew before. He called the next day and talked animatedly on the phone for an hour. Now we could be both touching and funny about each other onstage. And more important, we could be on the road together for months, because our two-hour Glendale chat went out on the Internet and picked up such a tremendous response that John asked me if I'd be interested in touring Florida with him. Sure, why not? I'd never been to Florida. This was pre Merde-a-Largo time, and the alligators hadn't yet come in to drain the swamps. With the prospect of some fine fall weather, and some pleasant places to visit, we could find an audience who were even older than we were. We called the show *John Cleese and Eric Idle, Together Again at Last . . . for the Very First Time*, and we based it on our first encounter in Glendale, adding some less familiar sketches from the *1948 Show*, inserting plenty of funny clips, and telling our joint story. We claimed to have met at Trump University and gone on from there . . .

In the second act, we separated. John did some of his solo tour material and then I came on and sang some tasteless songs. Oddly, this was the first time I had ever sung a solo set with just me and a guitar (*wot no band?*) and so it was in line with my own belief that you must always be trying something new. We finished the show together doing

Q&A, ad-libbing happily with the audience, before we ended with "Bright Side."

I loved being back onstage doing sketches with John. We could both make each other laugh and I'm afraid we did. We giggled a lot through Florida. Towards the end of our tour we engaged a large rock-and-roll bus, and it was great fun riding around reading, writing, kipping, and occasionally sipping champagne. We went north into the Carolinas and Georgia, ending up in Baltimore on Halloween night. Tania visited several times. Lily came to Orlando for a Harry Potter binge. Our crew were kind and very helpful and Simon Garner, an incredibly considerate Canadian gentleman, was the perfect tour manager. My favorite time was somewhere in Carolina, when we had a large and very funny lady "signing" for the partially hearing. I had begun to sing—"Isn't it awfully nice to have a penis?"—when I suddenly glanced at her and recognized the hand gestures she was making: unmistakable "dick" signs. I giggled. The audience, following my look, began to laugh too. Since the entire song is just a series of dick synonyms, I turned to face her, and continued singing directly to her. I tried desperately not to crack up as she found more and more elaborate hand gestures for that particular part of the male anatomy. She won. I collapsed in hysterics. She got an enormous round of applause from the audience. She was so funny I wanted to take her with us.

The whole tour went so well, and CAA paid so well, that John called a month later and asked me if I'd like to join him touring Australia and New Zealand. *Hell yeah.* So off we flew to summer in Sydney, everyone's favorite winter destination. After some promo, where John and I slipped easily into banter mode, I flew up to visit my son in the rain forest. He *does* have a house, but it sounds nicer like that. In fact, it couldn't *be* nicer. Carey practices Tibetan medicine on the Sunshine Coast and gave me a lot of meals and acupuncture. I once told him he'd let me down becoming a healer, as I had been hoping for a crack dealer. One of the funniest things he did was when the Dalai Lama visited the Chinrezig Institute, the nearby Buddhist center, Carey made a huge shrubbery with a plaque, which to this day says: SHRUBBERY SPONSORED BY ERIC IDLE & FAMILY FOR H. H. THE DALAI LAMA VISIT.

"We want . . . a shrubbery!"

Carey drove me to Surfers Paradise for our opening show, and then we went on to Brisbane, Sydney, and Melbourne. In Canberra we stayed for two nights in the wonderful Jamala Wildlife Lodge, where John and I had tea with a tiger, and bravely petted a cheetah.

Then on to Perth, Adelaide, and Wellington, where for our final show I played a gag on John. On a previous tour, he had dubbed

The Ascent of Mount Cleese. Without oxygen.

Palmerston North the "suicide capital of New Zealand." The locals were offended but, in 2006, encouraged by Fred Dagg—the pseudonymous character of John Clarke, a famous local comedian—they rather wittily named their rubbish dump after John, putting up an official sign at the Palmerston North refuse tip which says MT. CLEESE. On the drive to Wellington, I diverted and made a short film of me climbing it, with which I surprised him on the final night. I'm happy to say I'm the first Python to conquer Mount Cleese, and even Michael Palin hasn't been there.

After New Zealand, Tania and I flew home via Tahiti, where thanks to the vagaries of the international date line I celebrated three birthdays. (I don't have to add them *all* on, do I?)

Soon, John was back on the phone. This time he proposed a big U.S. tour, all the way from Vancouver, down the West Coast, through LA, San Diego, two nights in Vegas, on down through Arizona to El Paso, across the whole of Texas, ending up in New Orleans. Naturally we had a bus, and a spiffy one at that, but we actually *slept* in Four Seasons Hotels. It was rough, I'm telling you.

Before we left on this tour I recorded a TV show for the BBC with my pal Professor Brian Cox. He had been gently educating me in the mysteries of science since we met on *What About Dick?* and of course I turned my learnings into a musical. With songs by John Du Prez and choreography by the incomparable Arlene Phillips, we were back at the Beeb making another *Rutland Weekend Television Special* only forty-one years later. *The Entire Universe in One Hour as a Musical* is exactly that. It was broadcast on Boxing Day on BBC2 and again a year later when we sold it to PBS. It's a simple gag. Professor Brian comes in late from Patagonia, where he has been studying electromagnetism for a month, and hence out of cell phone range, to join Robin Ince in the studio at Elstree. He thinks he is coming in to give a simple lecture on the physics of the Universe, but no, in the meantime Arlene and I have changed it into a musical. A serious scientist trapped in a musical is a gag I like, and my proudest moment was getting Brian to climb into full drag to illustrate the infinite possibilities of the multiverse, a universe of infinitely extending universes. (Weren't we small enough?)

Say no more!

I can't think of many double professors of science who would un-complainingly climb into a red frock to illustrate a scientific principle. Perhaps it's our Oldham connection. Superbly complemented by Warwick Davis, the cast starred Hannah Waddingham, our first Lady of the Lake from *Spamalot* in the West End, and the brilliantly funny Noel Fielding (from the whimsically hilarious show *The Mighty Boosh*).

I don't think I can describe it, except as a nutty show, with science, song and dance, Albert Einstein, the Bee Gees singing about gravity, and a real astronaut (spacewalker Tim Peake, who had just returned from six months on the International Space Station). We ended up singing "The Galaxy Song," with Professor Hawking himself singing at the end. The show was great fun to do, before a live audience, but no sooner completed than I dashed off to join John Cleese on our big tour of the USA.

I liked the shape of the show we already had going, the double auto-biography, but I wondered why we couldn't just pick up and continue our story after the intermission, with the various Python breakups and all the coming-back-togethers such as *Brian, The Meaning of Life,* Aspen and O2. Even though it meant quite a bit of work, John thought this was a good idea, and we tried out this new Act Two for a few nights in Victoria, on Vancouver Island, where it immediately worked a lot better. I also wrote a new song to open the show, "Fuck Selfies!" which at least warned people where we stood:

> *Fuck "Selfies"*
> *And all those stupid gits*
> *Who want Selfies*
> *They just get on my tits*
> *Fuck grinning like a lunatic*
> *With people you don't know*
> *It takes them half an hour*
> *To get their fucking phones to go*
> *And then another fourteen other people*

Fucking show!
So, tell those selfish selfie pricks
Next time they bloody ask
To take their fucking selfie sticks
And shove 'em up their ass.

It's our kindness and sweetness people like . . .

Now that the whole show had a shape, it was more satisfactory. It had narrative. A beginning, a middle, and an end. It was our entwined life stories, plus a tale of Monty Python from start to finish. Mike Nichols would have been proud.

We had a blast on the road. We played a very strange hockey arena in Canada, which was, predictably, freezing. The show was going incredibly well, the dates flew by, and soon I was home in LA with two days off for the presidential election. It was supposed to be the triumph of the first woman president of the United States, but unfortunately Putin had other ideas. With the unexpected and unwelcome election of Donald J. Trump, our show became therapy. At Thousand Oaks Civic Arts Plaza the night after, the audience was still grieving. Laughter was tremendously important to them now. They laughed three times harder than before, and sang along to "Bright Side" with fervor. It was never more needed. I sang it with John on *Conan*, where I made a genuine ad-lib, live on the show, when I sang:

When you're feeling in the dumps
Forget about the Trumps
Just purse your lips and whistle, that's the thing

Sometimes jokes are just staring at you in the face, and that was one occasion. For the rest of the tour we sang that and the audience would cheer. The resistance was beginning. Across America our show was sad, glum, people coming out to be cheered up and set free by laughter. And really, laughter is the only sane response to pathological lying.

For two packed nights at the MGM Grand, we played *Vegas, baby,* staying in suites that were bigger than most private houses. In Arizona,

Alice Cooper came backstage to say hello ... He even invited us to Thanksgiving, which was most kind, but we had to move on. Texas was waiting, and after hooking up with old friends in Houston and playing all the "blue" cities, we flew to New Orleans for our final show. John and I had a final farewell lunch amongst the Christmas decorations, while outside a parade of leprechauns dressed as green Elvises with pointy ears and black pompadours drove past on scooters. We had done three tours in very quick succession and were still friends. In the Southeast of the States we had played twenty shows to 38,000 people. In our second tour, to Australia and New Zealand, we had played nine shows in seven cities to 36,000 people, and in our final U.S. tour, we had played thirty-four shows in twenty-three cities to 62,000 people. Our combined age was a hundred and fifty.

32

BREXIT THROUGH THE GIFT SHOP

After George introduced me to her in 1975, I got to see Joni Mitchell occasionally over the years; we spent New Year's Eve 2016 side by side in wheelchairs, and recently she came to my seventy-fifth birthday when my son was there: "Come on, Carey, get out your cane." One day I said to her, "You have to think of our generation as the survivors on the Raft of the Medusa. One by one we slide off the raft into the jaws of the waiting sharks."

The Raft of the Medusa, 1818–1819 oil painting by the French Romantic painter Théodore Géricault.

I was trying to cheer her up!

What I meant was, the end is inevitable, you have to embrace your fellow time travelers even as they slip away. Ours was an extraordinary generation, born into a devastated world, exhausted from six years of total war. Sixty million died. Nowadays the young think times are tough if they can't get an Internet connection. They're right; times are tough, but there was a time before it all began to go to shit, when it all really *was* shit. Our generation was born into that time. It was called World War II. We heard the sirens in the night and put on our foul-smelling Mickey Mouse gas masks and went down into the Anderson shelters. It was very loud and very terrifying. Then it stopped. For a bit. That was the gap in time our generation lived in. We thought we were hard done by, but we were wrong: we were lucky. We wouldn't have to march off to war. The peacetime conscription of the National Service stopped just before I was due to be enlisted. Senior boys at my boarding school would turn pale at breakfast as their call-up papers arrived, but it mercifully ended a few years before my turn. Phew! Not so good for the Yanks, of course. They were even more fucked over by Vietnam, and poor Gilliam had to serve his time in the New York Armory, where he would eventually film Robin Williams in *The Fisher King*. But from the bomb sites and the rationing, we skinny-shanked, undernourished, badly toothed British boys got to remake a shattered world. You're welcome . . .

So, what *were* we Pythons, we who were once so young and who are now so not? Were we friends, comrades, coworkers, teammates, gang members, rivals, siblings, brothers, brothers-in-law, or brothers-in-arms? I noticed we had become legends quite a while ago. We used to be icons, and before that stars, and before that celebrities, and before that merely TV comedians, but the Reaper keeps on Reaping and you go up a notch each time until you finally end up as myths, which is when you know you're dead. When I first noticed we had become legends I decided to keep a diary, in which I wrestled with the intimate problems of being a legend.

The Diary of a Legend.

Monday.
Got up. Was a legend. Had breakfast. Went back to bed.

Tuesday.
Got up. Still a legend. Fed dog. Went back to bed.

Wednesday.
Exhausted from being a legend. Stayed in bed.

Thursday.
Wife said you're not a legend, you're just a lazy old bastard.

Friday.
Decided to look for new wife.

Saturday.
Remembered John Cleese. Changed mind about looking for
new wife. Cheaper to stay with the old one.

Sunday.
Tired of being a legend. It's exhausting. I looked in the bathroom mirror and it appears fame has gone to my ass.

Monday.
Somebody in the pub said you're not a legend, you're not even
funny anymore, so piss off back to America.

Tuesday.
Pissed off back to America. They sent me back.

Wednesday.
Have decided to stop writing a diary about being a legend,
as I'm becoming the sort of person I would normally try and
avoid. I have decided instead to become a National Treasure.

Thursday.
They said: Fuck off, we have far too many National Treasures.
In fact, the U.K. is now National Treasure Island.

So, I'm not sure what we are. Perhaps we're collectibles. Survivors of the Sixties? British cultural icons? I don't know. We've even become a stamp.

I pay taxes in three countries and I can vote in none of them. I wasn't even allowed to vote against Brexit. The Russians had more say than I did. And of course, I can't vote in the States, though they coined the phrase "No taxation without representation." I was once coming home through LAX when a steely-eyed immigration officer peered suspiciously at me.

"How long have you been a green card holder?"

"Oh, I have had it for ages," I said. "More than twenty years."

"Then why aren't you an American?"

"Erm. Er . . . Well . . ."

I hesitated. What should I say? What was the correct thing to say?

"Because, sir, I am an Englishman. Born and raised in England under the bombs of Hitler. A member of one of its most prestigious universities, from a college founded in 1347. A man who watched England win the World Cup at Wembley in 1966 and Manchester United lift the European trophy in 1968. An Englishman, a proud Elizabethan, heir to the traditions of Shakespeare, Chaucer, Wilde, Wordsworth, Coleridge, and Dickens, a cricket-loving survivor of the Sixties and a member of one of the most admired comedy groups in the world. Is it not enough I live in your fair country and pay my taxes? Now you wish me to put my hand on my heart and pledge allegiance to a self-righteous, lying, tax-avoiding moron, and his racist, gay-bashing, environmentally dangerous, greedy-bastard, science-denying cronies, who reject evolution and the rights of women, and plunder the planet for profit to please their powerful funders, stealing the very air and clean water of their children, while tweeting insanely and lying through their teeth on propaganda TV channels that would have shamed Joseph Goebbels? No, sir! The French do not shrug at me sardonically and ask me why I am not French. The Norwegians do not stop me on their shores and insist I wear thick knitwear and a large red anorak and retire into the countryside suffering from Ibsen and ennui. The Australians don't force me into baggy swim pants to stand on planks in orange sunscreen hurtling across their shark-infested waters singing 'Advance Australia Fair.' No, sir. Enough, sir. I am a taxpayer, a member of your Academy, a Grammy winner, a Tony winner, a father of an American, a lover of America, married to an American wife with an American child, but *not*, sir, an American!"

Did I say any of that?

Are you kidding me? I fear all authority.

"Good question," I replied.

> *But in spite of all temptations*
> *To belong to other nations*
> *He remains an Englishman!*

I used to think those words of W. S. Gilbert pretty much described me, but of course, the more I return to the U.K. the less I recognize it. In my lifetime, it has changed beyond all recognition, particularly now it has become *Brexit Through the Gift Shop*. I feel like an old John le Carré character returning to a circus that has changed irrevocably.

I think, after all, I'm happiest being a foreigner. Perhaps there should be a Homo sapiens passport? I feel less and less connected to individual states, and more and more connected to human beings. Coming out of a Grammy MusiCares tribute to Paul McCartney, an evening I had found extremely moving and uplifting, I bumped into Smokey Robinson.

"That was so great," I said. "It made me proud to be white."

"Me too," he said.

Last year they tried to put Python in a museum. We were approached by London's Victoria and Albert Museum, who wanted to mount a big, six-month retrospective exhibition to celebrate fifty years of Monty Python. I warned the guys.

"Turn it down," I said. "Look at the others. Bowie: dead. Balenciaga: dead. Alexander McQueen: dead. Pink Floyd: almost dead. *Is that not telling you anything?* Run away now."

But they wouldn't listen to me.

"It's an honor," they said, which in England means "no money."

We should have been warned. The V&A immediately turned down our proposed title, *Monty Python: The Same Old Bollocks.* That title was very Python. In-your-face aggressive modesty. But they wouldn't accept it. We were polite and suggested another: *Monty Python Exposed.* But no, they weren't having that either. *What's this?* Fifty years later and we're still being cut by the establishment? Instead, they told us, they were going to call it *From Dali to Dead Parrots,* and it became clear they were doing an exhibition on Surrealism, and the so-called *roots* of our work. Pretentious nonsense. We're nothing to do with Dali or Duchamp. For me, Python has always been about comedy. *That* is the art. The Footlights motto is *Ars est celare artem.* "The art lies in concealing the art." A fine observation about performing. If you take us seriously you miss the joke, even though we were always deadly serious about being funny.

More important, the museum insisted they would have control and final say, so I was never prouder of Python than when we all said no. The museum couldn't believe it. Happily, we stuck to our guns. We are still a very gnarly gang. Un-clubbable. I like that. So, no museum for us in the future but certainly a mausoleum. Even if we don't all join Terry J. in an Old Jokes Home before then. Dear sweet Jonesy. He came to a Python meeting in October 2017 and sat quietly as we discussed business. At one point he yelled, "No. No. No!" and we all turned to look at his anxious face, but it was clear it was about the water he was being offered.

"Actually, when he says no, he means yes," said Michael seriously.

We dissolved into laughter. The meeting had turned into a Python sketch. Terry joined us for lunch, where he sat happily drinking red wine amidst the banter.

Laughter is still the best revenge. One day the sun will die, one day the galaxy will die, one day the entire Universe will die. I'm not feeling too good myself. So, what have I learned over my long and weird life? Well, firstly, that there are two kinds of people, and I don't much care for either of them. Secondly, when faced with a difficult choice, *either way* is often best. Thirdly, always leave a party when people begin to play the bongos.

Now I just wait for the inevitable question: "Didn't you used to be Eric Idle?" That and the delicious irony that I get to sing my own song at my own funeral. I have prepared some last words. Well, you can't be too careful, can you? In the Eighties when I was still comparatively young, a man sitting next to me in the Groucho Club said, "Oh, that's funny seeing you here, I'm just writing your obituary."

What?

I checked for vital signs, my wallet was still there, my dick was still there, my wife was still there.

"So far as I can tell," I said, "I'm not dead yet."

The young man explained that he was working for the *Daily Telegraph* and his job was to write obituaries of celebrities so that they would be ready to print at the drop of a hat.

"In that case," I said, "perhaps you'd like to know my last words?"

Indeed, he would.

"Say no more," I said.

He liked that. It's best to be prepared, and that does take care of the final words problem. Suppose you're having an off day and you can't think of anything funny, and you say something fatuous like "Pass the Kleenex." That would be embarrassing.

And my song goes on. I sang it at a Pembroke College fund-raiser in Cambridge in 2017 and they very kindly rewarded me with an honorary fellowship, which touched and moved me more than I can say. I sang it to the survivors of the England football team who won the World Cup fifty years before, back in 1966, when I had stood on the terraces at Wembley Stadium with Bill Oddie. I sang it at my daughter's graduation, where I was commencement speaker and Whitman College generously gave me an honorary degree. I have let Exit International use it, and, to the dismay of my wife and manager, I have turned down several large sums of money from advertisers to license it, so you will know I am either finally dead or destitute when you hear it on a car commercial. Not that I want to go, of course. I'll be like the rest of you, clinging on desperately and screaming for more morphine. Though I did want it to say on my tombstone: I'D LIKE A SECOND OPINION . . .

My funeral song will go on . . . and on . . . though obviously we don't. Dust to dust is about right. We dissipate into the carbon atoms we came from; technically, reincarnation is sort of correct, we get reassembled into other things. I'd like to be reassembled into a Tesla so my wife can still drive me.

I was born in the same place as my mother and I wonder if I will die in the same place as her, which would mean our home in LA. To be precise, in our guest room, but that's now become my wife's shoe closet. I think I wouldn't mind dying in there amongst the Jimmy Choos. I worship the ground she walks on anyway, so that would be appropriate. She, who sadly knows me best, thinks my last words will probably be "Fuck off," but that doesn't look good on a tombstone, so instead I would like on my grave:

Eric Idle
See Google

AND FINALLY . . .

I'd like to thank everyone I've forgotten. They know who they are. Without them I would not be half the man I used to be. I particularly want to thank Tania, Carey, and Lily, without whom I wouldn't even be a quarter of the man I used to be. They have taught me the meaning of love and family. So I'd also like to thank my extended Chicago family, my large Canadian family, and my London family, Nigel and the Wrays, for their love and kindness. I should thank all the Pythons of course. I know they were lucky to have me, but I learned a lot from them, even though wild horses wouldn't get me to confess it. A big legally binding thank-you to Tom Hoberman, my lawyer and friend of thirty-five years. Simon Green, my new agent, who had the fortitude to persist in encouraging me to write this book. My publishers, Tricia Boczkowski of Crown Archetype and Alan Samson of Orion Books, for listening to him when he asked them for money. Thanks also to Caspian Dennis for aiding in this task. I must thank my two fantastic assistants, the brilliant and hilarious Alana Gospodnetich, and my wonderful photographic assistant Stefanie Estes, who both helped me enormously, while encouragingly laughing at my jokes. Thank you to Kelly Bush and her IDPR team, including Chris Kanarick and Rachel Hunt, who supported this book early on; the photographer Robin von Swank made me look nice, and my dogdaughter Tasha Goldthwait dressed me up to look swanky for her. Michael Gorfaine fed me sushi and giggled at my anecdotes; and Steve Martin gave me forty years of friendship and advice. Thanks to Doctor Kipper for keeping me alive; Danny Ferrington for building me guitars; Kevin Nealon and Susan

Yeagley for being simply wonderful; Ed Begley and Rachelle; the magnificent Jim Beach; the adorable Olivia Harrison; Ian Miles; Holly Gilliam; Jane Tani; Ian Miles; John and Linda Goldstone; Tasha and Bobcat Goldthwait; Gavin and Yukimi de Becker; Arlene Phillips and Angus Ion; Adrienne Strong; Charles Wheeler; Salman; Joni; Jim and Annie; Jeff and Camelia, Joe and Margery; the Connollys; the Ashers; the Feigs; the Dysons; the Donners; Les Frenais; the E. Grants; Ruth Teale; Lyn Ashley; Sasha Smith; Sarah Polley; Bill Haber, producer extraordinaire; Steve Spiegel of TRW, who took a punt and turned it into a battleship; and Casey Nicholaw for just about everything. Merci to my summer friends in France: the Hopewells, Les Nicholas', Catriona and Jeremy, the Chaters, Dougie and Sylvie, Frank and Chrissie; my London chums, Brian and Gia, Noel and Birdy, Kathy Lette, the Beetles and Jeffrey Archer, who dine me and encourage me; my lovely shrink Barbara for keeping me relatively sane; and of course, my long-suffering musical partner of forty years, John Du Prez. Thank you all. It's been fun.

PHOTO CREDITS

Interior Art

Page xiv: Courtesy of Python (Monty) Pictures Limited

Page 3: Courtesy of the author

Page 5: Courtesy of the author

Page 6: Courtesy of the author

Page 22: With compliments from Scottish Television LTD Press and Publicity Department, Douglas 9999

Page 30: Cambridge News / BPM Media

Page 37: FremantleMedia Ltd / Shutterstock

Page 38: Courtesy of Python (Monty) Pictures Limited

Page 44: Courtesy of the author

Page 51: Courtesy of the author

Page 54: Courtesy of Python (Monty) Pictures Limited

Page 61: Drew Mara / Python (Monty) Pictures Limited

Page 64: © Donal F. Holway

Page 66: © Peter Baylis

Page 69: Trinity Mirror / Mirrorpix / Alamy Stock Photo

Page 70: © Catherine Nicolson

Page 73: Courtesy of the author

Page 77: Courtesy of the author

Page 79: © Bob Gruen

Page 80: © Carinthia West

Page 81: Courtesy of Python (Monty) Pictures Limited

Page 83: © Victoria Juvat

Page 84: © Catherine Nicolson

Page 87: Courtesy of the author

Page 88: Courtesy of the author

Page 95: Courtesy of the author

Page 97: Courtesy of the author

Page 103: Richard Avedon © Avedon Foundation

Page 104: Courtesy of Python (Monty) Pictures Limited

Page 107: Courtesy of the author

Page 110: © Lynn Goldsmith

Page 124, top: Courtesy of the author

Page 124, bottom: Courtesy of the author

Page 128: Courtesy of Python (Monty) Pictures Limited

Page 131: © Alan Kleinberg

Page 132: Courtesy of Ewe Mathuen

Page 134, top: © Alan Kleinberg

Page 134, bottom: © Alan Kleinberg

Page 139: © 1983 Celadine Films

Page 145: Courtesy of Python (Monty) Pictures Limited

Page 153: © Zoë Dominic

Page 157: Courtesy of the author

Page 158: NUNS ON THE RUN © 1990 Twentieth Century Fox. All rights reserved.

Page 159: © 1989 Harmony Gold Productions, Inc. All Rights Reserved.

Page 160: THE ADVENTURES OF BARON MUNCHAUSEN © 1989 Columbia Pictures Industries, Inc. All Rights Reserved. Courtesy of Columbia Pictures.

Page 165: © Alan Kleinberg

Page 166: © Alan Kleinberg

Page 168: Courtesy of the author

Page 170: © 1993 Universal Pictures

Page 171: © Brian Aris

Page 180: Courtesy of the author

Page 183: THE WIND IN THE WILLOWS © 1996 Allied Films Limited. All Rights Reserved. Courtesy of TriStar Pictures

Page 189: Courtesy of the author

Page 192: Courtesy of the author

Page 194: Courtesy of the author

Page 212: © Brigitte Lacombe

Page 227: Anwar Hussein Collection / ROTA / Contributor / Getty Images

Page 228: Frazer Harrison / Staff / Getty Images

Page 232, top: Leon Neal / AFP / Getty Images

Page 232, bottom: Jeff J Mitchell / Staff / Getty Images

Page 242: Geoff Robinson Photography / Shutterstock

Page 246: Courtesy of the author

Page 248: Courtesy of the author

Page 249: Courtesy of the author

Page 254: Steven Siewert / Fairfax Syndication

Page 257, top: Courtesy of the author

Page 257, bottom: Courtesy of the author

Page 259: © Vincent Graff for Radio Times / Immediate Media

Page 263: © RMN-Grand Palais / Art Resource, NY

Page 266: Monty Python stamp design © Royal Mail Group Limited. Images licensed courtesy of Python (Monty) Pictures Limited. All rights in the underlying images and the name "Monty Python" are reserved.

Insert

Page 1, top: Courtesy of the author

Page 1, bottom: © Victoria Juvrud

Page 2, top left: Courtesy of Python (Monty) Pictures Limited

Page 2, top right: Courtesy of the author

Page 2, bottom left: Courtesy of the author

Page 2, bottom right: © Carinthia West "Hanging Out Archive"

Page 3, top: Courtesy of the author

Page 3, middle left: Courtesy of the author

Page 3, middle right: Courtesy of the author

Page 3, bottom: Courtesy of the author

Page 4, top: Courtesy of the author

Page 4, middle left: Courtesy of the author

Page 4, middle right: Courtesy of the author

Page 4, bottom: Courtesy of the author

Page 5, top: Courtesy of the author

INDEX

Page numbers in *italics* refer to illustrations.

ABOUT THE AUTHOR

ERIC IDLE is a comedian, actor, author, and singer-songwriter who found immediate fame on television with the sketch-comedy show *Monty Python's Flying Circus*. Following its success, the group began making films that include *Monty Python and the Holy Grail* (1975), *Life of Brian* (1979), and *The Meaning of Life* (1983). Eric wrote, directed, and created *The Rutles,* the world's first-ever mockumentary, as well as the Tony Award–winning musical *Spamalot* (2005). He lives in Los Angeles.